ACP

Basic statistics

Statistiques de base

1987

Cataloguing data can be found at the end of this publication.
Une fiche bibliographique figure à la fin de l'ouvrage.

310 RT.

Luxembourg: Office des publications officielles
des Communautés européennes, 1987

ISBN 92-825-7382-6

Cat.: CA-47-86-575-2A-C

Printed in the FR of Germany

Contents

Table des matières

4

PART III — EDF AND EIB INTERVENTIONS UNDER THE LOMÉ II CONVENTION

PARTIE III — LES INTERVENTIONS DU FED ET DE LA BEI AU TITRE DE LA CONVENTION DE LOMÉ II

Tables

Tableaux

Introduction

This volume brings together the principal economic indicators of the ACP States for recent years. Most of the statistics have been taken from the developing countries data bank set up by the Statistical Office of the European Communities (Cronos system).

Three kinds of tables can be distinguished:
  (i) summary tables presenting the situation of ACP countries in a wider context;
  (ii) tables describing the situation in each country;
  (iii) tables related to the application of the agreements between the Community and the ACP countries.

In addition to the 66 countries who have signed the third Lomé Convention, this publication also includes the Mediterranean States which are linked to the European Community by special association agreements.

As for the previous edition, a 'paperback' format was chosen to encourage a wide readership and to give readers rapid acquaintance with the main trends in the ACP countries' economic development and the implementation of a number of the provisions in the Lomé Convention between the European Communities and the ACP States.

This publication is produced every year.
Remarks, comments or suggestions are welcome; the ambition of Eurostat being to provide a tool adapted to the needs of its users.

This volume was prepared by Mr Daniel Byk, Mrs Rosette Sprauer and Miss Josiane Libouton under the direction of Mr D. Heath, head of the division 'Analyses and developments'.

Luxembourg, May 1987

Introduction

Cette publication présente une synthèse des principaux indicateurs économiques des États ACP au cours des dernières années. La plupart des statistiques sont reprises de la banque de données des pays en développement (système Cronos) mise au point par l'Office statistique des Communautés européennes.

Trois types de tableaux sont à distinguer:
  — des tableaux de synthèse permettant de situer dans un contexte plus large la situation des pays ACP,
  — des tableaux décrivant la situation de chaque pays,
  — des tableaux relatifs à l'application des accords entre la Communauté et les pays ACP.

Outre les 66 pays signataires de la troisième convention de Lomé, figurent également les États de la Méditerranée qui sont liés à l'Europe communautaire par des accords d'association.

Comme pour l'édition précédente, le format «livre de poche» a été retenu pour permettre la diffusion vers un large public d'utilisateurs, qui pourront ainsi avoir rapidement connaissance des principales tendances de l'évolution de l'économie de ces pays et de l'application d'un certain nombre de dispositions prévues à la convention CE-ACP de Lomé.

Cette publication est réalisée annuellement.
Les remarques, commentaires ou suggestions sont les bienvenus, l'ambition d'Eurostat étant, avec cette publication, de mettre à disposition un instrument adapté aux besoins de ses utilisateurs.

Cette publication a été préparée par M. Daniel Byk, Mme Rosette Sprauer et Mlle Josiane Libouton, sous la direction de M. D. Heath, chef de la division «analyse et développement».

Luxembourg, mai 1987

Methodological notes and sources

The methodology as well as the detailed sources of the data contained in this publication can be provided on request. It may, however, be useful to repeat the general principles.

1. Data relating to GNP and per capita GNP were supplied by the World Bank. The per capita GNP growth rate is the true (annual) rate, whereas the GNP growth rate is the annual rate at current prices. GNP is calculated in accordance with the World Bank's own particular method: GNP data from countries expressed in local currency are converted into US dollars for the base period 1982-84 by applying an average rate of exchange. For earlier years the data are deflated by the true growth rate of the countries' GDP plus the rate of inflation in the USA. Reference to the rate of inflation in the USA enables comparisons to be made between the various countries. The GNP growth rate is therefore an indicator of growth of two kinds: the country's constant-price GDP and the rate of inflation in the USA rather than the rate of inflation in the country under consideration.

2. External trade statistics were supplied by the United Nations and the ACP States. The nomenclature used is the SITC rev. 1, although the exports/GDP ratio was calculated from national accounts data.

3. The financial indicators came from a variety of sources: balance of payments and international reserves data are from the IMF (BOP and IFS); details of the external public debt were supplied by the World Bank; lastly the ratio of debt service to exports, being a financial indicator, was calculated on the basis of export data extracted from the balance of payments.

Notes méthodologiques et sources

La méthodologie ainsi que les sources détaillées des données reprises dans cette publication peuvent être fournies sur demande. Il convient néanmoins d'en rappeler l'essentiel.

1. Les données concernant le PNB et le PNB/habitant proviennent de la Banque mondiale. Le taux de croissance du PNB/habitant est un taux réel (annuel). Au contraire, le taux de croissance du PNB est un taux courant (annuel). Le PNB est calculé par la Banque mondiale suivant une méthodologie très spécifique à cette institution: les données de PNB des pays exprimées en monnaie nationale sont converties en USD pour la période de base 1982-1984 par application d'une moyenne de taux de change. Pour les années antérieures, ces données sont déflatées de l'indice de croissance réelle du PIB du pays et du taux d'inflation des USA. L'utilisation du taux d'inflation des USA permet de rendre les différents pays comparables entre eux. Le taux de croissance du PNB reflète donc deux croissances: celle du PIB du pays à prix constant et le taux d'inflation des USA et non pas le taux d'inflation du pays considéré.

2. Les statistiques du commerce extérieur proviennent de l'ONU et des États ACP. La nomenclature utilisée est la CTCI rev. 1. Néanmoins, le ratio Exportations/PIB a été calculé à partir des chiffres de la comptabilité nationale.

3. Les indicateurs financiers ont des sources diverses: pour la balance des paiements et les réserves internationales, il s'agit du FMI (BOP et IFS). Pour la dette extérieure publique, il s'agit de la Banque mondiale.

Enfin, comme il s'agit d'un indicateur financier, le coefficient service de la dette/exportations a été calculé à partir des données d'exportations de la balance des paiements.

For a number of countries there are discrepancies between the changes in international reserves and in the net balance of payments; these are explained by differences in the concepts used.

4. Data relating to official development assistance (ODA) were supplied by the Development Assistance Committee (DAC). ODA data cover only the aid flows from the DAC (OECD's and not those from OPEC (Organization of Petroleum Exporting Countries). ODA figures are net of loan repayments.

5. For the first time, figures on food aid are being published this year. They are derived from data collected by the Development Aid Committee (OECD).

6. In addition, we have added a breakdown of GDP by origin and also an index of GDP price trends. These figures are from the World Bank.

For the following countries:
— Belize, Botswana, Ghana, Jamaica, Kenya, Liberia, Sierra Leone, Tanzania, Uganda, Zimbabwe, Algeria, Cyprus, Jordan, as the category 'non-defined origin GDP' is negative, the total of the categories 'origin of GDP' is greater than 100 %.

7. Agricultural production data came from the FAO, while data on industrial and mining production were taken from the United Nations' Statistical Yearbook.

8. Details of principal exports are given in millions of US dollars or as a percentage of total exports.

9. Statistics on the European Development Funds (EDFs) and the European Investment Bank (EIB) operations were taken from the report of the ACP-EEC Council of Ministers.
As the data obtained this year are incomplete, we have introduced the table 'The 5th EDF: Aid by type and beneficiary country' published in the annual report of the Court of Auditors.

10. In order to complete these data, this edition contains the rates of exchange from the US dollar, the ECU and the SDR into

Des différences conceptuelles expliquent que pour certains pays l'on puisse observer des divergences entre l'évolution des réserves internationales et celle du solde de la balance des paiements.

4. Les données d'aide publique au développement (APD) proviennent du CAD. Les données d'APD nettes ne reprennent pas les flux en provenance de l'OPEP (Organisation des pays exportateurs de pétrole), mais seulement ceux en provenance du CAD (Comité d'aide au développement de l'OCDE). Les données d'APD sont nettes des remboursements des prêts.

5. Tout comme l'année dernière, les données concernant l'aide alimentaire sont publiées. Elles proviennent de la collecte réalisée par le Comité d'aide au développement (OCDE).

6. En plus, nous avons introduit la répartition du PIB par origine, ainsi que l'indice d'évolution des prix du PIB. Ces données proviennent de la Banque mondiale.

Pour les pays suivants:
— Belize, Botswana, Ghana, Jamaïque, Kenya, Liberia, Sierra Leone, Tanzanie, Ouganda, Zimbabwe, Algérie, Chypre et Jordanie, le poste «Origine non définie du PIB» étant négatif, le total des trois postes repris dans «Origine du PIB» est supérieur à 100 %.

7. Les données de production proviennent de la FAO pour les produits agricoles et de l'ONU (Statistical Yearbook) pour les produits industriels et miniers.

8. Les principales exportations sont indiquées en millions de USD ou en pour cent des exportations totales.

9. Les statistiques concernant les interventions du FED et de la BEI ont pour source le Rapport du Conseil des ministres ACP-CE. Les informations obtenues cette année étant incomplètes, nous avons introduit le tableau «Le 5e FED: Aides par nature et par pays bénéficiaire», publié dans le rapport annuel de la Cour des comptes.

10. Pour compléter toutes ces données, cette édition comprend les taux de change du dollar

the national currencies of ACP and Mediterranean countries. A new table completes this edition: 'Population and density of ACP and Mediterranean countries'.

11. The ACP group consists of the signatory States of the Lomé III Convention.

12. The EC data from summary tables are concerning EUR 12.
For technical reasons the decimal point is represented by a comma in this publication.

américain, de l'Écu et du DTS vers les monnaies nationales des pays ACP et méditerranéens. Un nouveau tableau vient s'ajouter: «Population et densité des pays ACP et méditerranéens» pour les années 1983, 1984, 1985.

11. Le regroupement ACP comprend les pays signataires de Lomé III.

12. Les données CE des tableaux de synthèse concernent EUR 12.

Abbreviations:

EC: European Community
GNP: Gross national product
GDP: Gross domestic product
BOP: Balance of payments
IFS: International financial statistics
IMF: International Monetary Fund
EDF: European Development Fund
FAO: Food and Agriculture Organization of the United Nations
ODA: Official development assistance
DAC: Development Assistance Committee
SDR: Special drawing rights
EIB: European Investment Bank
SITC: Statistical international trade classification
OECD: Organization for Economic Cooperation and Development
OPEC: Organization of Petroleum Exporting Countries

Signification des sigles:

CE: Communauté européenne
PNB: produit national brut
PIB: produit intérieur brut
BOP: balance des paiements
IFS: statistiques internationales et financières
FMI: Fonds monétaire international
FED: Fonds européen de développement
FAO: Organisation des Nations unies pour l'alimentation et l'agriculture
APD: aide publique au développement
CAD: Comité d'aide au développement
DTS: droits de tirages spéciaux
BEI: Banque européenne d'investissement
CTCI: classification tarifaire du commerce international
OCDE: Organisation de coopération et de développement économiques
OPEP: Organisation des pays exportateurs de pétrole

ACP exchange rates USD 1 = x national currency units

Taux de conversion des ACP 1 USD = x unités monétaires nationales

ACP	1981	1982	1983	1984	1985	ACP
Angola	....	....	....	....	....	Angola
Antigua & Barbuda	2,7000	2,7000	2,7000	2,7000	2,7000	Antigua et Barbuda
Bahamas	1,0000	1,0000	1,0000	1,0000	1,0000	Bahamas
Barbados	2,0100	2,0100	2,0100	2,0100	2,0100	Barbade
Belize	2,0000	2,0000	2,0000	2,0000	2,0000	Belize
Benin	271,7300	328,6000	381,0600	436,9600	449,2600	Bénin
Botswana	0,8400	1,0300	1,1000	1,3000	1,9000	Botswana
Burkina Faso	271,7300	328,6000	381,0600	436,9600	449,2600	Burkina Faso
Burundi	90,0000	90,0000	92,9500	119,7100	120,6900	Burundi
Cameroon	271,7300	328,6000	381,0600	436,9600	449,2600	Cameroun
Cape Verde	48,6900	58,2900	71,6900	84,8800	91,6300	Cap-Vert
Central African Rep.	271,7300	328,6000	381,0600	436,9600	449,2600	République Centrafricaine
Chad	271,7300	328,6000	381,0600	436,9600	449,2600	Tchad
Comoros	271,7300	328,6000	381,0600	436,9600	449,2600	Comores
Congo	271,7300	328,6000	381,0600	436,9600	449,2600	Congo
Côte d'Ivoire	271,7300	328,6000	381,0600	436,9600	449,2600	Côte-d'Ivoire
Djibouti	177,7200	177,7200	177,7200	177,7200	177,7200	Djibouti
Dominica	2,7000	2,7000	2,7000	2,7000	2,7000	Dominique
Equatorial Guinea	184,6300	219,72	286,86	321,52	449,26	Guinée équatoriale
Ethiopia	2,0700	2,0700	2,0700	2,0700	2,0700	Éthiopie
Fiji	0,8500	0,9300	1,0200	1,0800	1,1500	Fidji
Gabon	271,7300	328,6000	381,0600	436,9600	449,2600	Gabon
Gambia	1,9900	2,2900	2,6400	3,5800	3,8900	Gambie
Ghana	2,7500	2,7500	8,8300	35,9900	54,3600	Ghana
Grenada	2,7000	2,7000	2,7000	2,7000	2,7000	Grenade
Guinea	20,9500	22,3700	23,0900	24,0900	24,3300	Guinée
Guinea-Bissau	37,3400	39,8700	42,1000	105,2900	159,6200	Guinée-Bissau
Guyana	2,8100	3,0000	3,0000	3,8300	4,2500	Guyane
Jamaica	1,7800	1,7800	1,9300	3,9400	5,5600	Jamaïque
Kenya	9,0500	10,9200	13,3100	14,4100	16,4300	Kenya
Kiribati	0,8700					Kiribati
Lesotho	0,8800	1,0900	1,1100	1,4700	2,2300	Lesotho
Liberia	1,0000	1,0000	1,0000	1,0000	1,0000	Liberia
Madagascar	271,7300	349,7400	430,4500	576,6400	662,4800	Madagascar
Malawi	0,8900	1,0600	1,1700	1,4100	1,7200	Malawi
Mali	271,7300	328,6000	381,0600	436,9600	449,2600	Mali
Mauritania	48,3000	51,7700	54,8100	63,8000	77,0800	Mauritanie
Mauritius	8,9400	10,8700	11,7100	13,8000	15,4400	Maurice
Mozambique						Mozambique

Niger	271,7300	328,6000	381,0600	436,9600	449,2600
Nigeria	0,6200	0,6700	0,7200	0,7700	0,8900
Papua New Guinea	92,8400	92,8400	94,3400	100,1700	101,2600
Rwanda	38,4000	41,0000	42,3300	44,1600	44,6600
Sao Tome & Principe					
Senegal	271,7300	328,6000	381,0600	436,9600	449,2600
Seychelles	6,3100	6,5500	6,7700	7,0600	7,1300
Sierra Leone	1,1600	1,2400	1,8800	2,5100	5,0900
Solomon	0,8700	0,9300	1,1500	1,2700	1,4800
Somalia	6,2900	10,7500	15,7900	20,0200	39,4900
St Kitts & Nevis	3,0000	3,0000	3,0000	3,0000	3,0000
St Lucia	2,7000	2,7000	2,7000	2,7000	2,7000
St Vincent & Gren.	2,7000	2,7000	2,7000	2,7000	2,7000
Sudan	0,5600	0,9500	1,3000	1,3000	2,3000
Suriname	1,7800	1,7800	1,7800	1,7800	
Swaziland	0,8800	1,0900	1,1100	1,4700	2,2000
Tanzania	8,2800	9,2800	11,1400	15,2900	17,4700
Togo	271,7300	328,6000	381,0600	436,9600	449,2600
Tonga	0,87				
Trinidad	2,4000	2,4000	2,4000	2,4000	2,4500
Tuvalu	0,8700				
Uganda	50,0500	94,0500	153,8600	359,7000	672,0200
Vanuatu	87,8300	96,2100	99,3700	99,2300	106,0300
Western Samoa	1,0300	1,2500	1,5500	1,8600	2,2400
Zaire	4,3800	5,7500	12,8900	36,1300	49,8700
Zambia	0,8700	0,9300	1,2600	1,8100	3,1400
Zimbabwe	0,6900	0,7600	1,0100	1,2600	1,6100
Mediterranean countries / Pays méditerranéens					
Algeria / Algérie	4,3200	4,5000	4,7900	4,9800	5,0300
Cyprus / Chypre	0,4200	0,4700	0,5300	0,5900	0,6100
Egypt / Egypte	0,7000	0,7000	0,7000	0,7000	0,7000
Israel / Israël	0,0100	0,0200	0,0600	0,2900	1,1800
Jordan / Jordanie	0,3300	0,3500	0,3600	0,3800	0,3900
Lebanon / Liban	4,3100	4,7400	4,5300	6,5100	16,4200
Libya / Libye	0,3000	0,3000	0,3000	0,3000	0,3000
Malta / Malte	0,3900	0,4100	0,4300	0,4600	0,4700
Morocco / Maroc	5,1700	6,0200	7,1100	8,8100	10,0600
Syria / Syrie	3,9200	3,9200	3,9200	3,9200	3,9200
Tunisia / Tunisie	0,4900	0,5900	0,6600	0,7800	0,8300
Turkey / Turquie	111,2200	162,5500	225,4600	366,6800	521,9800
Yugoslavia / Yougoslavie	34,9700	50,2800	92,8400	152,8200	270,1600

Source: International Monetary Fund: International financial statistics: exchange rate (rf: IFS code).
Source: Fonds monétaire international, International financial statistics, taux de change (rf: IFS code).

ACP exchange rates SDR 1 = x national currency units
Taux de conversion des ACP 1 DTS = x unités monétaires nationales

ACP	1981	1982	1983	1984	1985	ACP
Angola	..	..	..	..	..	Angola
Antigua & Barbuda	3,1400	2,9800	2,8300	2,6500	2,9700	Antigua et Barbuda
Bahamas	1,1600	1,1000	1,0500	0,9800	1,1000	Bahamas
Barbados	2,3400	2,2200	2,1100	1,9700	2,2100	Barbade
Belize	2,3300	2,2100	2,0900	1,9600	2,2000	Belize
Benin	334,5200	370,9200	436,9700	470,1100	415,2600	Bénin
Botswana	1,0200	1,1700	1,2100	1,5300	2,3100	Botswana
Burkina Faso	334,5200	370,9200	436,9700	470,1100	415,2600	Burkina Faso
Burundi	104,7600	99,2800	122,7000	122,7000	122,7000	Burundi
Cameroon	334,5200	370,9200	436,9700	470,1100	415,2600	Cameroun
Cape Verde	59,2000	69,5400	83,7300	91,1700	93,7800	Cap-Vert
Central African Rep.	334,5200	370,9200	436,9700	470,1100	415,2600	République Centrafricaine
Chad	334,5200	370,9200	436,9700	470,1100	415,2600	Tchad
Comoros	334,5200	370,9200	436,9700	470,1100	415,2600	Comores
Congo	334,5200	370,9200	436,9700	470,1100	415,2600	Congo
Côte d'Ivoire	334,5200	370,9200	436,9700	470,1100	415,2600	Côte-d'Ivoire
Djibouti	206,8600	196,0500	186,0600	174,2000	195,2100	Djibouti
Dominica	3,1400	2,9800	2,8300	2,6500	2,9700	Dominique
Equatorial Guinea	226,8600	277,1000	328,1100	340,7800	415,2600	Guinée équatoriale
Ethiopia	2,4100	2,2800	2,1700	2,0300	2,2700	Ethiopie
Fiji	1,0200	1,0400	1,0900	1,1200	1,2300	Fidji
Gabon	334,5200	370,9200	436,9700	470,1100	415,2600	Gabon
Gambia	2,4400	2,7300	2,8900	4,2400	3,8000	Gambie
Ghana	3,2000	3,0900	31,4100	49,0100	65,8900	Ghana
Grenada	3,1400	2,9800	2,8300	2,6500	2,9700	Grenade
Guinea	24,6800	24,6800	24,6800	24,6800	24,6600	Guinée
Guinea-Bissau	44,0000	44,0000	88,1100	126,0300	190,6900	Guinée-Bissau
Guyana	3,4900	3,3100	3,1400	4,8300	4,5600	Guyane
Jamaica	2,0700	1,9600	3,4300	..	6,0200	Jamaïque
Kenya	11,9500	14,0600	14,4200	15,1900	17,7400	Kenya
Kiribati	1,1100	1,1900	1,2800	1,9500	2,8100	Kiribati
Lesotho	1,1600	1,1000	1,0500	0,9800	1,1000	Lesotho
Liberia	..	..	..	..	..	Liberia
Madagascar	334,5200	405,6200	515,2700	645,0900	698,3600	Madagascar
Malawi	1,0500	1,2100	1,3600	1,5300	1,8400	Malawi
Mali	334,5200	370,9200	436,9700	470,1100	415,2600	Mali
Mauritania	56,9600	58,4200	59,7100	65,9600	84,6500	Mauritanie
Mauritius	12,0000	12,0000	13,3200	15,2900	15,7200	Maurice
Mozambique	..	..	..	..	..	Mozambique

Country						Pays
Niger	334,5200	370,9200	436,9700	470,1100	415,2600	Niger
Nigeria	0,7400	0,7400	0,7800	0,7900	1,1000	Nigéria
Papua New Guinea	0,7900	0,8200	0,9200	0,9200	1,1100	Papouasie-Nouvelle-Guinée
Rwanda	108,0600	102,4100	102,7100	102,7100	102,71	Rwanda
Sao Tome & Principe	45,2500	45,2500	45,2500	45,2500	45,2500	São Tomé et Principe
Senegal	334,5200	370,9200	436,9700	470,1100	415,2600	Sénégal
Seychelles	7,2300	7,2300	7,2300	7,2300	7,2300	Seychelles
Sierra Leone	1,3700	1,3600	2,6300	2,4600	5,7400	Sierra Leone
Solomon	1,0300	1,1500	1,2800	1,3200	1,7700	Salomon
Somalia	7,3300	16,5000	18,3800	25,4800	46,6800	Somalie
St Kitts & Nevis	3,1400	2,9800	2,8300	2,6500	2,9700	St-Christophe-et-Nevis
St Lucia	3,1400	2,9800	2,8300	2,6500	2,9700	Sainte-Lucie
St Vincent & Gren.	1,0500	1,4300	1,3600	1,2700	2,7500	St-Vincent et Grenadines
Sudan	2,0000	1,9700	1,8700	1,7500	1,9600	Soudan
Suriname	1,1100	1,1900	1,2800	1,9500	2,8100	Surinam
Swaziland						Swaziland
Tanzania	9,6900	10,5500	13,0400	17,7500	18,1200	Tanzanie
Togo	334,5200	370,9200	436,9700	470,1100	415,2600	Togo
Tonga						Tonga
Trinidad & Tobago	2,7900	2,6500	2,5100	2,3500	3,9500	Trinité et Tobago
Tuvalu						Tuvalu
Uganda	99,1100	116,7300	251,2700	509,7100	1 537,79	Ouganda
Vanuatu	106,2000	106,2000	106,2000	100,6000	110,0000	Vanuatu
Western Samoa	1,2800	1,3600	1,7000	2,1400	2,5300	Samoa occidentales
Zaire	6,3500	6,3500	31,5300	39,6500	61,2800	Zaïre
Zambia	1,0200	1,0200	1,2800	2,1600	6,2600	Zambie
Zimbabwe	0,8330	1,0100	1,1600	1,4700	1,8000	Zimbabwe
Mediterranean countries						**Pays méditerranéens**
Algeria	5,1000	5,1100	5,1500	5,0200	5,2400	Algérie
Cyprus	0,5000	0,5400	0,5800	0,6300	0,6000	Chypre
Egypt	0,8100	0,7700	0,7300	0,6900	0,7700	Égypte
Israel	0,0200	0,0400	0,1100	0,6300	1,6500	Israël
Jordan	0,3900	0,3900	0,3900	0,3900	0,3900	Jordanie
Lebanon	5,3800	4,2000	5,7500	8,7100	19,8800	Liban
Libya	0,3400	0,3300	0,3100	0,2900	0,3200	Libye
Malta	0,4500	0,4600	0,4700	0,4800	0,4700	Malte
Morocco	6,2100	6,9100	8,4400	9,3600	10,5700	Maroc
Syria	4,5700	4,3300	4,1100	3,8500	4,3100	Syrie
Tunisia	0,6000	0,6800	0,7600	0,8500	0,8300	Tunisie
Turkey	155,5300	206,0100	296,0800	435,9300	633,6300	Turquie
Yugoslavia	48,6800	68,9300	131,5700	207,5600	343,5900	Yougoslavie

Source: International Monetary Fund: International financial statistics: exchange rate (aa: IFS code).
Source: Fonds monétaire international, International financial statistics, taux de change (aa: IFS code).

ACP exchange rates ECU 1 = x national currency units

Taux de conversion des ACP 1 Écu = x unités monétaires nationales

ACP	1981	1982	1983	1984	1985	ACP
Angola	..	..	..	..	..	Angola
Antigua & Barbuda	3,0100	2,6500	2,4000	2,1300	2,0600	Antigua et Barbuda
Bahamas	1,1200	0,9500	0,8900	0,7900	0,7600	Bahamas
Barbados	2,2400	1,9700	1,7900	1,5900	1,5300	Barbade
Belize	2,2300	1,9600	1,7800	1,5800	1,5300	Belize
Benin	303,3700	321,9300	339,2300	344,7700	342,8300	Bénin
Botswana	0,9400	1,0100	0,9800	1,0300	1,4500	Botswana
Burkina Faso	303,3700	321,9300	339,2300	344,7700	342,8300	Burkina Faso
Burundi	100,4800	88,1700	82,7500	94,4500	92,1000	Burundi
Cameroon	303,3700	321,9300	339,2300	344,7700	342,8300	Cameroun
Cape Verde	54,3600	57,1100	63,8000	66,9700	69,9200	Cap-Vert
Central African Rep.	303,3700	321,9300	339,2300	344,7700	342,8300	République Centrafricaine
Chad	303,3700	321,9300	339,2300	344,7700	342,8300	Tchad
Comoros	303,3700	321,9300	339,2300	344,7700	342,8300	Comores
Congo	303,3700	321,9300	339,2300	344,7700	342,8300	Congo
Côte-d'Ivoire	303,3700	321,9300	339,2300	344,7700	342,8300	Côte-d'Ivoire
Djibouti	198,4200	174,1100	158,2100	140,2300	135,6200	Djibouti
Dominica	2,6100	2,6500	2,4000	2,1300	2,0600	Dominique
Equatorial Guinea	206,1300	215,2600	255,3700	253,6900	342,8300	Guinée équatoriale
Ethiopia	2,3100	2,0300	1,8400	2,1300	1,5800	Éthiopie
Fiji	0,9500	0,9100	0,9100	0,85	0,8800	Fidji
Gabon	303,3700	321,9300	339,2300	344,7700	342,8300	Gabon
Gambia	2,2200	2,2400	2,3500	2,8200	2,9700	Gambie
Ghana	3,0700	2,6900	7,8600	28,4000	41,4800	Ghana
Grenada	3,0100	2,6500	2,4000	2,1300	2,0600	Grenade
Guinea	23,3900	21,9200	20,5600	19,0100	18,5700	Guinée
Guinea-Bissau	41,6900	39,0600	37,4800	83,0800	121,8000	Guinée-Bissau
Guyana	3,1400	2,9400	2,6700	3,0200	3,2400	Guyane
Jamaica	1,9900	1,7400	1,7200	3,1100	4,2400	Jamaïque
Kenya	10,1000	10,7000	11,8500	11,3700	12,5400	Kenya
Kiribati	0,9700	..	..	..	..	Kiribati
Lesotho	0,9800	1,0700	0,9900	1,1600	1,7000	Lesotho
Liberia	1,1200	0,9600	0,8900	0,7900	0,7600	Liberia
Madagascar	303,3700	342,6400	383,2000	454,9900	505,5300	Madagascar
Malawi	0,9900	1,0400	1,0400	1,1100	1,3100	Malawi
Mali	303,3700	321,9300	339,2300	344,7700	342,8300	Mali
Mauritania	53,9200	50,7200	48,7900	50,3400	58,8200	Mauritanie
Mauritius	9,9800	10,6500	10,4200	10,8900	11,7800	Maurice
Mozambique	..	..	..	..	..	Mozambique

Country						Pays
Niger	303,3700	321,9300	339,2300	344,7700	342,8300	Niger
Nigeria	0,6900	0,6600	0,6400	0,6100	0,6800	Nigéria
Papua New Guinea	0,7500	0,7200	0,7500	0,7100	0,7600	Papouasie-Nouvelle-Guinée
Rwanda	103,6500	90,9600	83,9800	79,0400	77,2700	Rwanda
Sao Tome & Principe	42,8700	40,1700	37,6800	34,8400	34,0300	Sao Tomé et Principe
Senegal	303,3700	321,9300	339,2300	344,7700	342,8300	Sénégal
Seychelles	7,0400	6,4200	6,0300	5,7700	5,4400	Seychelles
Sierra Leone	1,3000	1,2100	1,6700	1,9800	3,8800	Sierra Leone
Solomon	0,9700	0,9500	1,0200	1,0000	1,1300	Salomon
Somalia	7,0200	10,5300	14,0600	15,8600	30,1300	Somalie
St Kitts & Nevis	3,3400	2,9300	2,6700	2,3600		St-Christophe-et-Nevis
St Lucia	3,0100	2,6500	2,4000	2,1300	2,0600	St-Lucie
St Vincent & Gren.	3,0100	2,6500	2,4000	2,1300	2,0600	St-Vincent-et-Grenadines
Sudan	0,6300	0,9300	1,1600	1,0300	1,7600	Soudan
Suriname	1,9900	1,7400	1,5800	1,4000	1,3600	Surinam
Swaziland	0,9800	1,0700	0,9900	1,1600	1,6900	Swaziland
Tanzania	9,2400	9,9900	9,9200	12,0600	13,3300	Tanzanie
Togo	303,3700	321,9300	339,2300	344,7700	342,8300	Togo
Tonga	0,9700					Tonga
Trinidad & Tobago	2,6800	2,3500	2,1400	1,8900	1,8700	Trinité et Tobago
Tuvalu	0,9700					Tuvalu
Uganda	55,8800	92,1400	136,9700	283,8100	512,8100	Ouganda
Vanuatu	98,0600	94,2600	88,4600	78,3000	80,9100	Vanuatu
Western Samoa	1,1500	1,1900	1,3800	1,4700	1,7100	Samoa occidentales
Zaire	4,8900	5,6300	11,4700	28,5100	38,0600	Zaire
Zambia	0,9700	0,9100	1,1200	1,4300	2,4000	Zambie
Zimbabwe	0,7700	0,7400	0,9000	0,9900	1,2300	Zimbabwe
Mediterranean countries						**Pays méditerranéens**
Algeria	4,8200	4,5000	4,2600	3,9300	3,8400	Algérie
Cyprus	0,4700	0,4600	0,4700	0,4700	0,4700	Chypre
Egypt	0,7800	0,6900	0,6200	0,5500	0,5300	Egypte
Israel	0,0100	0,0200	0,0500	0,2300	0,9000	Israël
Jordan	0,3700	0,3400	0,3400	0,3200	0,3000	Jordanie
Lebanon	4,8100	4,6400	4,0300	5,1400	12,5300	Liban
Libya	0,3300	0,2900	0,2700	0,2400	0,2300	Libye
Malta	0,4400	0,4000	0,3800	0,3600	0,3600	Malte
Morocco	5,7700	5,9000	6,3300	6,9600	7,6800	Maroc
Syria	4,3600	3,8400	3,4900	3,0900	2,9900	Syrie
Tunisia	0,5500	0,5800	0,6100	0,6200	0,6300	Tunisie
Turkey	124,1700	159,2500	200,7100	289,3200	398,3200	Turquie
Yugoslavia	39,0400	49,2600	82,6500	120,5800	206,1600	Yougoslavie

Source: International Monetary Fund: International financial statistics: exchange rate (rf: IFS code).
Source: Fonds monétaire international: International financial statistics, taux de change (rf: IFS code).

Population and density: 1983, 1984, 1985
Population et densité: 1983, 1984, 1985

ACP	Average population at 30 June (in thousands) Population moyenne au 30 juin (en milliers)			Number of inhabitants per km² Nombre d'habitants au km²			ACP
	1983	1984	1985	1983	1984	1985	
Angola	8 340	8 540	8 750	7	7	7	Angola
Antigua & Barbuda	80	80	80	182	182	182	Antigua et Barbuda
Bahamas	220	230	230	16	16	16	Bahamas
Barbados	250	250	250	581	581	581	Barbade
Belize	160	160	170	7	7	7	Belize
Benin	3 720	3 830	3 930	33	34	35	Bénin
Botswana	1 010	1 050	1 090	2	2	2	Botswana
Burkina Faso	6 410	6 530	6 640	23	24	24	Burkina
Burundi	4 420	4 540	4 720	159	163	170	Burundi
Cameroon	9 570	9 870	10 190	20	21	21	Cameroun
Cape Verde	310	320	330	77	79	82	Cap-Vert
Central African Rep.	2 460	2 520	2 610	4	4	4	Republique Centrafricaine
Chad	4 790	4 900	5 020	194	198	203	Tchad
Comoros	420	430	440	5	5	5	Comores
Congo	1 650	1 700	1 740	29	29	30	Congo
Côte d'Ivoire	9 300	9 460	9 810	17	19	20	Côte-d'Ivoire
Djibouti	380	410	430	107	107	107	Djibouti
Dominica	80	80	80	14	14	14	Dominique
Equatorial Guinea	380	380	390	34	35	35	Guinée equatoriale
Ethiopia	41 390	42 440	43 350	37	38	38	Ethiopie
Fiji	680	690	700	4	4	4	Fidji
Gabon	1 110	1 130	1 150	55	56	57	Gabon
Gambia	620	630	640	53	55	57	Gambie
Ghana	12 700	13 150	13 590	324	324	324	Ghana
Grenada	110	110	110	24	24	25	Grenade
Guinea	5 790	5 930	6 070	24	24	25	Guinée
Guinea-Bissau	860	880	890	4	4	4	Guinée-Bissau
Guyana	920	940	790	207	209	213	Guyane
Jamaica	2 270	2 300	2 340	32	34	35	Jamaïque
Kenya	18 770	19 540	20 330	85	85	85	Kenya
Kiribati	60	60	60	47	48	50	Kiribati
Lesotho	1 440	1 470	1 530	18	19	20	Lesotho
Liberia	2 040	2 110	2 190	16	17	17	Liberia
Madagascar	9 400	9 730	9 980				Madagascar

English							Français
Malawi	6 620	6 840	7 060	56	58	60	Malawi
Mali	7 740	7 970	8 210	6	6	7	Mali
Mauritania	1 780	1 830	1 890	2	2	2	Mauritanie
Mauritius	1 060	1 080	1 090	516	527	532	Maurice
Mozambique	13 260	13 600	13 990	17	17	17	Mozambique
Niger	5 770	5 940	6 110	5	5	5	Niger
Nigeria	89 020	92 040	95 200	96	100	103	Nigeria
Papua New Guinea	3 190	3 430	3 630	7	7	7	Papouasie-Nouvelle-Guinée
Rwanda	5 760	5 870	6 070	219	223	230	Rwanda
Sao Tome & Principe	90	90	110	94	94	115	São Tomé et Principe
Senegal	6 320	6 400	6 440	32	33	33	Sénégal
Seychelles	64	64	70	229	229	250	Seychelles
Sierra Leone	3 470	3 540	3 600	48	49	50	Sierra Leone
Solomon	250	260	270	9	9	9	Salomon
Somalia	4 420	4 540	4 650	7	7	7	Somalie
St Kitts & Nevis	40	50	50	111	139	139	St-Christophe-et-Nevis
St Lucia	130	130	130	210	210	210	St-Lucie
St Vincent & Grenadines	110	110	100	324	324	294	Saint-Vincent-et-Grenadines
Sudan	20 360	20 950	21 550	8	8	9	Soudan
Suriname	370	370	400	2	2	2	Surinam
Swaziland	610	630	650	35	36	37	Swaziland
Tanzania	20 410	21 060	21 730	22	22	23	Tanzanie
Togo	2 790	2 870	2 960	49	51	52	Togo
Tonga	100	100	100	143	143	143	Tonga
Trinidad & Tobago	1 150	1 170	1 180	224	228	230	Trinité et Tobago
Tuvalu	8	8	8				Tuvalu
Uganda	14 470	14 960	15 480	61	63	66	Ouganda
Vanuatu	120	130	140	8	9	9	Vanuatu
Western Samoa	160	160	160	56	56	56	Samoa occidentales
Zaire	28 160	29 670	30 360	12	13	13	Zaïre
Zambia	6 240	6 450	6 670	8	9	9	Zambie
Zimbabwe	7 740	7 980	8 380	20	20	21	Zimbabwe
Mediterranean countries							**Pays méditerranéens**
Algeria	20 520	21 050	21 720	9	9	9	Algérie
Cyprus	660	660	670	70	71	72	Chypre
Egypt	45 920	47 190	48 500	46	47	48	Egypte
Israel	4 110	4 160	4 230	198	200	204	Israël
Jordan	3 250	3 380	3 510	33	35	36	Jordanie
Lebanon	2 640	2 640	2 670	254	254	257	Liban
Libya	3 470	3 620	3 600	2	2	2	Libye
Malta	380	380	380	1 188	1 188	1 188	Malte
Morocco	20 880	21 410	21 940	47	48	49	Maroc
Syria	9 610	9 930	10 270	52	54	55	Syrie
Tunisia	6 840	7 030	7 260	42	43	44	Tunisie
Turkey	47 280	48 270	49 270	61	62	63	Turquie
Yugoslavia	22 800	22 960	23 120	89	90	90	Yougoslavie

The ACP countries
in the world

Les ACP
dans le monde

The 66 ACP States

Les 66 États ACP

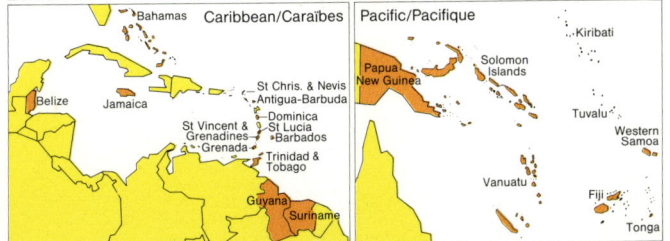

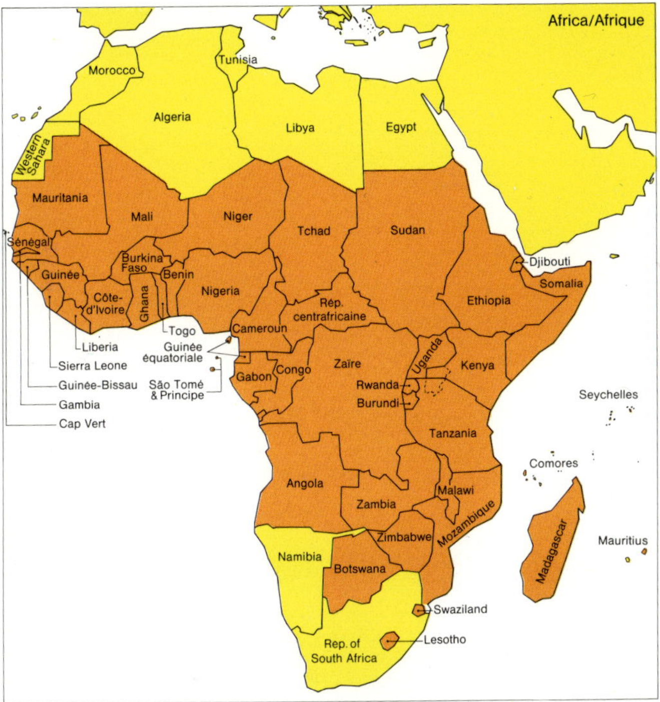
Africa/Afrique
Morocco
Tunisia
Algeria
Libya
Egypt
Western Sahara
Mauritania
Mali
Niger
Tchad
Sudan
Sénégal
Burkina Faso
Benin
Guinée
Côte-d'Ivoire
Ghana
Nigeria
Rép. centrafricaine
Djibouti
Somalia
Ethiopia
Togo
Cameroun
Liberia
Guinée équatoriale
Sierra Leone
Guinée-Bissau
São Tomé & Principe
Gambia
Cap Vert
Gabon
Congo
Zaïre
Uganda
Kenya
Rwanda
Burundi
Seychelles
Tanzania
Comores
Angola
Zambia
Malawi
Mozambique
Zimbabwe
Madagascar
Mauritius
Namibia
Botswana
Swaziland
Lesotho
Rep. of South Africa

Caribbean/Caraïbes
Bahamas
Belize
Jamaica
St Chris. & Nevis
Antigua-Barbuda
Dominica
St Lucia
St Vincent & Grenadines
Barbados
Grenada
Trinidad & Tobago
Guyana
Suriname

Pacific/Pacifique
Kiribati
Papua New Guinea
Solomon Islands
Tuvalu
Western Samoa
Vanuatu
Fiji
Tonga

Net official development assistance from DAC members

Aide publique au développement net des membres du CAD

100 = ODA to developing countries
APD aux pays en développement

Other developing countries
Autres pays en développement

ACP Pacific
ACP Pacifique

ACP Caribbean
ACP Caraïbes

ACP Africa
ACP Afrique

1977   1981   1985

Population (Mio), national accounts: GNP per capita (USD)

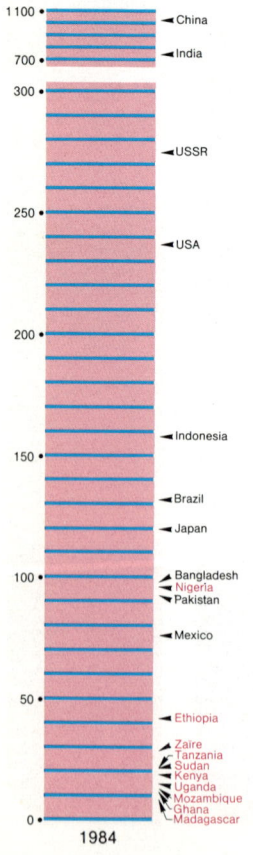

1 100 •	◄ China
700 •	◄ India
300 •	
	◄ USSR
250 •	◄ USA
200 •	
	◄ Indonesia
150 •	
	◄ Brazil
	◄ Japan
100 •	◄ Bangladesh
	◄ Nigeria
	◄ Pakistan
	◄ Mexico
50 •	◄ Ethiopia
	◄ Zaire
	◄ Tanzania
	◄ Sudan
	◄ Kenya
	◄ Uganda
	◄ Mozambique
	◄ Ghana
0 •	◄ Madagascar

1984

Population (Mio), comptes nationaux: PNB par habitant (USD)

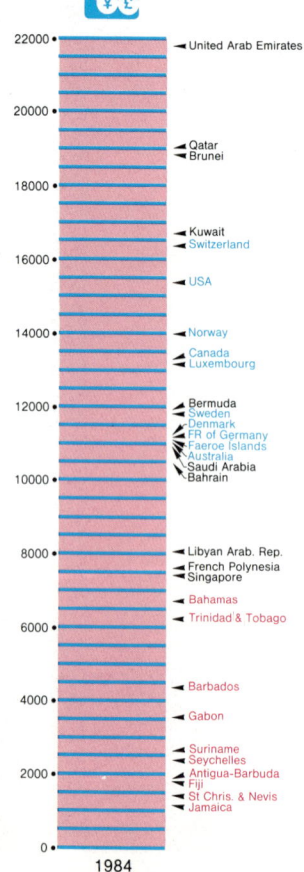

22000 •	◄ United Arab Emirates
20000 •	
	◄ Qatar
	◄ Brunei
18000 •	
	◄ Kuwait
	◄ Switzerland
16000 •	◄ USA
14000 •	◄ Norway
	◄ Canada
	◄ Luxembourg
12000 •	◄ Bermuda
	◄ Sweden
	◄ Denmark
	◄ FR of Germany
	◄ Faeroe Islands
	◄ Australia
	◄ Saudi Arabia
	◄ Bahrain
10000 •	
8000 •	◄ Libyan Arab. Rep.
	◄ French Polynesia
	◄ Singapore
	◄ Bahamas
6000 •	◄ Trinidad & Tobago
	◄ Barbados
4000 •	◄ Gabon
	◄ Suriname
	◄ Seychelles
2000 •	◄ Antigua-Barbuda
	◄ Fiji
	◄ St Chris. & Nevis
	◄ Jamaica
0 •	

1984

Population, national accounts: GNP per capita

Population, comptes nationaux: PNB par habitant

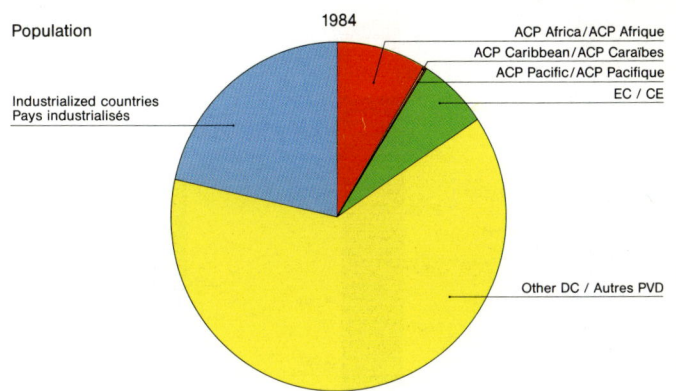

Population

1984

ACP Africa/ACP Afrique
ACP Caribbean/ACP Caraïbes
ACP Pacific/ACP Pacifique
EC / CE

Industrialized countries
Pays industrialisés

Other DC / Autres PVD

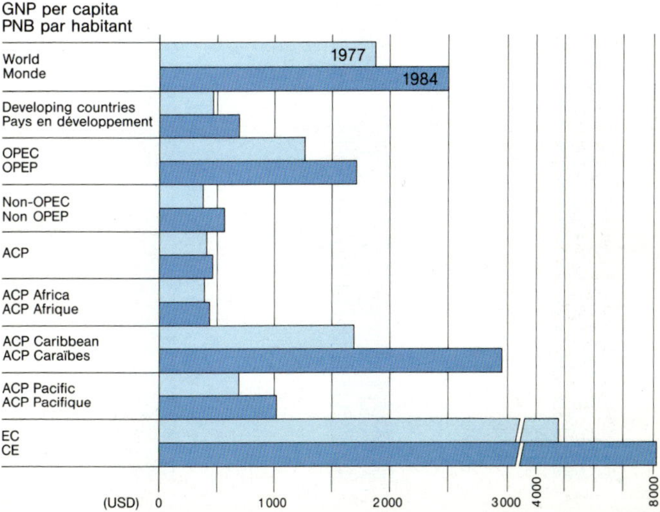

GNP per capita
PNB par habitant

	1977	1984
World / Monde		
Developing countries / Pays en développement		
OPEC / OPEP		
Non-OPEC / Non OPEP		
ACP		
ACP Africa / ACP Afrique		
ACP Caribbean / ACP Caraïbes		
ACP Pacific / ACP Pacifique		
EC / CE		

(USD) 0   1000   2000   3000   4000   8000

**Production: Bananas (fresh),
sugar (centrifugal), coffee (green)
1 000 t**

**Production: bananes fraîches,
sucre centrifugé, café vert
1 000 t**

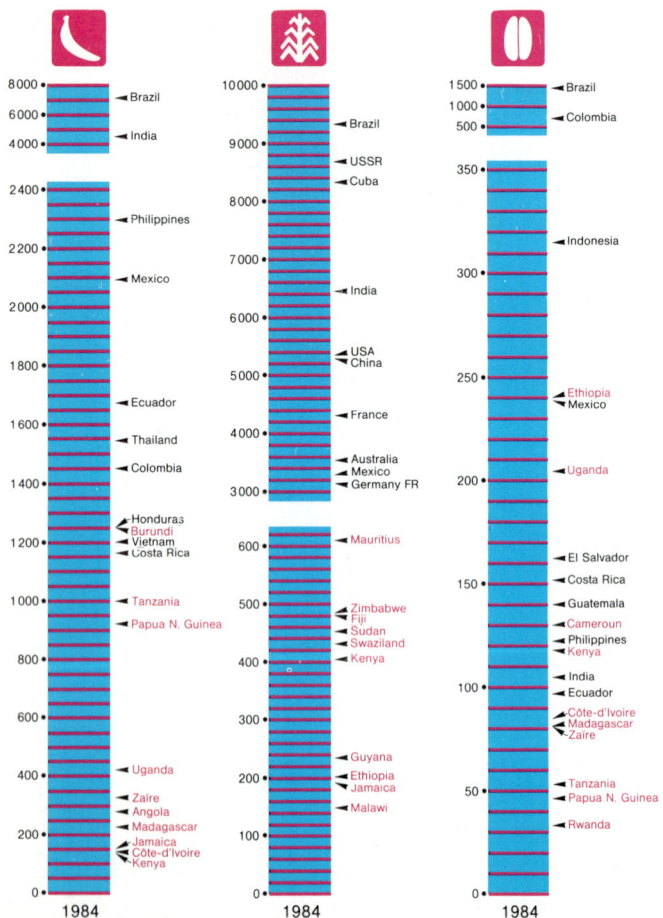

Bananas

8 000	◄ Brazil
6 000	◄ India
4 000	
2 400	◄ Philippines
2 200	◄ Mexico
2 000	
1 800	◄ Ecuador
1 600	◄ Thailand
1 400	◄ Colombia
1 200	◄ Honduras / Burundi / Vietnam / Costa Rica
1 000	◄ Tanzania
	◄ Papua N. Guinea
800	
600	
400	◄ Uganda
	◄ Zaire / Angola / Madagascar
200	◄ Jamaica / Côte-d'Ivoire / Kenya
0	**1984**

Sugar

10 000	
9 000	◄ Brazil
	◄ USSR
8 000	◄ Cuba
7 000	◄ India
6 000	
5 000	◄ USA / China
4 000	◄ France
3 000	◄ Australia / Mexico / Germany FR
600	◄ Mauritius
500	◄ Zimbabwe / Fiji / Sudan / Swaziland / Kenya
400	
300	
200	◄ Guyana / Ethiopia / Jamaica / Malawi
100	
0	**1984**

Coffee

1 500	◄ Brazil
1 000	◄ Colombia
500	
350	
	◄ Indonesia
300	
250	◄ Ethiopia / Mexico
200	◄ Uganda
	◄ El Salvador
150	◄ Costa Rica
	◄ Guatemala
	◄ Cameroun / Philippines / Kenya
100	◄ India / Ecuador
	◄ Côte-d'Ivoire / Madagascar / Zaire
50	◄ Tanzania / Papua N. Guinea
	◄ Rwanda
0	**1984**

30

**Production: Bananas (fresh),
sugar (centrifugal), coffee (green)**

**Production: bananes fraîches,
sucre centrifugé, café vert**

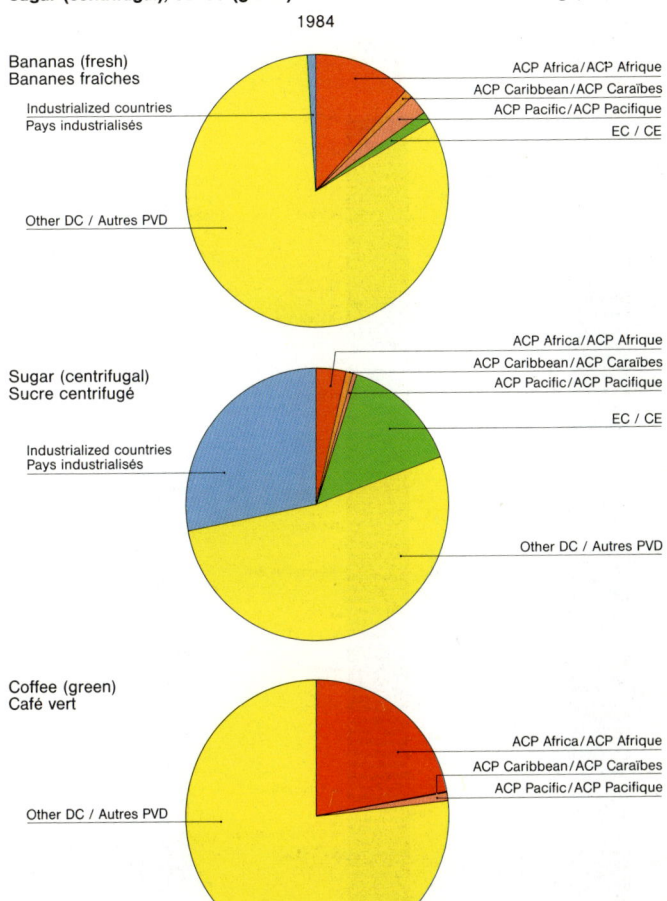

1984

Bananas (fresh)
Bananes fraîches

ACP Africa/ACP Afrique
ACP Caribbean/ACP Caraïbes
ACP Pacific/ACP Pacifique
EC / CE

Industrialized countries
Pays industrialisés

Other DC / Autres PVD

ACP Africa/ACP Afrique
ACP Caribbean/ACP Caraïbes
ACP Pacific/ACP Pacifique

EC / CE

Sugar (centrifugal)
Sucre centrifugé

Industrialized countries
Pays industrialisés

Other DC / Autres PVD

Coffee (green)
Café vert

ACP Africa/ACP Afrique
ACP Caribbean/ACP Caraïbes
ACP Pacific/ACP Pacifique

Other DC / Autres PVD

Production: Tea, cocoa beans, groundnuts (in shell), 1 000 t

Production: thé, fèves de cacao, arachides non décortiquées, 1 000 t

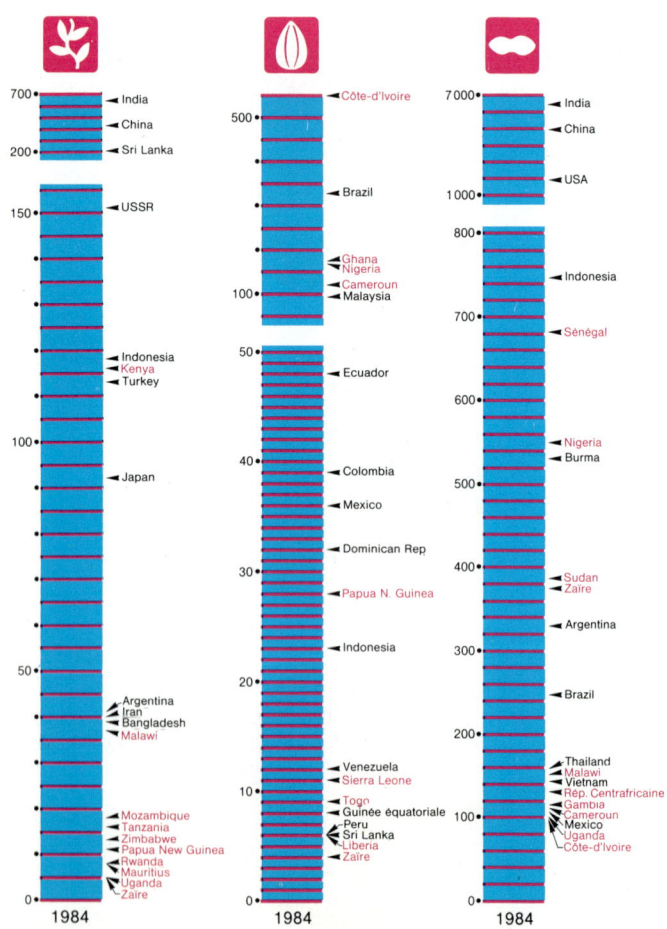

Tea
- 700 — India
- China
- 200 — Sri Lanka
- 150 — USSR
- Indonesia
- Kenya
- Turkey
- 100 — Japan
- 50 — Argentina
- Iran
- Bangladesh
- Malawi
- Mozambique
- Tanzania
- Zimbabwe
- Papua New Guinea
- Rwanda
- Mauritius
- Uganda
- Zaïre
- 0

1984

Cocoa beans
- 500 — Côte-d'Ivoire
- Brazil
- Ghana
- Nigeria
- 100 — Cameroun
- Malaysia
- 50 — Ecuador
- 40 — Colombia
- Mexico
- Dominican Rep
- 30 — Papua N. Guinea
- Indonesia
- 20 — Venezuela
- Sierra Leone
- 10 — Togo
- Guinée équatoriale
- Peru
- Sri Lanka
- Liberia
- Zaïre
- 0

1984

Groundnuts
- 7 000 — India
- China
- USA
- 1 000
- 800 — Indonesia
- 700 — Sénégal
- 600
- Nigeria
- 500 — Burma
- 400 — Sudan
- Zaïre
- Argentina
- 300 — Brazil
- 200 — Thailand
- Malawi
- Vietnam
- Rép. Centrafricaine
- Gambia
- 100 — Cameroun
- Mexico
- Uganda
- Côte-d'Ivoire
- 0

1984

Production: Tea, cocoa beans, groundnuts (in shell)

Production: thé, fèves de cacao arachides non décortiquées

1984

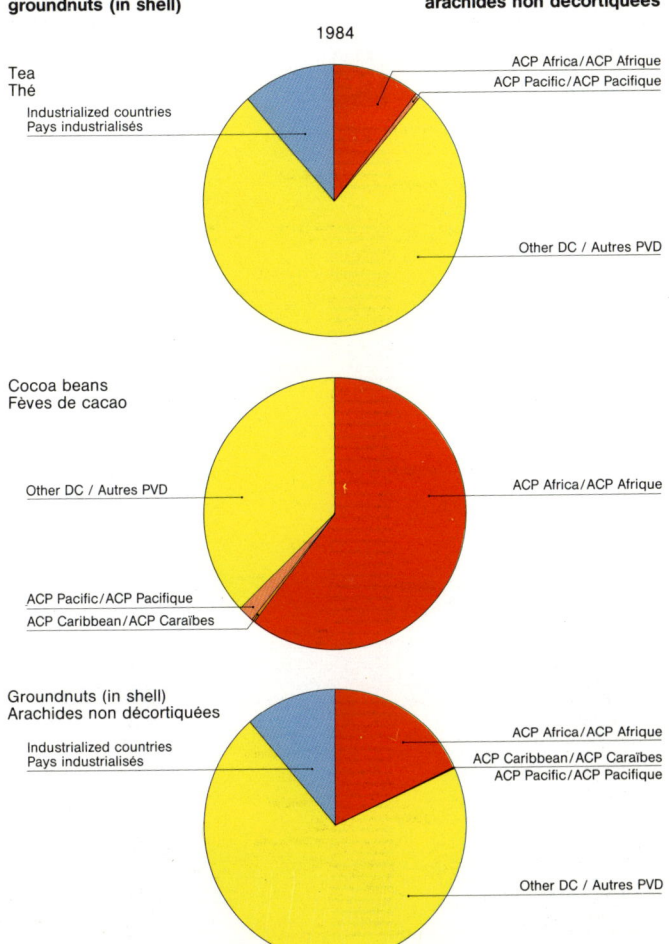

Tea
Thé

ACP Africa/ACP Afrique
ACP Pacific/ACP Pacifique

Industrialized countries
Pays industrialisés

Other DC / Autres PVD

Cocoa beans
Fèves de cacao

Other DC / Autres PVD

ACP Africa/ACP Afrique

ACP Pacific/ACP Pacifique
ACP Caribbean/ACP Caraïbes

Groundnuts (in shell)
Arachides non décortiquées

Industrialized countries
Pays industrialisés

ACP Africa/ACP Afrique
ACP Caribbean/ACP Caraïbes
ACP Pacific/ACP Pacifique

Other DC / Autres PVD

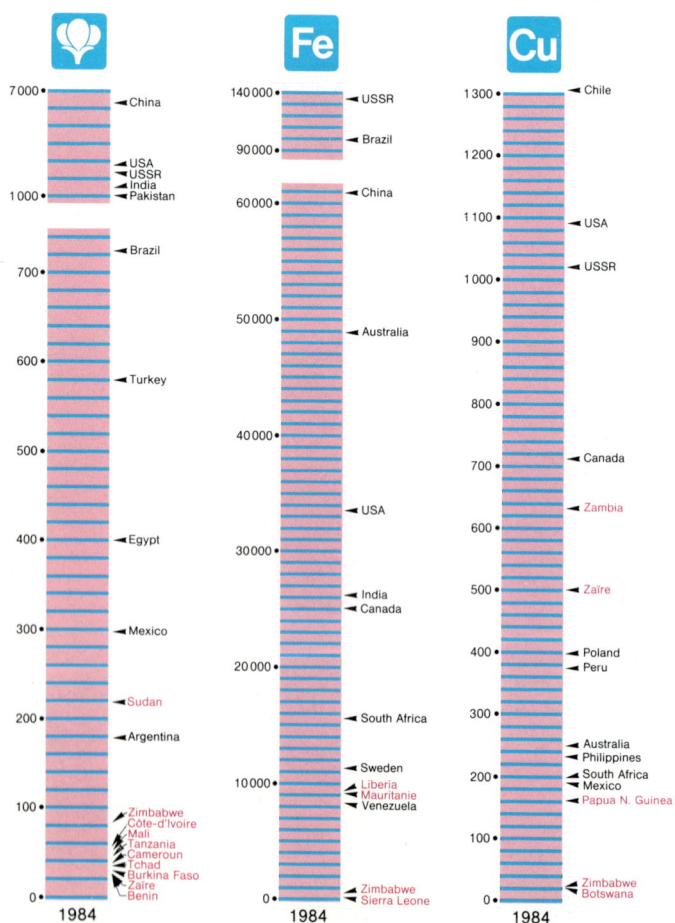

Production: Cotton (lint), iron ore (Fe content), copper ore (Cu content), 1 000 t

Production: fibres de coton, minerai de fer (Fe contenu), minerai de cuivre (Cu contenu), 1 000 t

Cotton (lint)

- 7 000 — China
- USA
- USSR
- India
- 1 000 — Pakistan
- Brazil
- 700 — Turkey
- 600 — Turkey
- 500 — Egypt
- 400 — Egypt
- 300 — Mexico
- Sudan
- 200 — Argentina
- 100 — Zimbabwe
- Côte-d'Ivoire
- Mali
- Tanzania
- Cameroun
- Tchad
- Burkina Faso
- Zaïre
- 0 — Benin

1984

Fe

- 140 000 — USSR
- 90 000 — Brazil
- 60 000 — China
- 50 000 — Australia
- 40 000 — USA
- 30 000 — India
- Canada
- 20 000 — South Africa
- Sweden
- Liberia
- Mauritanie
- 10 000 — Venezuela
- 0 — Zimbabwe
- Sierra Leone

1984

Cu

- 1 300 — Chile
- 1 200
- 1 100 — USA
- 1 000 — USSR
- 900
- 800
- 700 — Canada
- 600 — Zambia
- 500 — Zaïre
- 400 — Poland
- Peru
- 300 — Australia
- Philippines
- 200 — South Africa
- Mexico
- Papua N. Guinea
- 100
- 0 — Zimbabwe
- Botswana

1984

34

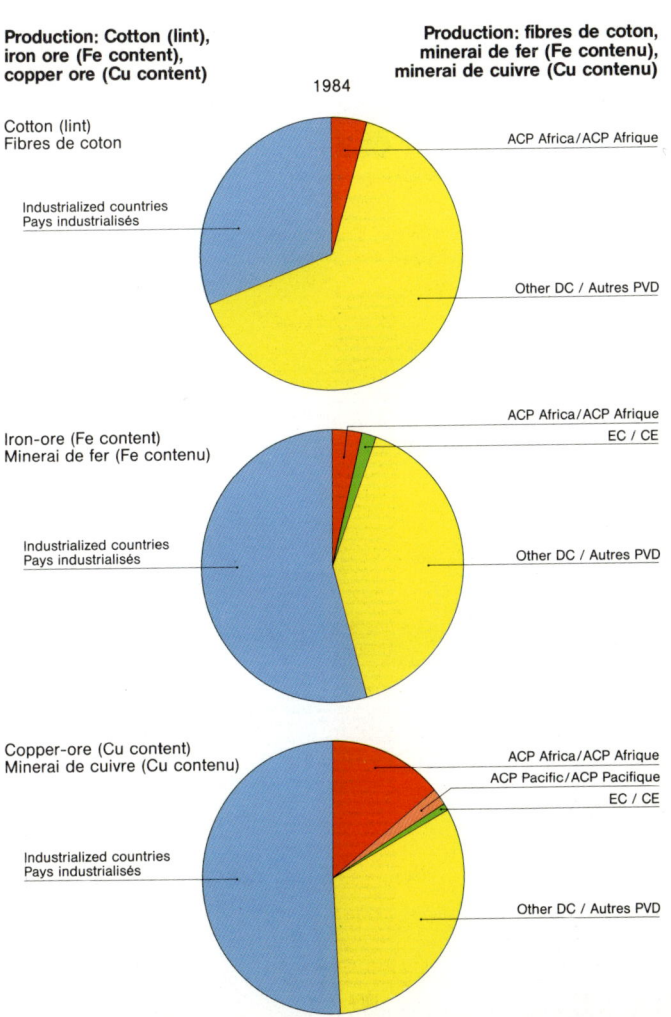

Production: Cotton (lint), iron ore (Fe content), copper ore (Cu content)

Production: fibres de coton, minerai de fer (Fe contenu), minerai de cuivre (Cu contenu)

1984

Cotton (lint)
Fibres de coton

ACP Africa/ACP Afrique

Industrialized countries
Pays industrialisés

Other DC / Autres PVD

Iron-ore (Fe content)
Minerai de fer (Fe contenu)

ACP Africa/ACP Afrique
EC / CE

Industrialized countries
Pays industrialisés

Other DC / Autres PVD

Copper-ore (Cu content)
Minerai de cuivre (Cu contenu)

ACP Africa/ACP Afrique
ACP Pacific/ACP Pacifique
EC / CE

Industrialized countries
Pays industrialisés

Other DC / Autres PVD

Production: Bauxite, phosphate rock, 1 000 t; crude petroleum, Mio t

Production: bauxite, phosphates naturels, 1 000 t; pétrole brut, Mio t

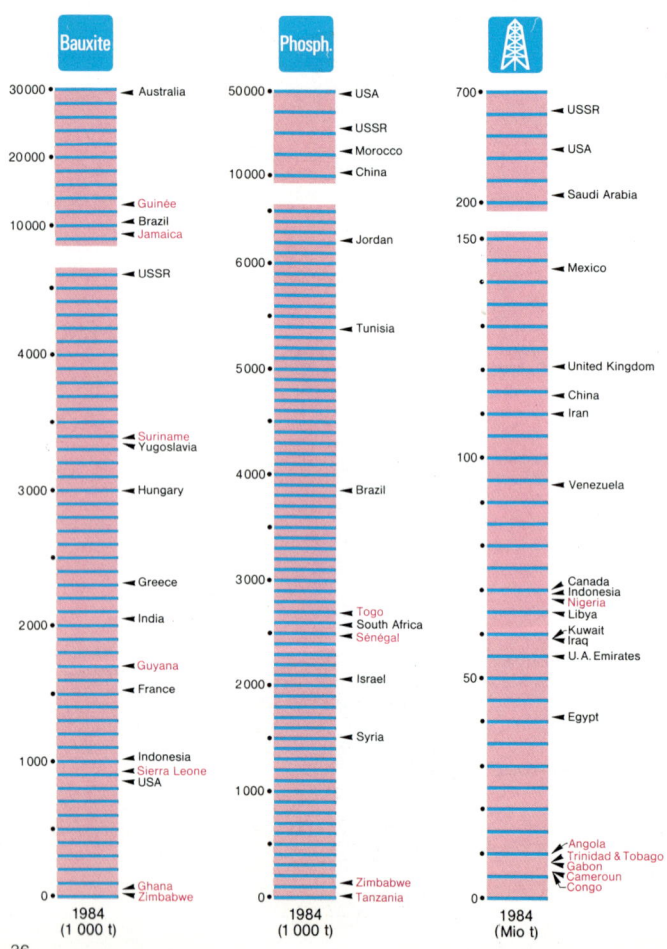

Bauxite (1984, 1 000 t)

- 30 000 — Australia
- 20 000
- Guinée
- 10 000 — Brazil
- Jamaica
- USSR
- 4 000
- Suriname / Yugoslavia
- 3 000 — Hungary
- Greece
- 2 000 — India
- Guyana
- France
- 1 000 — Indonesia
- Sierra Leone
- USA
- 0 — Ghana / Zimbabwe

Phosph. (1984, 1 000 t)

- 50 000 — USA
- USSR
- Morocco
- 10 000 — China
- Jordan
- 6 000
- Tunisia
- 5 000
- Brazil
- 3 000 — Togo / South Africa / Sénégal
- 2 000 — Israel
- Syria
- 1 000
- 0 — Zimbabwe / Tanzania

Pétrole (1984, Mio t)

- 700 — USSR
- USA
- 200 — Saudi Arabia
- 150 — Mexico
- United Kingdom
- China
- Iran
- 100 — Venezuela
- Canada / Indonesia / Nigeria / Libya / Kuwait / Iraq / U.A. Emirates
- 50 — Egypt
- Angola / Trinidad & Tobago / Gabon / Cameroun / Congo
- 0

36

Production: Bauxite, phosphate rock, crude petroleum

Production: bauxite, phosphates naturels, pétrole brut

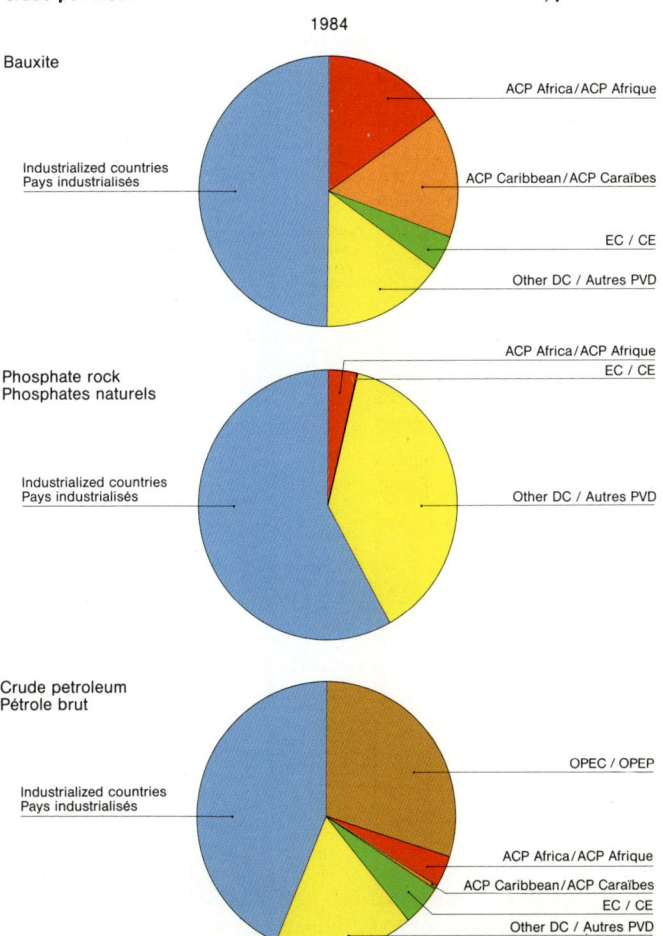

1984

Bauxite

ACP Africa / ACP Afrique

ACP Caribbean / ACP Caraïbes

EC / CE

Other DC / Autres PVD

Industrialized countries
Pays industrialisés

**Phosphate rock
Phosphates naturels**

ACP Africa / ACP Afrique
EC / CE

Other DC / Autres PVD

Industrialized countries
Pays industrialisés

**Crude petroleum
Pétrole brut**

OPEC / OPEP

ACP Africa / ACP Afrique

ACP Caribbean / ACP Caraïbes
EC / CE

Other DC / Autres PVD

Industrialized countries
Pays industrialisés

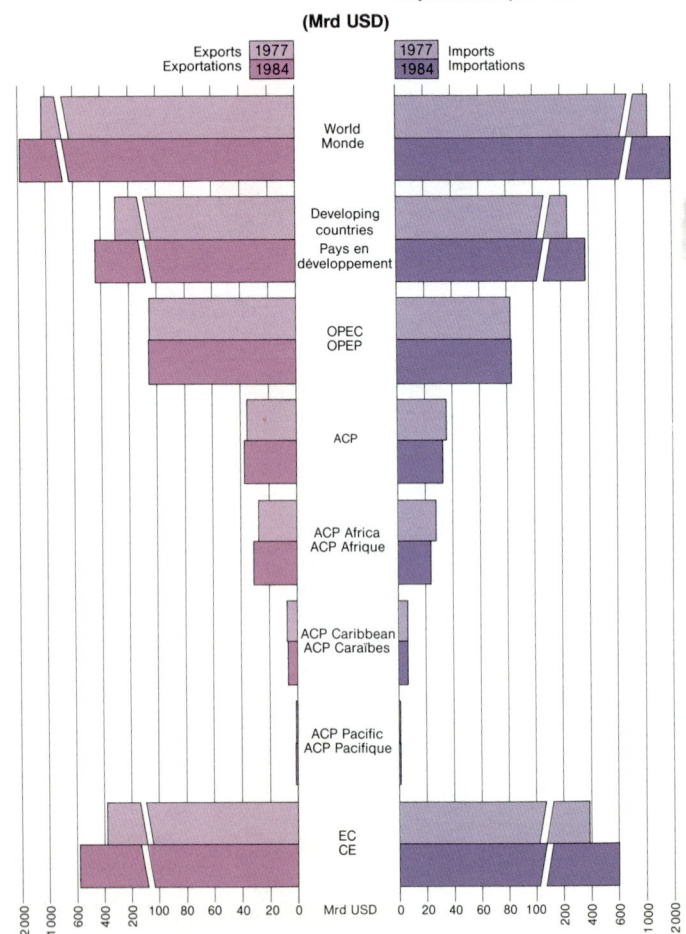

(Mrd USD)

Exports / Exportations — 1977 / 1984

Imports / Importations — 1977 / 1984

World / Monde

Developing countries / Pays en développement

OPEC / OPEP

ACP

ACP Africa / ACP Afrique

ACP Caribbean / ACP Caraïbes

ACP Pacific / ACP Pacifique

EC / CE

2000 1000 600 400 200 100 80 60 40 20 0   Mrd USD   0 20 40 60 80 100 200 400 600 1000 2000

External trade: EC imports, EC exports

Commerce extérieur: CE-importations, CE-exportations

(Mrd ECU)

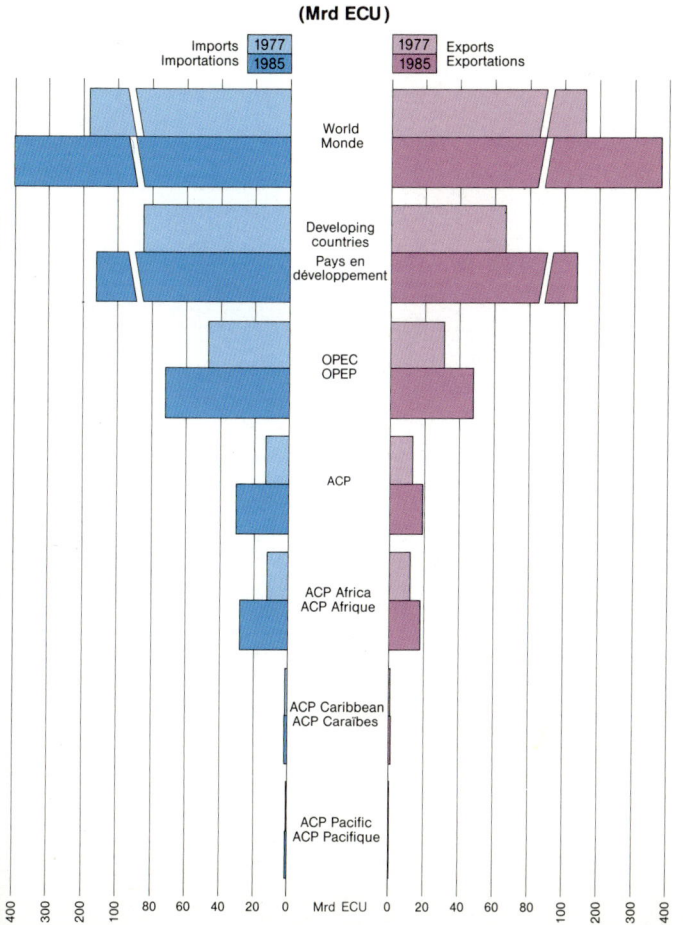

Imports / Importations — 1977, 1985

Exports / Exportations — 1977, 1985

World / Monde

Developing countries / Pays en développement

OPEC / OPEP

ACP

ACP Africa / ACP Afrique

ACP Caribbean / ACP Caraïbes

ACP Pacific / ACP Pacifique

400 300 200 100 80 60 40 20 0   Mrd ECU   0 20 40 60 80 100 200 300 400

Report. countries	1977		1981		1984		Pays déclarants
	‰	Mio	‰	Mio	‰	Mio	
World	1 000,0	4 421	1 000,0	4 628	1 000,0	4 763	**Monde**
Developing	669,6	2 960	695,4	3 218	718,7	3 423	Pays en voie de dév.
of which:							dont:
OPEC	71,0	313	75,6	350	79,8	380	OPEP
Non-OPEC	598,6	2 646	619,8	2 868	638,8	3 043	Non OPEP
ACP	77,9	344	83,2	385	88,6	422	ACP
of which:							dont:
Africa	75,8	335	81,1	375	86,4	411	Afrique
Caribbean	1,2	5	1,2	5	1,1	5	Caraïbes
Pacific	0,9	4	0,9	4	1,0	4	Pacifique
EC	71,0	314	68,9	319	67,3	321	CE

1984

Non-ACP countries Pays non ACP	‰	Mio	ACP countries Pays ACP	‰	Mio
1. China	216,0	1 029	1. Nigeria	20,2	96
2. India	157,2	749	2. Ethiopia	8,8	42
3. USSR	57,7	275	3. Zaïre	6,2	29
4. USA	49,7	237	4. Tanzania	4,5	21
5. Indonesia	33,3	158	5. Sudan	4,4	21
6. Brazil	27,8	132	6. Kenya	4,0	19
7. Japan	25,1	120	7. Uganda	3,1	15
8. Bangladesh	20,5	98	8. Mozambique	2,8	13
9. Pakistan	19,3	92	9. Ghana	2,5	12
10. Mexico	16,1	76	10. Madagascar	2,0	9
11. FR of Germany	12,8	61	11. Cameroun	2,0	9
12. Viet Nam	12,6	60	12. Côte-d'Ivoire	2,0	9
13. Italy	11,9	57	13. Angola	1,7	8
14. United Kingdom	11,8	56	14. Zimbabwe	1,7	8
15. France	11,5	54	15. Burkina Faso	1,6	7
16. Philippines	11,2	53	16. Mali	1,5	7
17. Thailand	10,4	50	17. Malawi	1,4	6
18. Turkey	10,1	48	18. Zambia	1,3	6
19. Egypt	9,6	45	19. Sénégal	1,3	6
20. Iran	9,1	43	20. Niger	1,3	6
Total	**733,7**	**3 493**	**Total**	**74,3**	**349**

GNP PER CAPITA
PNB PAR HABITANT

Reporting countries	1977	1981	1984	Pays déclarants
	USD	USD	USD	
World	**1 887**	**2 513**	**2 502**	**Monde**
Developing	476	713	691	Pays en voie de dév.
of which:				*dont:*
OPEC	1 275	1 788	1 719	OPEP
Non-OPEC	381	582	563	Non OPEP
ACP	415	515	469	ACP
of which:				*dont:*
Africa	392	482	435	Afrique
Caribbean	1 699	2 658	2 956	Caraïbes
Pacific	692	1 033	1 025	Pacifique
EC	4 780	8 060	8 115	CE

1984

Industrial countries Pays industrialisés	USD	Non-ACP countries Pays non ACP	USD	ACP countries Pays ACP	USD
1. Switzerland	16 370	U. A. Emirates	21 830	Bahamas	6 710
2. United States	15 540	Qatar	19 010	Trinidad & Tobago	6 240
3. Norway	13 970	Brunei	18 910	Barbados	4 380
4. Canada	13 310	Kuwait	16 720	Gabon	3 580
5. Luxembourg	13 200	Bermuda	11 920	Suriname	2 680
6. Sweden	11 880	Saudi Arabia	10 980	Seychelles	2 429
7. Denmark	11 200	Bahrain	10 490	Antigua-Barbuda	1 870
8. FR of Germany	11 160	Libyan Arab Rep.	8 060	St Kitts & Nevis	1 820
9. Faeroe Islands	11 080	French Polynesia	7 630	St Kitts & Nevis	1 460
10. Australia	11 060	Singapore	7 470	Jamaica	1 160
11. Iceland	11 040	Oman	6 910	Congo	1 140
12. Finland	10 800	Hong Kong	6 370	St Lucia	1 130
13. Japan	10 650	Netherlands Antilles	6 220	Belize	1 110
14. France	9 810	New Caledonia	5 890	Dominica	1 090
15. Netherlands	9 540	Guam	5 510	Maurice	1 080
16. Austria	9 160	American Samoa	5 250	Djibouti	970
17. Belgium	8 630	Guadeloupe	5 210	Botswana	940
18. United Kingdom	8 590	Israel	5 090	Grenada	920
19. New Zealand	7 740	Martinique	4 820	St Vincent	830
20. Greenland	6 930	Puerto Rico	4 650	Cameroun	810
21. Italy	6 430	Cyprus	3 790		
22. Ireland	4 980	Réunion	3 580		
23. Spain	4 450	Venezuela	3 480		
24. Gibraltar	4 420	Malta	3 360		
25. Greece	3 780	Iran	3 030		

BANANAS (FRESH)
BANANES FRAÎCHES

Report. countries	1977		1981		1984		Pays déclarants
	‰	1 000 t	‰	1 000 t	‰	1 000 t	
World	**1 000,0**	**35 441**	**1 000,0**	**39 139**	**1 000,0**	**39 189**	**Monde**
Developing	980,9	34 766	978,6	38 304	978,4	38 345	Pays en voie de dév.
of which:							dont:
ACP	148,5	5 264	152,4	5 965	153,5	6 017	ACP
of which:							dont:
Africa	112,8	4 000	118,3	4 630	119,1	4 668	Afrique
Caribbean	10,2	361	9,4	368	10,0	393	Caraïbes
Pacific	25,4	902	24,7	966	24,3	955	Pacifique
EC	11,9	422	13,3	522	12,4	486	CE

1984

Non-ACP countries Pays non ACP	‰	1 000 t	ACP countries Pays ACP	‰	1 000 t
1. Brazil	180,2	7 062	1. Burundi	31,8	1 250
2. India	118,0	4 626	2. Tanzania	25,5	1 000
3. Philippines	58,6	2 299	3. Papua New Guinea	23,4	920
4. Mexico	53,4	2 093	4. Uganda	10,7	420
5. Ecuador	42,8	1 677	5. Zaïre	8,2	325
6. Thailand	39,4	1 545	6. Angola	7,1	280
7. Colombia	36,9	1 450	7. Madagascar	5,7	224
8. Honduras	31,8	1 250	8. Jamaica	3,8	150
9. Viet Nam	30,6	1 200	9. Côte-d'Ivoire	3,7	148
10. Costa Rica	29,6	1 160	10. Kenya	3,6	142
11. Panama	26,9	1 055	11. Guinée	2,6	103
12. Indonesia	25,8	1 012	12. St Lucia	2,1	85
13. Venezuela	24,6	964	13. Rép. Centrafricaine	2,0	82
14. Bangladesh	17,6	689	14. Liberia	2,0	79
15. Guatemala	17,3	680	15. Malawi	1,9	77
16. China	12,8	503	16. Ethiopia	1,8	74
17. Malaysia	12,1	475	17. Mozambique	1,7	70
18. Spain	11,2	439	18. Cameroun	1,6	65
19. Dominican Rep.	8,4	330	19. Somalia	1,5	62
20. Paraguay	8,2	325	20. Zimbabwe	1,5	62
Total	**786,2**	**30 834**	**Total**	**142,2**	**5 618**

SUGAR (CENTRIFUGAL)
SUCRE CENTRIFUGÉ

Report. countries	1977		1981		1984		Pays déclarants
	‰	1 000 t	‰	1 000 t	‰	1 000 t	
World	**1 000,0**	**89 659**	**1 000,0**	**93 263**	**1 000,0**	**100 509**	**Monde**
Developing	544,7	48 840	547,0	51 020	576,3	57 927	Pays en voie de dév.
of which:							*dont:*
ACP	45,0	4 038	49,5	4 624	49,3	4 962	ACP
of which:							*dont:*
Africa	29,9	2 686	35,5	3 318	36,8	3 700	Afrique
Caribbean	11,0	989	8,9	835	7,4	745	Caraïbes
Pacific	4,0	362	5,0	470	5,1	517	Pacifique
EC	152,8	13 704	183,5	17 118	143,4	14 418	CE

1984

	Non-ACP countries Pays non ACP	‰	1 000 t		ACP countries Pays ACP	‰	1 000 t
1.	Brazil	92,8	9 331	1.	Maurice	6,0	609
2.	USSR	86,4	8 685	2.	Zimbabwe	4,8	484
3.	Cuba	82,8	8 331	3.	Fiji	4,7	480
4.	India	63,9	6 430	4.	Sudan	4,5	454
5.	USA	53,3	5 363	5.	Swaziland	4,2	429
6.	China	52,7	5 298	6.	Kenya	4,0	404
7.	France	42,8	4 305	7.	Guyana	2,3	237
8.	Australia	35,3	3 548	8.	Ethiopia	1,9	201
9.	Mexico	32,8	3 297	9.	Jamaica	1,9	193
10.	FR of Germany	31,3	3 151	10.	Malawi	1,4	149
11.	South Africa	25,4	2 560	11.	Zambia	1,4	141
12.	Philippines	24,8	2 498	12.	Tanzania	1,3	131
13.	Thailand	23,3	2 350	13.	Côte-d'Ivoire	1,2	126
14.	Poland	18,6	1 878	14.	Belize	1,0	104
15.	Indonesia	17,6	1 777	15.	Barbados	0,9	100
16.	Turkey	16,4	1 655	16.	Madagascar	0,7	80
17.	Argentina	15,3	1 544	17.	Cameroun	0,7	73
18.	United Kingdom	13,9	1 400	18.	Trinidad & Tobago	0,6	69
19.	Italy	13,7	1 385	19.	Zaïre	0,6	60
20.	Pakistan	12,5	1 258	20.	Nigeria	0,5	58
	Total	**755,6**	**76 044**		**Total**	**44,6**	**4 582**

COFFEE (GREEN)
CAFÉ VERT

Report. countries	1977		1981		1984		Pays déclarants
	‰	1 000 t	‰	1 000 t	‰	1 000 t	
World	**1 000,0**	**4 408**	**1 000,0**	**6 036**	**1 000,0**	**5 185**	**Monde**
Developing	999,7	4 407	999,8	6 035	999,8	5 184	Pays en voie de dév.
of which:							*dont:*
ACP	290,0	1 278	219,0	1 322	233,0	1 208	ACP
of which:							*dont:*
Africa	280,1	1 234	209,6	1 265	233,3	1 158	Afrique
Caribbean	1,2	5	0,9	5	0,6	3	Caraïbes
Pacific	8,6	38	8,4	51	8,9	46	Pacifique

1983

Non-ACP countries Pays non ACP		‰	1 000 t	ACP countries Pays ACP		‰	1 000 t
1.	Brazil	273,9	1 420	1.	Ethiopia	46,2	240
2.	Colombia	133,7	693	2.	Uganda	39,3	204
3.	Indonesia	60,8	315	3.	Cameroun	25,0	130
4.	Mexico	46,2	239	4.	Kenya	22,8	118
5.	El Salvador	31,2	162	5.	Côte-d'Ivoire	16,4	85
6.	Costa Rica	29,1	151	6.	Madagascar	15,6	81
7.	Guatemala	27,0	140	7.	Zaïre	15,6	81
8.	Philippines	23,5	122	8.	Tanzania	10,2	53
9.	India	20,2	105	9.	Papua New Guinea	8,9	46
10.	Ecuador	18,7	97	10.	Rwanda	6,4	33
11.	Peru	16,8	87	11.	Angola	5,2	27
12.	Honduras	14,0	72	12.	Burundi	5,0	26
13.	Dominican Rep.	13,9	72	13.	Rép. Centrafricaine	2,8	15
14.	Venezuela	11,7	61	14.	Guinée	2,8	14
15.	Nicaragua	9,7	50	15.	Zimbabwe	2,2	11
16.	Haiti	6,9	36	16.	Liberia	2,2	11
17.	Cuba	4,2	22	17.	Eq. Guinea	1,3	6
18.	Thailand	3,4	18	18.	Bénin	0,5	3
19.	Bolivia	3,3	17	19.	Nigeria	0,5	3
20.	China	3,2	17	20.	Togo	0,5	2
	Total	**751,4**	**3 896**		**Total**	**229,4**	**1 189**

TEA
THÉ

Report. countries	1977		1981		1984		Pays déclarants
	‰	1 000 t	‰	1 000 t	‰	1 000 t	
World	**1 000,0**	**1 750**	**1 000,0**	**1 874**	**1 000,0**	**2 185**	**Monde**
Developing	878,6	1 538	869,8	1 630	886,1	1 937	Pays en voie de dév.
of which:							*dont:*
ACP	113,5	198	108,6	203	112,4	245	ACP
of which:							*dont:*
Africa	109,5	191	103,7	194	107,1	234	Afrique
Pacific	3,9	7	4,9	9	5,2	11	Pacifique

1984

Non-ACP countries Pays non ACP	‰	1 000 t	ACP countries Pays ACP	‰	1 000 t
1. India	295,0	645	1. Kenya	53,1	116
2. China	200,5	438	2. Malawi	17,0	37
3. Sri Lanka	95,2	208	3. Mozambique	8,2	18
4. USSR	69,1	151	4. Tanzania	7,5	16
5. Indonesia	54,3	118	5. Zimbabwe	5,9	13
6. Turkey	52,0	113	6. Papua New Guinea	5,0	11
7. Japan	42,3	92	7. Rwanda	3,9	8
8. Argentina	18,9	41	8. Maurice	3,6	8
9. Iran	18,2	40	9. Uganda	2,3	5
10. Bangladesh	17,9	39	10. Zaïre	2,2	5
11. Taiwan	11,1	24	11. Burundi	1,5	3
12. Viet Nam	11,0	24	12. Cameroun	1,0	2
13. Brazil	4,3	9			
14. South Africa	2,2	5			
15. Malaysia	1,6	3			
16. Ecuador	1,2	2			
17. Peru	0,9	2			
18. Thailand	0,9	2			
19. Bolivia	0,7	1			
Total	**897,3**	**1 957**	**Total**	**111,2**	**242**

COCOA BEANS
FÈVES DE CACAO

Report. countries	1977		1981		1984		Pays déclarants
	‰	1 000 t	‰	1 000 t	‰	1 000 t	
World	**1 000,0**	**1 464**	**1 000,0**	**1 737**	**1 000,0**	**1 765**	**Monde**
Developing	1000,0	1 464	1 000,0	1 737	1 000,0	1 765	Pays en voie de dév.
of which:							*dont:*
ACP	671,6	983	639,8	1 111	629,2	1 110	ACP
of which:							*dont:*
Africa	644,3	943	614,4	1 067	606,0	1 069	Afrique
Caribbean	5,6	8	4,6	8	4,3	7	Caraïbes
Pacific	21,6	31	20,7	36	18,9	33	Pacifique

1984

Non-ACP countries Pays non ACP	‰	1 000 t	ACP countries Pays ACP	‰	1 000 t
1. Brazil	186,9	329	1. Côte-d'Ivoire	311,6	550
2. Malaysia	53,8	95	2. Ghana	98,0	173
3. Ecuador	27,5	48	3. Nigeria	96,3	170
4. Colombia	22,0	39	4. Cameroun	68,5	121
5. Mexico	20,4	36	5. Papua New Guinea	16,0	28
6. Dominican Rep.	18,6	32	6. Sierra Leone	6,4	11
7. Indonesia	13,5	23	7. Togo	5,5	9
8. Venezuela	6,9	12	8. Eq. Guinea	4,5	8
9. Peru	3,8	6	9. Liberia	3,4	6
10. Sri Lanka	3,7	6	10. Zaïre	2,4	4
11. Philippines	2,8	5	11. Guinée	2,2	4
12. Haiti	2,6	4	12. São Tomé & Principe	1,9	3
13. Costa Rica	1,9	3	13. Madagascar	1,6	3
14. Bolivia	1,6	3	14. Jamaica	1,5	2
15. Cuba	1,0	1	15. Grenada	1,4	2
16. Guatemala	1,0	1	16. Western Samoa	1,1	2
17. Panama	0,8	1	17. Gabon	1,1	2
18. Honduras	0,5	1	18. Solomon Islands	0,9	1
			19. Congo	0,9	1
			20. Trinidad & Tobago	0,9	1
Total	**369,3**	**645**	**Total**	**626,1**	**1 101**

GROUNDNUTS (IN SHELL)
ARACHIDES NON DÉCORTIQUÉES

Report. countries	1977		1981		1984		Pays déclarants
	‰	1 000 t	‰	1 000 t	‰	1 000 t	
World	**1 000,0**	**17 367**	**1 000,0**	**20 721**	**1 000,0**	**20 061**	**Monde**
Developing	880,0	15 283	890,1	18 445	889,5	17 845	Pays en voie de dév.
of which:							*dont:*
ACP	250,2	4 345	217,5	4 507	182,5	3 661	ACP
of which:							*dont:*
Africa	249,8	4 339	217,1	4 499	182,0	3 653	Afrique
Caribbean	0,1	2	0,2	4	0,1	4	Caraïbes
Pacific	0,1	3	0,1	4	0,2	4	Pacifique

1984

Non-ACP countries Pays non ACP	‰	1 000 t	ACP countries Pays ACP	‰	1 000 t
1. India	320,5	6 430	1. Sénégal	34,0	682
2. China	244,3	4 902	2. Nigeria	27,4	550
3. USA	99,6	1 998	3. Sudan	19,2	386
4. Indonesia	37,2	747	4. Zaïre	18,7	375
5. Burma	26,4	531	5. Malawi	8,4	170
6. Argentina	16,3	328	6. Rép. Centrafricaine	6,4	130
7. Brazil	12,3	248	7. Gambia	5,6	114
8. Thailand	8,9	179	8. Cameroun	5,4	110
9. Viet Nam	8,0	162	9. Uganda	4,9	100
10. Mexico	5,2	105	10. Côte-d'Ivoire	4,8	98
11. Taiwan	4,3	87	11. Ghana	4,4	90
12. South Africa	3,7	75	12. Tchad	4,4	90
13. Pakistan	3,5	71	13. Burkina Faso	4,1	83
14. Japan	2,5	51	14. Guinée	4,0	81
15. Turkey	2,3	47	15. Burundi	3,9	80
16. Australia	2,3	47	16. Mozambique	3,4	70
17. Haiti	2,2	45	17. Tanzania	2,9	59
18. Philippines	2,1	42	18. Bénin	2,8	57
19. Dominican Rep.	2,0	42	19. Mali	2,6	54
20. Paraguay	1,8	37	20. Madagascar	1,5	31
Total	**805,4**	**16 174**	**Total**	**168,8**	**3 410**

COTTON (LINT)
FIBRES DE COTON

Report. countries	1977		1981		1984		Pays déclarants
	‰	1 000 t	‰	1 000 t	‰	1 000 t	
World	**1 000,0**	**13 965**	**1 000,0**	**15 277**	**1 000,0**	**18 267**	**Monde**
Developing	560,5	7 827	558,0	8 525	691,5	12 632	Pays en voie de dév.
of which:							dont:
ACP	46,6	651	37,4	572	44,2	808	ACP
of which:							dont:
Africa	46,6	651	37,4	572	44,2	808	Afrique
Caribbean	–	–	–	–	–	–	Caraïbes

1984

Non-ACP countries Pays non ACP	‰	1 000 t	ACP countries Pays ACP	‰	1 000 t
1. China	342,5	6 258	1. Sudan	11,9	219
2. USA	154,7	2 826	2. Zimbabwe	4,5	84
3. USSR	128,2	2 343	3. Côte-d'Ivoire	3,1	58
4. India	79,1	1 446	4. Mali	2,9	54
5. Pakistan	55,2	1 008	5. Tanzania	2,6	47
6. Brazil	39,5	723	6. Cameroun	2,0	38
7. Turkey	31,7	580	7. Tchad	1,9	35
8. Egypt	21,8	400	8. Burkina Faso	1,6	29
9. Mexico	16,4	299	9. Zaïre	1,4	26
10. Argentina	9,8	179	10. Bénin	1,4	26
11. Syria	8,6	158	11. Ethiopia	1,2	22
12. Greece	7,7	142	12. Sénégal	1,1	21
13. Australia	7,7	141	13. Uganda	1,0	19
14. Colombia	6,9	126	14. Nigeria	0,8	16
15. Iran	6,1	112	15. Zambia	0,8	15
16. Paraguay	5,7	105	16. Mozambique	0,8	15
17. Peru	5,1	94	17. Madagascar	0,6	12
18. Israel	4,7	87	18. Rép. Centrafricaine	0,6	12
19. Nicaragua	4,6	85	19. Swaziland	0,6	11
20. Guatemala	3,2	58	20. Angola	0,6	11
Total	**939,2**	**17 170**	**Total**	**41,4**	**770**

IRON ORE (Fe content)
MINERAI DE FER (Fe contenu)

Report. countries	1977		1981		1984		Pays déclarants
	‰	1 000 t	‰	1 000 t	‰	1 000 t	
World	**1 000,0**	**511 869**	**1 000,0**	**534 620**	**1 000,0**	**523 209**	**Monde**
Developing	366,0	187 388	393,7	210 525	440,8	230 649	Pays en voie de dév.
of which:							*dont:*
ACP	37,0	18 976	37,0	19 817	36,8	19 274	ACP
of which:							*dont:*
Africa	37,0	18 976	37,0	19 817	36,8	19 274	Afrique
EC	36,0	18 451	22,5	12 001	17,1	8 959	CE

1984

Non-ACP countries Pays non ACP	‰	1 000 t	ACP countries Pays ACP	‰	1 000 t
1. USSR	257,6	134 809	1. Liberia	17,8	9 359
2. Brazil	189,3	99 072	2. Mauritania	17,3	9 100
3. China	116,5	60 960	3. Zimbabwe	1,1	591
4. Australia	93,5	48 946	4. Sierra Leone	0,4	224
5. USA	64,2	33 640			
6. India	50,0	26 188			
7. Canada	47,8	25 050			
8. South Africa	29,9	15 677			
9. Sweden	21,7	11 378			
10. Venezuela	15,9	8 348			
11. Mexico	10,1	5 307			
12. France	8,9	4 679			
13. Chile	8,2	4 341			
14. Spain	6,4	3 360			
15. Korea DPR	6,2	3 250			
16. Norway	4,7	2 500			
17. Peru	4,5	2 405			
18. Turkey	4,3	2 282			
19. Algeria	3,7	1 975			
20. Yugoslavia	3,5	1 861			
Total	**946,9**	**496 028**	**Total**	**36,6**	**19 274**

COPPER ORE (Cu content)
MINERAI DE CUIVRE (Cu contenu)

Report. countries	1977		1981		1984		Pays déclarants
	‰	1 000 t	‰	1 000 t	‰	1 000 t	
World	**1 000,0**	**8 062**	**1 000,0**	**8 414**	**1 000,0**	**8 308**	**Monde**
Developing	427,8	3 449	426,4	3 588	484,0	4 021	Pays en voie de dév.
of which:							*dont:*
ACP	172,5	1 391	155,4	1 308	161,6	1 343	ACP
of which:							*dont:*
Africa	149,9	1 208	135,8	1 142	142,0	1 180	Afrique
Pacific	22,6	182	19,6	165	19,5	162	Pacifique
EC	5,3	43	6,8	57	7,8	65	CE

1984

Non-ACP countries Pays non ACP	‰	1 000 t	ACP countries Pays ACP	‰	1 000 t
1. Chile	157,1	1 305	1. Zambia	76,1	633
2. USA	131,3	1 091	2. Zaïre	60,3	501
3. USSR	122,7	1 020	3. Papua New Guinea	19,5	162
4. Canada	85,7	712	4. Zimbabwe	2,7	22
5. Poland	47,9	398	5. Botswana	2,5	21
6. Peru	45,1	375			
7. Australia	29,9	249			
8. Philippines	28,0	233			
9. South Africa	23,8	198			
10. Mexico	22,9	190			
11. China	21,6	180			
12. Iran	18,7	156			
13. Yugoslavia	16,4	136			
14. Sweden	10,8	90			
15. Indonesia	9,9	82			
16. Bulgaria	8,7	73			
17. Spain	7,6	63			
18. India	5,7	47			
19. Japan	5,1	43			
20. Turkey	4,6	38			
Total	**803,5**	**6 679**	**Total**	**161,1**	**1 339**

BAUXITE
BAUXITE

Report. countries	1977		1981		1984		Pays déclarants
	‰	1 000 t	‰	1 000 t	‰	1 000 t	
World	**1 000,0**	**80 146**	**1 000,0**	**88 407**	**1 000,0**	**90 931**	**Monde**
Developing	479,7	38 448	485,5	42 924	460,0	41 837	Pays en voie de dév.
of which:							dont:
OPEC	16,2	1 301	13,6	1 203	11,0	1 003	OPEP
Non-OPEC	463,4	37 147	471,9	41 721	449,0	40 834	Non – OPEP
ACP	393,1	31 510	357,6	31 623	305,7	27 799	ACP
of which:							dont:
Africa	148,1	11 876	153,9	13 614	153,7	13 985	Afrique
Caribbean	244,9	19 634	203,7	18 009	151,9	13 814	Caraïbes
EC	62,2	4 984	57,9	5 120	42,3	3 849	CE

1984

Non-ACP countries Pays non ACP	‰	1 000 t	ACP countries Pays ACP	‰	1 000 t
1. Australia	322,2	29 300	1. Guinée	142,8	12 986
2. Brazil	113,8	10 355	2. Jamaica	96,0	8 735
3. USSR	50,5	4 600	3. Suriname	37,1	3 375
4. Yugoslavia	36,8	3 347	4. Guyana	18,7	1 704
5. Hungary	32,9	2 994	5. Sierra Leone	10,1	924
6. Greece	25,4	2 313	6. Ghana	0,5	52
7. India	22,4	2 045	7. Zimbabwe	0,2	23
8. France	16,7	1 527			
9. Indonesia	11,0	1 003			
10. USA	9,4	856			
11. Malaysia	6,9	635			
12. Romania	5,0	460			
13. Turkey	3,3	306			
14. Spain	0,1	10			
Total	**656,4**	**59 751**	**Total**	**305,4**	**27 799**

PHOSPHATE ROCK
PHOSPHATES NATURELS

Report. countries	1977		1981		1984		Pays déclarants
	‰	1 000 t	‰	1 000 t	‰	1 000 t	
World	**1 000,0**	**119 064**	**1 000,0**	**145 349**	**1 000,0**	**149 028**	**Monde**
Developing	315,1	37 526	360,9	52 457	418,4	62 367	Pays en voie de dév.
of which:							dont:
ACP	43,7	5 205	28,6	4 161	35,7	5 326	ACP
of which:							dont:
Africa	40,1	4 786	28,6	4 161	35,7	5 326	Afrique
EC	0,7	84	0,0	12	0,2	40	CE

1984

Non-ACP countries Pays non ACP	‰	1 000 t	ACP countries Pays ACP	‰	1 000 t
1. USA	330,1	49 197	1. Togo	18,0	2 696
2. USSR	214,0	31 900	2. Sénégal	16,6	2 481
3. Morocco	143,2	21 351	3. Zimbabwe	0,8	134
4. China	79,1	11 800	4. Tanzania	0,1	15
5. Jordan	41,6	6 213			
6. Tunisia	36,1	5 385			
7. Brazil	25,8	3 855			
8. South Africa	17,3	2 585			
9. Israel	13,8	2 065			
10. Syria	10,1	1 515			
11. Nauru	9,1	1 358			
12. Egypt	6,9	1 043			
13. Algeria	6,7	1 000			
14. India	5,9	884			
15. Mexico	3,4	518			
16. Korea DPR	3,3	500			
17. Viet Nam	1,3	200			
18. Turkey	0,6	96			
19. Colombia	0,1	28			
Total	**948,4**	**141 493**	**Total**	**35,5**	**5 326**

CRUDE PETROLEUM
PÉTROLE BRUT

Report. countries	1977		1981		1984		Pays déclarants
	‰	Mio t	‰	Mio t	‰	Mio t	
World	**1 000,0**	**2 970**	**1 000,0**	**2 794**	**1 000,0**	**2 708**	**Monde**
Developing	621,4	1 846	549,1	1 534	512,6	1 388	Pays en voie de dév.
of which:							*dont:*
OPEC	521,1	1 547	404,6	1 130	327,6	887	OPEP
Non-OPEC	100,3	298	144,5	403	184,9	501	Non OPEP
ACP	45,8	136	37,8	105	41,0	111	ACP
of which:							*dont:*
Africa	41,8	124	34,3	96	37,8	102	Afrique
Caribbean	3,9	11	3,5	9	3,2	8	Caraïbes
EC	16,2	48	35,4	99	51,3	139	CE

1984

Non-ACP countries Pays non ACP	‰	Mio t	ACP countries Pays ACP	‰	Mio t
1. USSR	226,2	612	1. Nigeria	25,2	68
2. USA	161,7	438	2. Angola	3,8	10
3. Saudi Arabia	86,5	234	3. Trinidad & Tobago	3,2	8
4. Mexico	52,9	143	4. Gabon	3,0	8
5. United Kingdom	44,7	121	5. Cameroun	2,3	6
6. China	42,2	114	6. Congo	2,2	6
7. Iran	40,9	110	7. Zaïre	0,5	1
8. Venezuela	34,8	94	8. Côte-d'Ivoire	0,4	1
9. Canada	26,0	70			
10. Indonesia	25,5	69			
11. Libya	24,2	65			
12. Kuwait	22,1	59			
13. Iraq	21,9	59			
14. U. A. Emirates	20,6	55			
15. Egypt	15,1	41			
16. Norway	12,9	35			
17. Algeria	10,4	28			
18. India	10,3	27			
19. Argentina	9,0	24			
Total	**887,9**	**2 398**	**Total**	**40,6**	**108**

EXPORTS TO WORLD
EXPORTATIONS VERS LE MONDE

Report. countries	1977		1981		1984		Pays déclarants
	‰	Mio USD	‰	Mio USD	‰	Mio USD	
World	**1 000,0**	**1 126 999**	**1 000,0**	**1 975 399**	**1 000,0**	**1 903 599**	**Monde**
Developing	260,1	293 230	263,9	521 429	231,5	440 830	Pays en voie de dév.
of which:							*dont:*
OPEC	133,4	150 409	130,2	257 369	82,9	157 932	OPEP
Non-OPEC	126,7	142 822	133,6	264 064	148,6	282 899	Non OPEP
ACP	31,4	35 400	27,0	53 418	19,9	37 931	ACP
of which:							*dont:*
Africa	24,3	27 453	21,2	42 067	15,9	30 278	Afrique
Caribbean	6,2	7 057	5,0	10 063	3,3	6 338	Caraïbes
Pacific	0,7	889	0,6	1 287	0,6	1 315	Pacifique
EC (¹)	337,1	379 956	308,1	608 743	305,6	581 850	CE (¹)

(¹) EUR 10.

1984

Non-ACP countries Pays non ACP	‰	Mio USD	ACP countries Pays ACP	‰	Mio USD
1. USA	114,4	217 888	1. Nigeria	7,4	14 124
2. FR of Germany	89,8	171 014	2. Côte-d'Ivoire	1,4	2 698
3. Japan	89,1	169 748	3. Bahamas	1,2	2 346
4. United Kingdom	49,4	94 226	4. Trinidad & Tobago	1,1	2 173
5. France	48,9	93 114	5. Angola	1,0	2 029
6. USSR	48,1	91 719	6. Gabon	0,9	1 801
7. Canada	45,6	86 862	7. Kenya	0,5	1 083
8. Italy	38,5	73 430	8. Zaïre	0,5	1 004
9. Netherlands	34,4	65 648	9. Zimbabwe	0,5	1 003
10. Belgium/Luxembourg	27,1	51 704	10. Cameroun	0,5	988
11. Saudi Arabia	19,3	36 834	11. Papua New Guinea	0,4	911
12. Sweden	15,3	29 315	12. Jamaica	0,3	738
13. Korea (Rep.)	15,3	29 247	13. Zambia	0,3	685
14. Hong Kong	14,8	28 317	14. Sudan	0,3	628
15. Brazil	14,1	27 005	15. Ghana	0,2	571
16. Switzerland	13,5	25 814	16. Sénégal	0,2	534
17. China	13,0	24 871	17. Liberia	0,2	449
18. German D. Rep.	13,0	24 836	18. Ethiopia	0,2	417
19. Singapore	12,6	24 055	19. Uganda	0,2	399
20. Australia	12,5	23 861	20. Barbados	0,2	391
Total	**728,7**	**1 389 508**	**Total**	**17,5**	**34 972**

IMPORTS FROM WORLD
IMPORTATIONS PROVENANCE MONDE

Report. countries	1977		1981		1984		Pays déclarants
	‰	Mio USD	‰	Mio USD	‰	Mio USD	
World	**1 000,0**	**1 165 899**	**1 000,0**	**2 035 299**	**1 000,0**	**1 992 800**	**Monde**
Developing	216,1	252 062	238,3	485 068	193,6	385 861	Pays en voie de dév.
of which:							*dont:*
OPEC	71,6	83 583	71,0	144 510	42,1	84 033	OPEP
Non-OPEC	144,5	168 479	167,3	340 561	151,4	301 828	Non OPEP
ACP	31,4	36 644	27,2	55 500	16,9	33 790	ACP
of which:							*dont:*
Africa	24,2	28 220	21,0	42 829	12,4	24 777	Afrique
Caribbean	6,4	7 473	5,2	10 674	3,6	7 368	Caraïbes
Pacific	0,8	950	0,9	1 995	0,8	1 644	Pacifique
EC (¹)	337,8	393 891	318,5	648 372	302,7	603 415	CE (¹)

(¹) EUR 10.

1984

Non-ACP countries Pays non ACP	‰	Mio USD	ACP countries Pays ACP	‰	Mio USD
1. USA	163,4	325 726	1. Nigeria	4,7	9 392
2. FR of Germany	76,2	152 017	2. Bahamas	1,5	3 025
3. Japan	68,3	136 142	3. Trinidad & Tobago	0,9	1 919
4. United Kingdom	52,7	105 176	4. Kenya	0,7	1 547
5. France	51,9	103 445	5. Côte-d'Ivoire	0,7	1 511
6. Italy	42,3	84 337	6. Jamaica	0,5	1 171
7. USSR	40,4	80 553	7. Sudan	0,5	1 146
8. Canada	37,1	74 004	8. Cameroun	0,5	1 087
9. Netherlands	31,1	61 981	9. Zimbabwe	0,5	1 052
10. Belgium/Luxembourg	27,7	55 252	10. Sénégal	0,5	1 010
11. Saudi Arabia	16,9	33 696	11. Papua New Guinea	0,4	969
12. Korea (Rep.)	15,3	30 608	12. Ethiopia	0,4	942
13. Switzerland	14,7	29 376	13. Gabon	0,3	726
14. Singapore	14,3	28 655	14. Zaïre	0,3	692
15. Spain	14,3	28 606	15. Barbados	0,3	658
16. Hong Kong	14,3	28 567	16. Angola	0,3	636
17. Sweden	13,2	26 340	17. Zambia	0,3	608
18. China	13,1	26 184	18. Ghana	0,2	591
19. Australia	11,7	23 425	19. Mozambique	0,2	487
20. German D. Rep.	11,5	22 940	20. Maurice	0,2	473
Total	**730,4**	**1 457 030**	**Total**	**13,9**	**29 642**

EC IMPORTS
CE-IMPORTATIONS

Report. countries	1977		1981		1985		Pays déclarants
	‰	Mio ECU	‰	Mio ECU	‰	Mio ECU	
World (¹)	**1 000,0**	**181 613**	**1 000,0**	**318 259**	**1 000,0**	**406 417**	**Monde (¹)**
Developing	470,6	85 476	465,1	148 033	397,4	161 520	Pays en voie de dév.
of which:							*dont:*
OPEC	261,6	47 513	269,7	85 850	177,6	72 202	OPEP
Non-OPEC	209,0	37 963	195,3	62 183	219,7	89 317	Non OPEP
ACP	74,3	13 500	58,8	18 724	74,1	30 134	ACP
of which:							*dont:*
Africa	68,3	12 421	53,3	16 969	69,1	28 101	Afrique
Caribbean	3,9	716	4,1	1 315	3,3	1 352	Caraïbes
Pacific	1,9	363	1,3	440	1,6	680	Pacifique

(¹) Extra-EC trade/Commerce extra CE.

1985

Non-ACP countries Pays non ACP	‰	Mio ECU	ACP countries Pays ACP	‰	Mio ECU
1. USA	169,6	68 941	1. Nigeria	28,0	11 392
2. Japan	70,3	28 585	2. Cameroun	6,2	2 550
3. Switzerland	58,2	23 687	3. Côte-d'Ivoire	6,1	2 517
4. USSR	50,9	20 710	4. Zaïre	3,5	1 435
5. Sweden	48,2	19 595	5. Gabon	3,0	1 224
6. Norway	43,5	17 716	6. Angola	2,6	1 087
7. Austria	31,6	12 861	7. Kenya	1,7	723
8. Libya	29,4	11 950	8. Liberia	1,5	638
9. Algeria	28,5	11 605	9. Zimbabwe	1,4	594
10. Brazil	25,7	10 473	10. Papua New Guinea	1,4	583
11. South Africa	23,2	9 455	11. Congo	1,3	539
12. Saudi Arabia	21,1	8 610	12. Maurice	1,0	431
13. Finland	18,6	7 570	13. Trinidad & Tobago	1,0	411
14. Canada	18,6	7 569	14. Guinée	0,9	393
15. Iraq	17,2	7 017	15. Ghana	0,9	369
16. Iran	16,5	6 729	16. Zambia	0,8	357
17. Mexico	12,6	5 129	17. Uganda	0,7	324
18. Australia	12,1	4 952	18. Sénégal	0,7	323
19. Kuwait	11,8	4 831	19. Bahamas	0,7	305
20. Hong Kong	11,8	4 819	20. Mauritania	0,7	290
Total	**719,4**	**292 804**	**Total**	**64,1**	**26 485**

EC EXPORTS
CE-EXPORTATIONS

Report. countries	1977		1981		1985		Pays déclarants
	‰	Mio ECU	‰	Mio ECU	‰	Mio ECU	
World (¹)	1 000,0	162 316	1 000,0	265 348	1 000,0	378 650	**Monde (¹)**
Developing	410,6	66 652	456,3	121 085	363,2	137 543	Pays en voie de dév.
of which:							*dont:*
OPEC	191,9	31 153	212,3	56 334	128,3	48 598	OPEP
Non-OPEC	218,7	35 499	244,0	64 751	234,9	88 945	Non OPEP
ACP	82,1	13 341	76,9	20 421	50,7	19 200	ACP
of which:							*dont:*
Africa	77,9	12 656	72,2	19 168	47,8	18 124	Afrique
Caribbean	3,8	625	4,3	1 164	2,4	945	Caraïbes
Pacific	0,3	60	0,3	88	0,3	130	Pacifique

(¹) Extra-EC trade/Commerce extra CE.

1985

Non-ACP countries Pays non ACP	‰	Mio ECU	ACP countries Pays ACP	‰	Mio ECU
1. USA	225,8	85 523	1. Nigeria	11,8	4 470
2. Switzerland	77,1	29 219	2. Cameroun	3,3	1 286
3. Sweden	54,9	20 812	3. Côte-d'Ivoire	2,7	1 045
4. Austria	47,7	18 086	4. Angola	2,3	883
5. USSR	33,0	12 509	5. Zaïre	2,1	808
6. Saudi Arabia	29,0	11 013	6. Gabon	2,0	770
7. Japan	27,6	10 474	7. Sudan	1,8	687
8. Canada	26,1	9 915	8. Kenya	1,7	660
9. Norway	25,3	9 591	9. Liberia	1,6	638
10. Algeria	19,4	7 378	10. Ethiopia	1,6	610
11. Australia	19,0	7 196	11. Sénégal	1,5	581
12. China	18,9	7 179	12. Congo	1,3	527
13. Egypt	17,2	6 526	13. Tanzania	1,1	443
14. Finland	17,0	6 454	14. Ghana	1,0	383
15. Yugoslavia	15,6	5 914	15. Zimbabwe	0,8	306
16. India	15,2	5 762	16. Togo	0,7	295
17. South Africa	15,0	5 688	17. Trinidad & Tobago	0,7	286
18. Turkey	14,2	5 400	18. Mali	0,7	265
19. Iran	14,1	5 351	19. Zambia	0,7	265
20. Hong Kong	12,0	4 551	20. Guinée	0,6	246
Total	**724,1**	**274 541**	**Total**	**40,0**	**15 454**

Report. countries	1977		1981		1985		Pays déclarants
	‰	Mio USD	‰	Mio USD	‰	Mio USD	
Developing	1 000,0	16 908	1 000,0	27 220	1 000,0	27 817	Pays en voie de dév.
of which:							*dont:*
ACP	246,3	4 165	302,5	8 236	334,1	9 295	ACP
of which:							*dont:*
Africa	215,1	3 638	269,4	7 334	309,2	8 601	Afrique
Caribbean	10,7	181	14,7	400	11,2	311	Caraïbes
Pacific	20,4	346	18,4	501	13,7	381	Pacifique

1985

Non-ACP countries Pays non ACP	‰	Mio USD	ACP countries Pays ACP	‰	Mio USD
1. Israel	71,1	1 978	1. Sudan	40,5	1 127
2. Egypt	63,2	1 759	2. Ethiopia	25,5	709
3. India	52,8	1 469	3. Tanzania	17,4	484
4. Bangladesh	41,0	1 141	4. Kenya	15,7	438
5. China	33,7	939	5. Mali	13,6	379
6. Morocco	29,9	833	6. Somalia	12,7	353
7. Pakistan	26,9	750	7. Zambia	11,7	326
8. Syria	22,9	639	8. Zaïre	11,6	324
9. Indonesia	21,6	603	9. Niger	10,9	304
10. Jordan	19,7	549	10. Mozambique	10,7	300
11. Philippines	17,4	486	11. Sénégal	10,5	294
12. Sri Lanka	17,4	485	12. Papua New Guinea	9,3	258
13. Thailand	17,2	480	13. Zimbabwe	8,5	236
14. Réunion	13,7	383	14. Mauritania	7,3	204
15. Burma	12,7	355	15. Ghana	7,3	204
16. El Salvador	12,4	345	16. Burkina Faso	7,0	197
17. Peru	11,3	316	17. Uganda	6,6	183
18. Martinique	10,5	293	18. Madagascar	6,5	182
19. Yemen AR	10,3	287	19. Tchad	6,5	181
20. Costa Rica	10,1	280	20. Rwanda	6,4	180
Total	**515,8**	**14 370**	**Total**	**246,2**	**6 863**

Benef. countries	1977	1981	1984	Pays bénéficiaires
	USD	USD	USD	
Developing *of which:*	5,72	8,46	7,46	Pays en voie de dév. *dont:*
ACP *of which:*	12,11	21,40	19,74	ACP *dont:*
Africa	10,86	19,56	18,45	Afrique
Caribbean	36,20	80,00	59,20	Caraïbes
Pacific	86,50	125,25	112,50	Pacifique

1984

Non-ACP countries Pays non ACP	USD	ACP countries Pays ACP	USD
1. Falkland Islands	4 025	1. Granada	250
2. St Pierre & Miquelon	2 940	2. Djibouti	248
3. St Helena	1 666	3. Seychelles	236
4. Pacific Islands	1 236	4. Cape Verde	199
5. Turks & Caicos Islands	1 145	5. Tonga	156
6. Fr. Polynesia	1 012	6. Western Samoa	126
7. Fr. Guyana	879	7. São Tomé & Principe	125
8. New Caledonia	870	8. Botswana	97
9. Martinique	749	9. Comoros	95
10. Réunion	641	10. Papua New Guinea	93
11. Bahrain	498	11. Mauritania	93
12. Guadeloupe	397	12. Belize	87
13. Gibraltar	365	13. Gambia	85
14. Israel	301	14. Somalia	80
15. Jordan	206	15. Solomon Islands	74
16. Wallis and Futuna	145	16. Jamaica	74
17. Costa Rica	89	17. Gabon	66
18. Syria	86	18. Lesotho	66
19. Honduras	68	19. Liberia	63
20. Oman	56	20. Guinea Bissau	62

**Principal economic and social
indicators by ACP State**

**Principaux indicateurs économiques
et sociaux par État ACP**

ANGOLA

Population 1985:	8 750 000	→ Taux de croissance 1970-85: 3,0 %
PNB 1985:	6 930,0 Mio USD	→ Taux de croissance 1970-85: 2,5 %
PNB/h 1985:	690,0 USD	→ Taux de croissance 1970-81: −6,2 %

Exportations 1984:	2 029,0 Mio USD	Importations 1984: 636,0 Mio USD
Exportations vers la CE 1983:	239,8 Mio USD	Importations de la CE 1983: 269,2 Mio USD
Élèves: enseign. primaire 1982:	1 178 430	Élèves: enseign. secondaire 1982: 131 918
Personnes/lit d'hôpital 1982:	322	Personnes/médecin 1982: 15 404

	Unités	1981	1982	1983	1984
Commerce extérieur					
Exportations	75 = 100	188,6	140,5	156,1	204,1
Importations	75 = 100	313,2	193,4	145,7	140,8
Balance commerciale	Mio USD	460,1	523,1	893,7	1 393,0
Exportations/importations	%	132,5	159,9	235,9	319,0
Balance commerciale avec la CE	Mio USD	− 84,7	− 126,8	− 29,4	
Export. vers la CE/import. de la CE	%	82,3	61,0	89,1	
Exportations/PIB	%	51,5	47,8	45,0	
Aide publique au développement					
APD net total	Mio USD	61,0	60,0	75,3	95,0
APD net bilatéral	Mio USD	39,4	40,6	46,6	60,7
APD net CE/bilatéral	%	28,2	49,3	67,1	57,2
APD net multilatéral	Mio USD	21,6	19,5	28,7	34,3
APD net FED/multilatéral	%	14,6	8,3	8,9	25,5
Aide alimentaire					
Céréales	000 t	25,5	25,3	43,4	61,9
Produits laitiers	000 t	2,6	3,7	1,2	5,8
Total	Mio USD	11,6	10,2	15,5	25,2
Origine du PIB					
Agriculture, forêts, pêche	%	42,4	47,4	49,1	
Industrie	%	30,5	24,5	21,7	
Services	%	27,1	28,1	29,2	
Indice d'évolution des prix	75 = 100	286,0	304,8	313,8	

Productions et exportations	Unités	1981	1982	1983	1984
Principales productions					
Céréales, total	000 t	330	330	357	342
Maïs	000 t	250	250	275	260
Tubercules et racines	000 t	2 120	2 170	2 170	2 170
Huile de palme	000 t	40	40	40	40
Café vert	000 t	21	17	22	27
Bananes	000 t	280	280	280	280
Lait de vache	000 t	147	148	148	148
Viande de bovins	000 t	51	52	53	53
Bois rond	000 m³	9 027	9 044	9 061	9 078
Pêche	000 t	131	112	111	71
Pétrole brut	000 t	7 158	6 410	8 304	10 284
Gaz naturel	Térajoule	3 500	3 500	4 000	5 000
Poisson salé	000 t	27	28	27	22
Poisson en conserve	000 t	3	4	4	3
Principales exportations					
CTCI 071.1 Café	Mio USD	73,7	68,2	42,7	
	%	4,0	4,9	2,8	
CTCI 331 Pétrole brut part. raffiné	Mio USD	1 326,3	1 250,6	1 364,3	
	%	71,7	89,6	87,9	
CTCI 667 Pierres précieuses, semi-précieuses	Mio USD	161,2	7,7	0.3	
	%	8,7	0,6	0,0	

ANTIGUA & BARBUDA

Population 1985:	80 000 →	Rate of growth 1970-85:	0,9 %
GNP 1985:	160,0 Mio USD →	Rate of growth 1970-85:	7,9 %
GNP/capita 1985:	2 030,0 USD →	Rate of growth 1970-81:	− 0,4 %

Total exports 1983:	10,1 Mio USD	Total imports 1983:	34,1 Mio USD
Exports to EC 1983:	0,0 Mio USD	Imports from EC 1983:	2,1 Mio USD
Pupils: primary school 1983:	11 394	Pupils: secondary school 1977:	5 706
Pers. by hospital bed 1980:	120	Pers. by doctor 1980:	2 313

	Units	1981	1982	1983	1984
External trade					
Total exports	75 = 100	43,9	52,1	36,5	
Total imports	75 = 100	63,7	51,3	50,7	
Balance of trade	Mio USD	− 30,6	− 20,0	− 24,0	
Exports/imports	%	28,5	41,9	29,7	
Balance of trade with EC	Mio USD	− 1,7	− 1,2	− 2,1	
Exports to EC/imports from EC	%	19,7	14,2	2,2	
Exports/GDP	%	72,0	64,7	64,8	
Financial indicators					
Overall balance of payments	Mio SDR	− 0,3	1,1	1,3	5,6
International reserves	Mio USD	7,3	8,5	9,9	15,4
External public debt	Mio USD				
Debt service/exports	%				
Official development assistance					
Total net ODA	Mio USD				
Bilateral net ODA	Mio USD				
Net ODA: EC/bilateral	%				
Multilateral net ODA	Mio USD	2,4	2,7	2,0	1,3
Multilateral: EDF/multilateral	%				
Index of price changes	75 = 100	169,3	177,7	180,2	189,5
Main products					
Bananas	000 t	1,0	1,0		
Cow milk	000 t	6,0	6,0	6,0	6,0
Fishing	000 t	2,0	2,0	2,0	2,0

Population 1985:	230 000 →	Rate of growth 1970-85:			2,0 %
GNP 1985:	1 670,0 Mio USD →	Rate of growth 1970-85:			10,7 %
GNP/capita 1985:	7 150,0 USD →	Rate of growth 1970-81:			− 2,1 %

Total exports 1985:	1 426,0 Mio USD	Total imports 1985:	2 420,0 Mio USD
Exports to EC 1979:	521,4 Mio USD	Imports from EC 1979:	218,7 Mio USD
Pupils: primary school 1982:	32 664	Pupils: secondary school 1975:	30 610
Pers. by hospital bed 1980:	256	Pers. by doctor 1980:	1 218

	Units	1981	1982	1983	1984
External trade					
Total exports	75 = 100	153,2	98,1	158,3	93,5
Total imports	75 = 100	155,8	113,1	119,8	112,2
Balance of trade	Mio USD	− 360,0	− 591,0	− 740,0	− 679,0
Exports/imports	%	91,4	80,6	122,9	77,6
Balance of trade with EC	Mio USD				
Exports to EC/imports from EC	%				
Exports/GDP	%				
Financial indicators					
Overall balance of payments	Mio SDR	4,2	10,7	9,2	36,6
International reserves	Mio USD	100,2	113,5	122,0	161,1
External public debt	Mio USD	272,4	267,3	252,1	226,2
Debt service/exports	%	31,0	24,8	22,0	21,2
Official development assistance					
Total net ODA	Mio USD	2,0	1,9	0,9	10,9
Bilateral net ODA	Mio USD	0,1	0,1	0,1	8,0
Net ODA: EC/bilateral	%	100,0	36,4	10,0	0,5
Multilateral net ODA	Mio USD	1,9	1,8	0,8	2,8
Multilateral: EDF/multilateral	%	3,6	9,9	15,5	31,3
Main products					
Tomatoes	000 t	8,0	8,0	8,0	8,0
Bananas	000 t	8,0	8,0	8,0	8,0
Roundwood	000 m³	115,0	115,0	115,0	115,0
Fishing	000 t	4,0	5,0	5,0	5,0
Motor spirit	000 t	43,0	40,0	40,0	40,0
Light oils	000 t	1 666,0	1 600,0	1 550,0	800,0
Heavy oils	000 t	4 250,0	4 100,0	4 050,0	3 100,0
Main exports					
SITC 112.4 Alcoholic beverages	Mio USD	23,9	24,1	22,4	42,4
	%	0,6	1,0	0,6	1,8
SITC 332 Petroleum products	Mio USD	1 549,7	1 319,2	1 791,9	
	%	40,3	53,6	45,1	
SITC 541 Medicinal, pharm. products	Mio USD	78,9	78,8	91,6	
	%	2,1	3,2	2,3	

BARBADOS

Population 1985:	250 000 →	Rate of growth 1970-85:	0,3 %
GNP 1985:	1 180,0 Mio USD →	Rate of growth 1970-85:	9,9 %
GNP/capita 1985:	4 680,0 USD →	Rate of growth 1970-81:	3,0 %

Total exports 1985:	352,0 Mio USD	Total imports 1985:	607,0 Mio USD
Exports to EC 1983:	22,1 Mio USD	Imports from EC 1983:	69,2 Mio USD
Pupils: primary school 1983:	30 907	Pupils: secondary school 1983:	27 715
Pers. by hospital bed 1982:	120	Pers. by doctor 1982:	1 167

	Units	1981	1982	1983	1984
External trade					
Total exports	75 = 100	227,9	245,0	274,8	365,0
Total imports	75 = 100	273,2	254,1	203,0	304,4
Balance of trade	Mio USD	− 346,7	− 286,9	− 144,4	− 267,1
Exports/imports	%	41,4	47,8	67,1	59,4
Balance of trade with EC	Mio USD	− 77,5	− 56,8	− 47,1	
Exports to EC/imports from EC	%	21,4	32,1	32,0	
Exports/GDP	%	59,4	61,4	62,4	64,3
Financial indicators					
Overall balance of payments	Mio SDR	2,0	− 0,2	− 10,0	− 13,2
International reserves	Mio USD	100,6	121,6	123,3	132,5
External public debt	Mio USD	311,2	314,4	352,0	397,3
Debt service/exports	%	12,5	12,6	10,9	7,8
Official development assistance					
Total net ODA	Mio USD	17,2	12,9	19,0	8,7
Bilateral net ODA	Mio USD	4,0	2,0	11,6	5,1
Net ODA: EC/bilateral	%	29,4	44,4	3,6	9,9
Multilateral net ODA	Mio USD	13,2	10,9	7,4	3,7
Multilateral: EDF/multilateral	%	1,1	5,2	3,3	11,7
Food aid					
Cereals	t	300,00	100,00		
Dairy products	t	100,00	100,00		
Total	Mio USD	0,3	0,1		
Origin of GDP					
Agriculture, forestry, fisheries	%	7,6	6,8	7,1	6,8
Industry	%	22,3	21,8	23,2	23,7
Services	%	70,2	71,4	69,7	69,5
Index of price changes	75 = 100	221,7	233,9	245,7	262,5

BARBADOS

Production and exports	Unités	1981	1982	1983	1984
Main products					
Tubers and roots	000 t	9	10	10	7
Centrifugal sugar	000 t	94	86	85	100
Fishing	000 t	3	3	7	7
Natural gas (Mio tera cal.)	TeraJ	314	336	450	672
Motor spirit	000 t	44	42	43	42
Light oils	000 t	45	43	42	40
Heavy oils	000 t	94	101	91	105
Main exports					
SITC 061.1 Sugar	Mio USD	25,6	22,9	19,2	28,5
	%	10,5	8,7	5,4	7,3
SITC 061.5 Molasses	Mio USD	4,1	17,8	3,5	4,2
	%	1,7	6,8	1,0	1,1
SITC 112.4 Alcoholic beverages	Mio USD	2,4	2,9	2,4	3,2
	%	1,0	1,1	0,7	0,8
SITC 332 Petroleum products [1]	Mio USD	70,4	47,3		
	%	28,8	18,0		
SITC 729 Electric machinery	Mio USD	35,4	59,9		
	%	14,5	22,8		
SITC 841 Clothing [2]	Mio USD	26,9	33,3		
	%	11,0	12,7		
[1] Imports of petroleum	Mio USD	90,4	84,3		
[2] Imports of clothing	Mio USD	19,0	16,7		

Population 1985:	170 000 →	Rate of growth 1970-85:	2,3 %
GNP 1985:	180,0 Mio USD →	Rate of growth 1970-84:	9,7 %
GNP/capita 1985:	1 130,0 USD →	Rate of growth 1970-81:	3,1 %

Total exports 1983:	77,3 Mio USD	Total imports 1984:	130,1 Mio USD
Exports to EC 1984:	18,6 Mio USD	Imports from EC 1984:	20,5 Mio USD
Pupils: primary school 1982:	37 158	Pupils: secondary school 1982:	6 308
Pers. by hospital bed 1980:	232	Pers. by doctor 1980:	3 239

	Units	1981	1982	1983	1984
External trade					
Total exports	75 = 100	166,3	148,2	119,0	115,2
Total imports	75 = 100	176,3	139,4	93,1	147,0
Balance of trade	Mio USD	− 44,4	− 23,9	− 2,5	− 52,8
Exports/imports	%	71,6	80,6	97,0	59,4
Balance of trade with EC	Mio USD	0,0	3,8	4,2	− 1,8
Exports to EC/imports from EC	%	100,1	115,2	125,6	91,1
Exports/GDP	%	56,4	53,0	53,4	55,5
Financial indicators					
Overall balance of payments	Mio SDR				
International reserves	Mio USD	10,3	9,8	9,3	6,1
External public debt	Mio USD	56,7	78,3	84,3	78,1
Debt service/exports	%				
Official development assistance					
Total net ODA	Mio USD	11,4	12,1	15,1	14,0
Bilateral net ODA	Mio USD	8,4	6,8	12,3	12,5
Net ODA: EC/bilateral	%	95,8	75,0	33,5	57,2
Multilateral net ODA	Mio USD	3,0	5,3	2,8	1,4
Multilateral: EDF/multilateral	%	32,5	25,7	7,5	2,8
Origin of GDP					
Agriculture, forestry, fisheries	%	24,9	27,3	27,6	:
Industry	%	21,7	19,8	20,1	:
Services	%	56,3	55,7	55,0	:
Index of price changes	75 = 100	153,0	147,2	152,7	158,2

BELIZE

Production and exports	Units	1981	1982	1983	1984
Main products					
Cereals, total	000 t	32	29	21	21
Maize	000 t	21	21	15	16
Rice, paddy	000 t	11	8	6	6
Centrifugal sugar	000 t	99	108	116	105
Bananas	000 t	14	14	14	14
Oranges	000 t	43	43	31	46
Roundwood	000 m³	117	122	144	164
Sawn wood	000 m³	38	42	33	38
Fishing	000 t	1	1	2	2
Main exports					
SITC 053 Fruit preserved, prepared	Mio USD	9,8	9,8	6,4	
	%	8,8	9,8	8,0	
SITC 061.1 Sugar	Mio USD	22,6	22,0	20,5	
	%	20,2	22,1	25,7	
SITC 061.2 Refined sugar	Mio USD	20,4	15,8	12,2	
	%	18,3	15,9	15,3	

Population 1985:	3 930 000	→	Taux de croissance 1970-85:		2,5 %
PNB 1985:	1 080,0 Mio USD	→	Taux de croissance 1970-85:		7,6 %
PNB/h 1985	270,0 USD	→	Taux de croissance 1970-81:		0,9 %

Exportations 1983:	79,4 Mio USD	Importations 1983:	348,5 Mio USD
Exportations vers la CE 1983:	36,4 Mio USD	Importations de la CE 1983:	170,6 Mio USD
Élèves: enseign. primaire 1982:	428 185	Élèves: enseign. secondaire 1980:	87 648
Personnes/lit d'hôpital 1982:	704	Personnes/médecin 1982:	17 500

	Unités	1981	1982	1983	1984
Commerce extérieur					
Exportations	75 = 100	89,4	93,2	173,6	
Importations	75 = 100	342,9	242,4	177,6	
Balance commerciale	Mio USD	− 631,7	− 432,9	− 269,1	
Exportations/importations	%	6,1	9,0	22,8	
Balance commerciale avec la CE	Mio USD	− 262,7	− 273,6	− 134,2	
Export. vers la CE/import. de la CE	%	8,0	4,9	21,3	
Exportations/PIB	%	28,3	27,6	20,2	18,1
Indicateurs financiers					
Balance des paiements	Mio DTS				
Réserves internationales	Mio USD	57,6	4,9	3,7	2,5
Dette extérieure publique	Mio USD	790,8	871,2	857,8	878,3
Service de la dette/exportations	%	10,8	11,3		
Aide publique au développement					
APD net total	Mio USD	81,6	80,6	86,4	77,6
APD net bilatéral	Mio USD	46,3	41,3	43,4	39,5
APD net CE/bilatéral	%	73,2	77,7	74,8	78,8
APD net multilatéral	Mio USD	35,3	39,3	43,0	38,1
APD net FED/multilatéral	%	25,8	17,2	18,2	17,2
Aide alimentaire					
Céréales	000 t	9,6	7,3	8,1	10,9
Produits laitiers	000 t	0,6	0,6	0,7	1,3
Total	Mio UDS	4,1	2,2	3,5	5,3
Origine du PIB					
Agriculture, forêts, pêche	%	39,1	39,4	39,8	42,9
Industrie	%	11,4	11,6	:	:
Services	%	38,9	38,5	:	:
Indice d'évolution des prix	75 = 100	181,0	204,5	237,5	250,8

Productions et exportations	Unités	1981	1982	1983	1984
Principales productions					
Céréales, total	000 t	363	353	353	481
Sorgho	000 t	57	60	57	82
Maïs	000 t	287	273	282	379
Riz, paddy	000 t	9	9	5	8
Haricots, pois, lentilles	000 t	31	32	32	40
Tomates	000 t	34	25	33	32
Tubercules et racines	000 t	1 283	1 321	1 243	1 473
Arachides non décortiquées	000 t	52	35	34	58
Palmistes	000 t	27	24	20	18
Huile de palme	000 t	30	30	33	34
Bananes	000 t	13	13	13	13
Noix de coco	000 t	20	20	20	20
Oranges	000 t	12	12	12	13
Fibres de coton	000 t	5	10	13	26
Coton à graines	000 t	14	32	45	88
Lait de vache	000 t	13	13	13	15
Viande de bovins	000 t	12	12	13	13
Bois rond	000 m³	3 887	3 998	4 113	4 234
Pêche	000 t	24	24	21	20
Poisson salé	000 t	2	2	2	2
Principales exportations					
CTCI 072.1 Fèves de cacao	Mio USD	10,2	0,9	6,7	
	%	24,9	2,0	8,4	
CTCI 081.3 Tourteaux	Mio USD	0,0	2,1	:	
	%	0,0	4,9	:	
CTCI 263.1 Coton brut	Mio USD	5,9	4,5	5,2	
	%	14,4	10,4	6,5	
CTCI 422.4 Huile de palme	Mio USD	1,8	4,0	0,8	
	%	4,4	9,3	1,0	

BOTSWANA

Population 1985: 1 090 000 → Rate of growth 1970-85: 4,3 %
GNP 1985: 900,0 Mio USD → Rate of growth 1970-85: 14,8 %
GNP/capita 1985: 840,0 USD → Rate of growth 1970-81: 9,3 %

Total exports 1982: 456,0 Mio USD | Total imports 1982: 686,0 Mio USD
Exports to EC 1979: 63,4 Mio USD | Imports from EC 1979: 15,5 Mio USD
Pupils: primary school 1984: 209 345 | Pupils: secondary school 1983: 25 010
Pers. by hospital bed 1980: 344 | Pers. by doctor 1980: 7 378

	Units	1981	1982	1983	1984
External trade					
Total exports	75 = 100	281,7	321,1		
Total imports	75 = 100	367,1	315,2		
Balance of trade	Mio USD	− 399,0	− 230,0		
Exports/imports	%	50,1	66,5		
Balance of trade with EC	Mio USD				
Exports to EC/imports from EC	%				
Exports/GDP	%	50,7	44,3	60,5	60,9
Financial indicators					
Overall balance of payments	Mio SDR	− 62,8	49,7	115,7	121,4
International reserves	Mio USD	253,4	293,0	395,7	474,3
External public debt	Mio USD	309,7	402,3	525,7	534,3
Debt service/exports	%	3,0	3,5	4,2	4,9
Official development assistance					
Total net ODA	Mio USD	96,9	101,5	103,6	102,7
Bilateral net ODA	Mio USD	75,9	89,4	83,0	75,1
Net ODA: EC/bilateral	%	44,9	46,1	45,2	36,7
Multilateral net ODA	Mio USD	21,0	12,2	20,6	27,6
Multilateral: EDF/multilateral	%	32,3	14,3	10,4	24,7
Food aid					
Cereals	000 t	13,9	4,0	11,0	27,3
Dairy products	000 t	1 200,0	700,0	0,0	1 209,0
Total	Mio USD	5,8	2,3	3,9	12,7
Origin of GDP					
Agriculture, forestry, fisheries	%	11,5	11,1	7,3	6,3
Industry	%	40,3	35,5	42,9	45,7
Services	%	52,4	59,1	54,9	53,4
Index of price changes	75 = 100	184,5	177,9	192,0	198,7

BOTSWANA

Poduction and exports	Units	1981	1982	1983	1984
Main products					
Cereals, total	000 t	53	18	15	8
Sorghum	000 t	28	4	5	6
Maize	000 t	21	12	8	2
Pulses, total	000 t	18	18	15	13
Tubers and roots	000 t	7	8	8	7
Cow milk	000 t	91	95	98	95
Beef and buffalo meat	000 t	43	47	41	41
Roundwood	000 m³	791	794	796	798
Fishing	000 t	1	1	1	2
Copper ore	000 t	18	18	20	21
Nickel ore	000 t	18	16	18	19
Diamonds	000 ca	4 961	7 769	8 322	7 100
Coal	000 t	380	414	396	396

BURKINA FASO

Population 1985:	6 640 000	→ Taux de croissance 1970-84:	1,4 %
PNB 1985:	1 080,0 Mio USD	→ Taux de croissance 1970-85:	5,6 %
PNB/h 1985:	140,0 USD	→ Taux de croissance 1970-81:	1,5 %

Exportations 1984:	80,1 Mio USD	Importations 1984:	255,5 Mio USD
Exportations vers la CE 1983:	16,4 Mio USD	Importations de la CE 1983:	129,1 Mio USD
Élèves: enseign. primaire 1983:	276 732	Élèves: enseign. secondaire 1983:	35 904
Personnes/lit d'hôpital 1982:	1 762	Personnes/médecin 1982:	55 858

	Unités	1981	1982	1983	1984
Commerce extérieur					
Exportations	75 = 100	172,3	129,1	130,9	183,9
Importations	75 = 100	223,2	228,9	190,1	168,9
Balance commerciale	Mio USD	− 262,6	− 290,0	− 230,5	− 175,4
Exportations/importations	%	22,2	16,2	19,8	31,3
Balance commerciale avec la CE	Mio USD	− 146,5	− 143,8	− 112,7	
Export. vers la CE/import. de la CE	%	14,3	14,2	12,7	
Exportations/PIB	%	16,7	15,7	16,8	18,0
Indicateurs financiers					
Balance des paiements	Mio DTS	12,0	− 0,1		
Réserves internationales	Mio USD	70,8	61,8	85,0	106,3
Dette extérieure publique	Mio USD	565,3	671,0	699,7	696,8
Service de la dette/exportations	%	11,3	15,4		
Aide publique au développement					
APD net total	Mio USD	216,8	212,8	183,5	188,6
APD net bilatéral	Mio USD	158,0	150,8	128,4	134,2
APD net CE/bilatéral	%	67,5	72,2	67,0	51,7
APD net multilatéral	Mio USD	58,8	62,0	55,1	54,3
APD net FED/multilatéral	%	32,3	31,5	28,0	31,3
Aide alimentaire					
Céréales	000 t	51,9	55,8	43,0	91,2
Produits laitiers	000 t	9,5	2,7	5,1	6,0
Total	Mio USD	40,4	18,6	20,1	32,9
Origine du PIB					
Agriculture, forêts, pêche	%	42,3	40,4	41,2	42,5
Industrie	%	15,5	16,6	:	:
Services	%	42,2	42,9	40,3	37,8
Indice d'évolution des prix	75 = 100	189,9	207,9	225,3	248,2

BURKINA FASO

Productions et exportations	Unités	1981	1982	1983	1984
Principales productions					
Céréales, total	000 t	1 270	1 210	1 119	1 089
Sorgho	000 t	659	609	611	594
Millet	000 t	443	441	391	372
Maïs	000 t	119	111	71	77
Riz, paddy	000 t	45	43	40	41
Haricots, pois, lentilles	000 t	175	178	176	155
Tubercules et racines	000 t	88	95	99	101
Arachides non décortiquées	000 t	78	71	82	83
Sucre centrifugé brut	000 t	26	28	28	26
Fibres de coton	000 t	22	29	30	30
Coton à graines	000 t	57	58	76	80
Lait de vache	000 t	82	84	85	87
Viande de bovins	000 t	21	25	28	27
Bois rond	000 m³	6 139	6 282	6 427	6 586
Pêche	000 t	8	7	7	7
Principales exportations					
CTCI 001.1 Bovins	Mio USD	5,9	2,3	1,3	
	%	7,8	4,1	2,3	
CTCI 001.2 Ovins et caprins	Mio USD	5,1	3,2	0,9	0,2
	%	6,8	5,7	1,6	:
CTCI 001.4 Volailles	Mio USD	2,1	1,6	0,9	
	%	2,8	2,8	1,5	
CTCI 221.8 Graines oléagineuses	Mio USD	12,3	8,7	8,0	1,4
	%	16,3	15,5	14,0	:
CTCI 263.1 Coton brut	Mio USD	30,5	23,6	31,2	20,0
	%	40,7	41,9	54,7	:

BURUNDI

Population 1985:	4 720 000	→ Taux de croissance 1970-85:	1,8 %
PNB 1985:	1 110,0 Mio USD	→ Taux de croissance 1970-85:	8,5 %
PNB/h 1985:	240,0 Mio USD	→ Taux de croissance 1970-81:	1,1 %

Exportations 1985:	110,0 Mio USD	Importations 1985:	186,0 Mio USD
Exportations vers la CE 1983:	58,2 Mio USD	Importations de la CE 1983:	82,3 Mio USD
Élèves: enseign. primaire 1983:	301 278	Élèves: enseign. secondaire 1983:	26 415
Personnes/lit d'hôpital 1982:	857	Personnes/médecin 1982:	45 432

	Unités	1981	1982	1983	1984
Commerce extérieur					
Exportations	75 = 100	312,6	475,6	314,5	310,0
Importations	75 = 100	182,1	219,5	312,4	296,6
Balance commerciale	Mio USD	− 15,4	12,7	− 96,5	− 88,0
Exportations/importations	%	86,5	109,2	50,8	52,7
Balance commerciale avec la CE	Mio USD	− 2,4	− 2,0	− 24,1	
Export. vers la CE/import. de la CE	%	93,7	96,5	70,7	
Exportations/PIB	%	8,9	10,5	9,1	
Indicateurs financiers					
Balance des paiements	Mio DTS				
Réserves internationales	Mio USD	61,3	29,5	26,9	19,7
Dette extérieure publique	Mio USD	455,1	521,1	555,4	586,9
Service de la dette/exportations	%				
Aide publique au développement					
APD net total	Mio USD	122,0	126,7	139,9	141,2
APD net bilatéral	Mio USD	67,0	81,3	75,8	83,3
APD net CE/bilatéral	%	80,4	76,7	75,6	60,6
APD net multilatéral	Mio USD	55,0	45,4	64,1	57,8
APD net FED/multilatéral	%	46,4	15,8	19,5	17,2
Aide alimentaire					
Céréales	000 t	7,7	7,5	4,6	10,5
Produits laitiers	000 t	1,6	1,3	1,0	3,0
Total	Mio USD	6,6	3,4	2,6	8,0
Origine du PIB					
Agriculture, forêts, pêche	%	61,2	57,8	57,9	:
Industrie	%	13,9	15,2	:	:
Services	%	20,4	22,1	21,2	:
Indice d'évolution des prix	75 = 100	192,3	205,0	228,4	263,5

BURUNDI

Productions et exportations	Unités	1981	1982	1983	1984
Principales productions					
Céréales, total	000 t	453	429	418	360
Sorgho	000 t	243	230	220	160
Millet	000 t	39	34	35	35
Maïs	000 t	146	144	148	139
Riz, paddy	000 t	15	9	9	18
Haricots, pois, lentilles	000 t	327	332	313	261
Tubercules et racines	000 t	1 070	1 073	1 088	1 174
Arachides non décortiquées	000 t	77	79	80	80
Café vert	000 t	44	20	36	26
Thé	000 t	2	2	2	2
Bananes	000 t	1 239	1 220	1 210	1 250
Fibres de coton	000 t	2	2	2	2
Lait de vache	000 t	27	25	26	24
Viande de bovins	000 t	6	6	6	6
Bois rond	000 m³	3 191	3 274	3 365	3 466
Pêche	000 t	12	12	12	12
Minerai d'or	kg	3	3	8	9
Principales exportations					
CTCI 071.1 Café	Mio USD	62,4	78,3	74,2	
	%	87,5	89,4	74,6	
CTCI 074.1 Thé	Mio USD	2,4	2,8	0,6	
	%	3,3	3,2	0,6	
CTCI 263.1 Coton brut	Mio USD	1,3	2,4	2,8	
	%	1,8	2,8	2,8	

CAMEROUN

Population 1985:	10 190 000	→ Taux de croissance 1970-85:			2,8 %
PNB 1985:	8 300,0 Mio USD	→ Taux de croissance 1970-85:			10,9 %
PNB/h 1985:	810,0 USD	→ Taux de croissance 1970-81:			4,4 %

Exportations 1984:	988,4 Mio USD	Importations 1984:		1 087,1 Mio USD
Exportations vers la CE 1983:	1 072,6 Mio USD	Importations de la CE 1983:		1 155,4 Mio USD
Élèves: enseign. primaire 1983:	1 563 582	Élèves: enseign. secondaire 1983:		288 728
Personnes/lit d'hôpital 1982:	372	Personnes/médecin 1982:		13 681

	Unités	1981	1982	1983	1984
Commerce extérieur					
Exportations	75 = 100	439,6	230,5	411,6	221,5
Importations	75 = 100	239,1	207,8	198,5	181,7
Balance commerciale	Mio USD	531,6	− 214,2	649,3	− 98,7
Exportations/importations	%	137,2	82,8	154,7	90,9
Balance commerciale avec la CE	Mio USD	277,0	− 350,8	− 82,9	
Export. vers la CE/import. de la CE	%	132,9	58,3	92,8	
Exportations/PIB	%	28,5	28,0	28,5	31,7
Indicateurs financiers					
Balance des paiements	Mio DTS	− 51,7	− 2,5	106,8	− 92,1
Réserves internationales	Mio USD	85,2	67,2	159,1	53,8
Dette extérieure publique	Mio USD	2 595,3	2 643,2	2 500,5	2 444,4
Service de la dette/exportations	%	17,2	21,9	15,9	14,3
Aide publique au développement					
APD net total	Mio USD	198,7	212,4	128,9	186,5
APD net bilatéral	Mio USD	133,9	151,7	103,1	162,3
APD net CE/bilatéral	%	77,3	88,7	79,4	71,0
APD net multilatéral	Mio USD	64,7	60,7	25,8	24,2
APD net FED/multilatéral	%	15,3	27,7	20,1	29,3
Aide alimentaire					
Céréales	000 t	10,4	4,2	3,6	2,0
Produits laitiers	000 t	1,2	0,9	0,5	0,1
Total	Mio USD	5,5	1,8	1,6	0,5
Origine du PIB					
Agriculture, forêts, pêche	%	27,2	27,0	23,2	22,0
Industrie	%	27,6	30,2	33,1	34,6
Service	%	39,5	36,9	:	:
Indice d'évolution des prix	75 = 100	297,1	345,7	427,5	505,7

Productions et exportations	Unités	1981	1982	1983	1984
Principales productions					
Millet	000 t	835	979	959	981
Céréales, total	000 t	351	380	361	400
Maïs	000 t	431	503	500	500
Riz, paddy	000 t	51	95	97	80
Haricots, pois, lentilles	000 t	109	113	115	114
Tubercules et racines	000 t	2 099	1 817	2 030	2 115
Arachides non décortiquées	000 t	130	141	120	110
Huile de palme	000 t	71	72	65	77
Sucre centrifugé brut	000 t	66	68	59	74
Fèves de cacao	000 t	118	105	111	121
Café vert	000 t	109	130	68	130
Bananes	000 t	70	51	57	66
Ananas	000 t	33	31	30	32
Caoutchouc naturel	000 t	18	16	16	18
Fibres de coton	000 t	31	29	37	38
Coton à graines	000 t	80	72	102	67
Lait de vache	000 t	43	44	45	46
Viande de bovins	000 t	51	48	47	48
Bois rond	000 m³	10 285	10 307	10 391	10 408
Bois scié	000 m³	468	468	426	426
Panneaux à base de bois	000 m³	73	73	73	73
Pêche	000 t	59	60	54	52
Poisson salé	000 t	4	4	4	4
Aluminium	000 t	65	79	77	87
Pétrole brut	000 t	4 340	5 331	5 689	6 475
Principales exportations					
CTCI 071.1 Café	Mio USD	189,8	160,3	195,5	
	%	16,9	15,6	18,1	
CTCI 072.1 Fèves de cacao	Mio USD	145,7	124,3	131,1	
	%	13,0	12,1	12,1	
CTCI 072.32 Beurre de cacao	Mio USD	19,7	13,1	15,7	6,7
	%	1,8	1,3	1,4	0,8
CTCI 242.31 Bois brut	Mio USD	52,7	45,2	33,9	
	%	4,7	4,4	3,1	
CTCI 263.1 Coton brut	Mio USD	41,2	36,9	36,6	13,6
	%	3,7	3,6	3,4	1,5
CTCI 331.01 Huile brute de pétrole	Mio USD	431,7	481,9	427,8	
	%	38,5	46,8	39,5	
CTCI 684 Aluminium (¹)	Mio USD	17,6	16,8	70,8	
	%	1,6	1,6	6,5	
CTCI 684.1 Aluminium brut	Mio USD	31,2	0,0	59,7	28,2
	%	2,8	0,0	5,5	3,2
(¹) Importations d'alumine	000 t	155,0	73,7	154,2	

CAPE VERDE

Population 1985:	330 000 →	Rate of growth 1970-85:			1,3 %
GNP 1985:	140,0 Mio USD →	Rate of growth:			– %
GNP/capita 1985:	430,0 USD →	Rate of growth:			– %

Total exports 1984:	2,6 Mio USD	Total imports 1983:	71,5 Mio USD
Exports to EC 1984:	0,6 Mio USD	Imports from EC 1983:	25,1 Mio USD
Pupils: primary school 1980:	57 587	Pupils: secondary school 1978:	6 600
Pers. by hospital bed 1982:	512	Pers. by doctor 1982:	6 353

	Units	1981	1982	1983	1984
External trade					
Total exports	75 = 100	188,2	126,3	131,4	108,7
Total imports	75 = 100	195,5	140,3	174,5	
Balance of trade	Mio USD	– 75,6	– 54,5	– 68,4	
Exports/imports	%	5,6	5,3	4,4	
Balance of trade with EC	Mio USD	– 23,1	– 17,8	– 23,8	
Exports to EC/imports from EC	%	2,5	5,1	5,1	
Exports/GDP	%	35,3	40,0	43,7	46,2
Financial indicators					
Overall balance of payments	Mio SDR				
International reserves	Mio USD				
External public debt	Mio USD	92,3	112,1	132,5	151,2
Debt service/exports	%				
Official development assistance					
Total net ODA	Mio USD	50,3	54,9	59,9	63,9
Bilateral net ODA	Mio USD	36,2	44,1	45,6	40,6
Net ODA: EC/bilateral	%	45,9	44,8	50,7	56,6
Multilateral net ODA	Mio USD	14,1	10,7	14,3	23,3
Multilateral: EDF/multilateral	%	48,0	29,4	24,9	32,5
Food aid					
Cereals	000 t	41,6	14,2	57,2	43,4
Dairy products	000 t	1,6	0,6	1,5	2,3
Total	Mio USD	15,5	8,0	17,7	17,6
Origin of GDP					
Agriculture, forestry, fisheries	%	23,7	21,5	20,0	23,3
Industry	%	25,2	28,2	:	:
Services	%	51,1	50,3	:	:
Index of price changes	75 = 100	181,2	219,2	265,2	314,1
Main products					
Maize	000 t	3	4	3	3
Pulses, total	000 t	1	3	2	5
Tubers and roots	000 t	17	8	7	9
Bananas	000 t	6	3	3	3
Coconuts	000 t	10	10	10	10
Fishing	000 t	11	10	13	9
Main exports					
SITC 031 Fish	Mio USD	2,1	:	:	1,4
	%	46,4	:	:	2,9

COMORES

Population 1985:	440 000	→ Taux de croissance 1970-85:	3,3 %		
PNB 1985:	110,0 Mio USD	→ Taux de croissance 1970-85:	6,1 %		
PNB/h 1985:	280,0 USD	→ Taux de croissance 1970-77:	− 3,6 %		

Exportations 1983:	18,9 Mio USD	Importations 1983:	45,5 Mio USD
Exportations vers la CE 1977:	6,2 Mio USD	Importations de la CE 1977:	7,1 Mio USD
Élèves: enseign. primaire 1980:	59 709	Élèves: enseign. secondaire 1980:	13 798
Personnes/lit d'hôpital 1980:	458	Personnes/médecin 1980:	16 000

	Unités	1981	1982	1983	1984
Commerce extérieur					
Exportations	75 = 100	126,2	221,0	199,3	
Importations	75 = 100	145,9	137,3	195,3	
Balance commerciale	Mio USD	− 22,0	− 11,0	− 26,6	
Exportations/importations	%	35,3	65,6	41,6	
Balance commerciale avec la CE	Mio USD				
Export. vers la CE/import. de la CE	%				
Exportations/PIB	%				
Indicateurs financiers					
Balance des paiements	Mio DTS	3,3	3,4	2,3	− 6,3
Réserves internationales	Mio USD				
Dette extérieure publique	Mio USD	96,6	157,0	184,9	186,7
Service de la dette/exportations	%	3,5	5,2	8,8	38,0
Aide publique au développement					
APD net total	Mio USD	46,6	38,9	38,2	41,0
APD net bilatéral	Mio USD	30,4	24,5	21,4	22,7
APD net CE/bilatéral	%	52,1	52,7	53,4	67,0
APD net multilatéral	Mio USD	16,2	14,4	16,7	18,3
APD net FED/multilatéral	%	28,7	29,0	13,7	15,2
Aide alimentaire					
Céréales	000 t	2,7	10,2	4,2	8,6
Produits laitiers	000 t	0,9	1,0	0,0	0,4
Total	Mio USD	2,7	3,4	2,0	2,8
Principales productions					
Céréales, total	000 t	19	20	21	21
Maïs	000 t	5	5	6	6
Riz, paddy	000 t	14	14	15	15
Tubercules et racines	000 t	103	104	105	107
Bananes	000 t	32	33	34	34
Noix de coco	000 t	43	45	46	46
Pêche	000 t	4	4	4	4
Principales exportations					
CTCI 075 Épices	Mio USD	17,5	18,6	14,8	
	%	83,7	86,5	82,2	
CTCI 551 Huiles essentielles	Mio USD	3,4	2,9	2,8	
	%	16,3	13,5	15,6	

Population 1985:	1 740 000	→ Taux de croissance 1970-85:			2,5 %
PNB 1985:	1 910,0 Mio USD	→ Taux de croissance 1970-85:			10,4 %
PNB/h 1985:	1 020,0 USD	→ Taux de croissance 1970-81:			3,5 %

Exportations 1983:	1 141,5 Mio USD	Importations 1983:		540,2 Mio USD
Exportations vers la CE 1983:	180,6 Mio USD	Importations de la CE 1983:		409,8 Mio USD
Élèves: enseign. primaire 1982:	422 874	Élèves: enseign. secondaire 1981:		190 668
Personnes/lit d'hôpital 1982:	212	Personnes/médecin 1982:		5 328

	Unités	1981	1982	1983	1984
Commerce extérieur					
Exportations	75 = 100	631,1	707,3	638,7	
Importations	75 = 100	405,0	503,7	327,8	
Balance commerciale	Mio USD	460,5	434,0	601,3	
Exportations/importations	%	169,0	152,3	211,3	
Balance commerciale avec la CE	Mio USD	− 31,1	− 201,2	− 229,2	
Export. vers la CE/import. de la CE	%	93,1	63,4	44,1	
Exportations/PIB	%	58,0	54,2	54,6	
Indicateurs financiers					
Balance des paiements	Mio DTS	39,5	− 77,0	− 30,1	− 8,3
Réserves internationales	Mio USD	123,4	37,0	7,4	4,1
Dette extérieure publique	Mio USD	1 564,3	1 805,9	1 898,4	1 803,8
Service de la dette/exportations	%	15,2	17,6	22,6	19,7
Aide publique au développement					
APD net total	Mio USD	81,0	93,1	108,4	97,9
APD net bilatéral	Mio USD	55,3	66,3	81,9	77,7
APD net CE/bilatéral	%	71,3	81,8	62,6	82,2
APD net multilatéral	Mio USD	25,7	26,8	26,5	20,2
APD net FED/multilatéral	%	18,9	6,2	24,2	36,6
Aide alimentaire					
Céréales	t	1 070,0	7 500,0	270,0	500,0
Produits laitiers	t	111,0	117,0	15,0	17,0
Total	Mio USD	0,6	2,6	0,1	0,2
Origine du PIB					
Agriculture, forêts, pêche	%	7,9	6,9	7,0	:
Industrie	%	50,8	52,0	54,5	:
Services	%	37,2	36,8	:	:
Indice d'évolution des prix	75 = 100	209,8	243,9	266,2	277,6

Productions et exportations	Unités	1981	1982	1983	1984
Principales productions					
Manioc	000 t	530	650	600	610
Céréales, total	000 t	8	8	9	9
Maïs	000 t	6	6	7	7
Haricots, pois, lentilles	000 t	4	7	7	7
Tomates	000 t	8	8	9	9
Tubercules et racines	000 t	698	700	650	650
Arachides non décortiquées	000 t	15	15	15	15
Huile de palme	000 t	15	15	15	15
Sucre centrifugé brut	000 t	16	28	21	31
Fèves de cacao	000 t	2	2	2	2
Café vert	000 t	3	2	3	2
Bananes	000 t	31	32	32	32
Ananas	000 t	103	104	105	105
Bois rond	000 m³	2 177	2 192	2 238	2 357
Bois scié	000 m³	73	66	66	60
Panneaux à base de bois	000 m³	71	67	79	71
Pêche	000 t	29	30	32	31
Pétrole brut	000 t	4 283	4 481	5 365	6 007
Gaz naturel	térajoule	60	60	60	60
Poisson salé	000 t	4	4	4	4
Principales exportations					
CTCI 072.1 Fèves de cacao	Mio USD	6,2	3,7	2,8	
	%	0,5	0,3	0,2	
CTCI 242.31 Bois brut	Mio USD	75,5	60,9	42,2	
	%	6,7	4,8	3,7	
CTCI 331.01 Huile brute de pétrole	Mio USD	899,5	1 066,2	920,0	
	%	79,7	84,3	80,6	
CTCI 667.2 Diamants	Mio USD	43,0	46,1	32,5	
	%	3,8	3,6	2,8	

CÔTE-D'IVOIRE

Population 1985 :	9 810 000	→ Taux de croissance 1970-85 :	4,2 %
PNB 1985 :	6 250,0 Mio USD	→ Taux de croissance 1970-85 :	6,2 %
PNB/h 1985 :	620,0 USD	→ Taux de croissance 1970-81 :	1,0 %

Exportations 1985 :	2 668,9 Mio USD	Importations 1985 :	1 733,8 Mio USD
Exportations vers la CE 1983 :	1 150,4 Mio USD	Importations de la CE 1983 :	997,4 Mio USD
Élèves : enseign. primaire 1982 :	1 134 915	Élèves : enseign. secondaire 1979 :	214 298
Personnes/lit d'hôpital 1982 :	589	Personnes/médecin 1982 :	15 234

	Unités	1981	1982	1983	1984
Commerce extérieur					
Exportations	75 = 100	214,6	193,6	175,0	228,3
Importations	75 = 100	212,4	193,8	161,0	134,1
Balance commerciale	Mio USD	142,1	104,2	254,2	1 187,0
Exportations/importations	%	105,9	104,8	114,0	178,6
Balance commerciale avec la CE	Mio USD	329,9	207,6	153,0	
Export. vers la CE/import. de la CE	%	128,4	119,2	115,3	
Exportations/PIB	%	36,8	37,6	35,4	45,6
Indicateurs financiers					
Balance des paiements	Mio DTS	− 325,6	− 330,0	− 266,0	− 299,0
Réserves internationales	Mio USD	17,8	2,2	19,7	5,4
Dette extérieure publique	Mio USD	6 026,4	6 094,1	5 863,1	5 530,6
Service de la dette/exportations	%	44,6	45,1	40,9	24,8
Aide publique au développement					
APD net total	Mio USD	123,7	136,7	155,3	127,5
APD net bilatéral	Mio USD	91,1	102,3	140,3	113,9
APD net CE/bilatéral	%	92,4	93,8	95,8	90,1
APD net multilatéral	Mio USD	32,5	34,5	15,0	13,6
APD net FED/multilatéral	%	80,5	85,5	66,6	71,9
Aide alimentaire					
Produits laitiers	t	34	39	41	35
Total	Mio USD	0,1	0,2	0,2	0,1
Origine du PIB					
Agriculture, forêts, pêche	%	27,0	25,9	27,0	28,4
Industrie	%	23,5	23,4	24,3	25,6
Services	%	:	:	:	:
Indice d'évolution des prix	75 = 100	330,9	341,7	346,6	353,4

CÔTE-D'IVOIRE

Productions et exportations	Unités	1981	1982	1983	1984
Principales productions					
Céréales, total	000 t	822	928	842	1 014
Maïs	000 t	375	423	435	468
Riz, paddy	000 t	390	450	360	490
Tubercules et racines	000 t	3 675	4 008	3 891	4 068
Arachides non décortiquées	000 t	85	90	80	98
Coprah	000 t	19	33	38	42
Palmistes	000 t	37	39	39	33
Huile de palme	000 t	160	176	176	151
Sucre centrifugé brut	000 t	135	166	187	127
Fèves de cacao	000 t	465	360	411	550
Café vert	000 t	367	248	271	85
Bananes	000 t	151	150	130	148
Ananas	000 t	296	230	207	229
Noix de coco	000 t	165	235	260	290
Caoutchouc naturel	000 t	23	26	29	35
Fibres de coton	000 t	56	56	66	58
Coton à graines	000 t	135	133	157	142
Bois rond	000 m³	11 546	11 863	12 111	12 190
Bois scié	000 m³	611	748	718	646
Panneaux à base de bois	000 m³	139	130	166	154
Pâte de bois	000 t	271	271	271	271
Pêche	000 t	80	92	94	84
Poisson salé	000 t	15	15	15	13
Poisson en conserve	000 t	26	29	26	23
Essence	000 t	233	240	250	245
Huiles légères	000 t	416	190	512	450
Huiles lourdes	000 t	590	580	518	510
Engrais azotés	000 t	2	3	4	6
Engrais phosphatés	000 t	3	3	2	3
Principales exportations					
CTCI 032.01 Cons. poissons	Mio USD	46,0	45,2	52,0	
	%	1,8	2,0	2,5	
CTCI 051 Fruits frais et noix non ol.	Mio USD	84,9	62,6	49,0	
	%	3,3	2,7	2,4	
CTCI 071.1 Café	Mio USD	445,8	466,2	414,2	
	%	17,6	20,4	20,0	
CTCI 072.1 Fèves de cacao	Mio USD	734,6	499,6	422,3	
	%	29,0	21,8	20,4	
CTCI 072.31 Pâte de cacao	Mio USD	48,3	47,8	54,7	
	%	1,9	2,1	2,6	
CTCI 072.32 Beurre de cacao	Mio USD	72,9	62,4	46,8	
	%	2,9	2,7	2,3	
CTCI 231.1 Caoutchouc naturel brut	Mio USD	23,1	21,5	28,3	
	%	0,9	0,9	1,4	
CTCI 242.31 Bois brut	Mio USD	270,9	212,2	196,0	
	%	10,7	9,3	9,5	
CTCI 243.31 Bois scié	Mio USD	55,5	57,4	62,9	
	%	2,2	2,5	3,0	
CTCI 263.1 Coton brut	Mio USD	66,2	55,2	82,8	68,5
	%	2,6	2,4	4,0	2,5
CTCI 332 Produits pétroliers	Mio USD	191,0	242,2	195,7	
	%	7,5	10,6	9,5	
CTCI 422.2 Huile de palme	Mio USD	35,4	30,0	23,9	
	%	1,4	1,3	1,2	
CTCI 652.2 Tissus de coton mercerisés	Mio USD	38,7	32,0	5,8	
	%	1,5	1,4	0,3	

DJIBOUTI

Population 1985:	430 000	→ Taux de croissance 1970-85:			11,0 %
PNB 1985:	340,0 Mio USD	→ Taux de croissance 1970-85:			12,3 %
PNB/h 1985:	970,0 USD	→ Taux de croissance			–

Exportations 1983:	33,6 Mio USD	Importations 1983:	252,4 Mio USD
Exportations vers la CE 1983:	8,5 Mio USD	Importations de la CE 1983:	112,7 Mio USD
Élèves: enseign. primaire 1983:	21 847	Élèves: enseign. secondaire 1983:	6 331
Personnes/lit d'hôpital 1982:	286	Personnes/médecin 1982:	2 196

	Unités	1981	1982	1983	1984
Commerce extérieur					
Exportations	75 = 100	188,0	183,8	210,2	
Importations	75 = 100	162,3	199,5	172,6	
Balance commerciale	Mio USD	– 207,3	– 262,4	– 218,8	
Exportations/importations	%	12,7	10,1	13,3	
Balance commerciale avec la CE	Mio USD	– 108,8	– 102,4	– 104,2	
Export. vers la CE/import. de la CE	%	2,0	1,2	7,6	
Exportations/PIB	%				
Indicateurs financiers					
Balance des paiements	Mio DTS				
Réserves internationales	Mio USD				
Dette extérieure publique	Mio USD	75,1	101,8	142,6	179,3
Service de la dette/exportations	%				
Aide publique au développement					
APD net total	Mio USD	64,5	58,7	65,5	102,0
APD net bilatéral	Mio USD	50,0	46,1	52,7	81,8
APD net CE/bilatéral	%	65,0	89,3	71,5	48,9
APD net multilatéral	Mio USD	14,6	12,6	12,8	20,2
APD net FED/multilatéral	%	30,3	19,1	11,8	12,4
Aide alimentaire					
Céréales	000 t	9,3	5,9	8,5	14,1
Produits laitiers	000 t	0,8	0,5	0,1	0,1
Total	Mio USD	5,4	2,1	2,2	3,6
Principales productions					
Viande de bovins	000 t	2	2	1	1

Population 1985:	80 000 →	Rate of growth 1970-85:		0,9 %
GNP 1985:	90,0 Mio USD →	Rate of growth 1970-85:		7,4 %
GNP/capita 1985:	1 160,0 USD →	Rate of growth 1970-81:		– 3,0 %

Total exports 1983:	31,2 Mio USD	Total imports 1983:	26,0 Mio USD
Exports to EC 1983:	19,2 Mio USD	Imports from EC 1983:	14,0 Mio USD
Pupils: primary school 1983:	13 283	Pupils: secondary school 1983:	7 622
Pers. by hospital bed 1980:	234	Pers. by doctor 1980:	7 800

	Units	1981	1982	1983	1984
External trade					
Total exports	75 = 100	168,0	281,5	273,5	
Total imports	75 = 100	238,3	138,5	124,5	
Balance of trade	Mio USD	– 30,5	3,2	5,2	
Exports/imports	%	38,6	111,2	120,2	
Balance of trade with EC	Mio USD	– 2,6	4,9	5,2	
Exports to EC/imports from EC	%	79,0	131,7	136,9	
Exports/GDP	%	37,9	45,0	45,5	40,3
Financial indicators					
Overall balance of payments	Mio SDR	– 7,1	– 1,4	– 4,0	5,6
International reserves	Mio USD	3,1	4,3	1,5	5,2
External public debt	Mio USD				
Debt service/exports	%				
Official development assistance					
Total net ODA	Mio USD				
Bilateral net ODA	Mio USD				
Net ODA: EC/bilateral	%				
Multilateral net ODA	Mio USD	9,4	11,2	5,4	5,5
Multilateral: EDF/multilateral	%				
Food aid					
Cereals	000 t	0,0	1 568	0,0	520
Total	Mio USD	0,0	370	0,0	290
Origin of GDP					
Agriculture, forestry, fisheries	%	24,0	23,6	22,7	22,9
Industry	%	22,6	22,7	20,8	20,5
Services	%	:	:	:	:
Index of price changes	75 = 100	312,2	340,8	367,4	396,3
Main products					
Tubers and roots	000 t	24	25	25	25
Copra	000 t	1	2	3	2
Bananas	000 t	35	35	37	38
Coconuts	000 t	6	11	17	13
Oranges	000 t	2	2	3	3
Fishing	000 t	2	2	1	1
Main exports					
SITC 051.2 Citrus fruits	Mio USD	0,4	0,8	0,5	
	%	2,3	2,4	1,6	
SITC 051.3 Bananas	Mio USD	9,2	10,1	17,2	
	%	48,2	31,6	55,1	
SITC 422.3 Copra and coconut oil	Mio USD	0,1	1,1	:	
	%	0,6	3,5	:	

ETHIOPIA

Population 1985:	43 350 000	→ Rate of growth 1970-85:	3,8 %
GNP 1985:	4 630,0 Mio USD	→ Rate of growth 1970-85:	7,5 %
GNP/capita 1985:	110,0 USD	→ Rate of growth 1970-81:	0,9 %

Total exports 1985:	337,8 Mio USD	Total imports 1985:	988,6 Mio USD
Exports to EC 1985:	165,1 Mio USD	Imports from EC 1985:	351,6 Mio USD
Pupils: primary school 1982:	2 511 050	Pupils: secondary school 1973:	191 700
Pers. by hospital bed 1982:	2 787	Pers. by doctor 1982:	72 582

	Units	1981	1982	1983	1984
External trade					
Total exports	75 = 100	164,9	176,3	184,2	181,9
Total imports	75 = 100	250,8	267,0	199,7	320,6
Balance of trade	Mio USD	− 359,1	− 380,6	− 164,4	− 525,2
Exports/imports	%	51,3	51,5	72,0	44,3
Balance of trade with EC	Mio USD	− 168,1	− 162,7	− 96,6	− 152,6
Exports to EC/imports from EC	%	41,8	44,6	60,5	53,1
Exports/GDP	%	13,0	11,7	11,7	
Financial indicators					
Overall balance of payments	Mio SDR	92,9	− 70,1	− 51,4	− 58,6
International reserves	Mio USD	266,7	181,8	125,9	44,3
External public debt	Mio USD	1 437,3	1 489,2	1 919,6	2 247,7
Debt service/exports	%	15,7	16,5	18,9	20,4
Official development assistance					
Total net ODA	Mio USD	245,0	199,7	339,3	363,6
Bilateral net ODA	Mio USD	94,5	77,0	163,4	187,9
Net ODA: EC/bilateral	%	37,8	50,5	25,5	51,5
Multilateral net ODA	Mio USD	150,5	122,7	175,9	175,6
Multilateral: EDF/multilateral	%	27,6	21,9	26,9	33,0
Food aid					
Cereals	000 t	124,2	130,9	155,2	273,7
Dairy products	000 t	6,9	5,7	3,5	11,1
Total	Mio USD	54,0	38,3	40,7	90,7
Origin of GDP					
Agriculture, forestry, fisheries	%	50,0	48,6	48,4	
Industry	%	15,5	15,8	15,7	
Services	%	28,7	29,6	29,9	
Index of price changes	75 = 100	134,4	137,3	140,0	

ETHIOPIA

Production and exports	Units	1981	1982	1983	1984
Main products					
Cereals, total	000 t	5 382	6 718	5 527	4 188
Wheat	000 t	716	917	666	675
Sorghum	000 t	1 203	1 356	1 202	515
Millet	000 t	197	240	199	190
Maize	000 t	1 184	1 603	1 533	1 060
Pulses, total	000 t	918	1 026	811	804
Tomatoes	000 t	47	48	49	49
Tubers and roots	000 t	1 468	1 520	1 574	1 182
Unshelled groundnuts	000 t	36	33	31	28
Centrifugal sugar	000 t	167	158	195	201
Raw coffee	000 t	202	202	220	240
Bananas	000 t	73	73	74	74
Cotton lint	000 t	27	27	20	22
Seed cotton	000 t	89	89	67	73
Cow milk	000 t	600	605	610	595
Sheep milk	000 t	58	58	60	61
Goat milk	000 t	95	95	95	95
Beef and buffalo meat	000 t	214	215	216	214
Roundwood	000 m³	28 626	29 569	30 353	31 154
Fishing	000 t	4	4	4	4
Gold ore	kg	373	373	435	467
Main exports					
SITC 054 Vegetables and tubers	Mio USD	14,9	19,5	15,8	
	%	3,9	4,8	3,7	
SITC 061.2 Refined sugar	Mio USD	2,1	3,1	:	
	%	0,6	0,8	:	
SITC 071.1 Coffee	Mio USD	227,0	248,7	261,8	
	%	60,0	61,5	62,0	
SITC 081.3 Oil seed cake	Mio USD	3,8	3,2	8,2	
	%	1,0	0,8	1,9	
SITC 211.1 Bovine hides	Mio USD	6,9	7,2	4,0	
	%	1,8	1,8	0,9	
SITC 211.4 Goat skins	Mio USD	12,9	10,2	:	
	%	3,4	2,5	:	
SITC 211.6 Sheep skins	Mio USD	27,8	23,8	:	
	%	7,3	5,9	:	
SITC 221 Oil seeds	Mio USD	14,0	12,0	6,5	
	%	3,7	3,0	1,5	
SITC 263 Cotton	Mio USD	8,4	10,5	:	
	%	2,2	2,6	:	
SITC 292.4 Plants, seeds, (for pharm. industry)	Mio USD	8,6	15,9	25,0	
	%	2,3	3,9	5,9	
SITC 332 Residual fuel oil	Mio USD	29,9	30,9	:	
	%	7,9	7,6	:	

FIJI

Population 1985:	700 000	→ Rate of growth 1970-85:		2,0 %
GNP 1985:	1 190,0 Mio USD	→ Rate of growth 1970-85:		8,4 %
GNP/capita 1985:	1 700,0 USD	→ Rate of growth 1970-81:		3,0 %

Total exports 1985:	236,0 Mio USD	Total imports 1984:		442,0 Mio USD
Exports to EC 1983:	75,1 Mio USD	Imports from EC 1983:		39,4 Mio USD
Pupils: primary school 1981:	116 318	Pupils: secondary school 1981:		48 608
Pers. by hospital bed 1981:	364	Pers. by doctor 1980:		2 222

	Units	1981	1982	1983	1984
External trade					
Total exports	75 = 100	186,8	169,0	140,1	149,0
Total imports	75 = 100	236,1	192,2	180,7	167,9
Balance of trade	Mio USD	− 333,4	− 244,4	− 259,9	− 211,4
Exports/imports	%	47,2	52,4	46,2	52,9
Balance of trade with EC	Mio USD	26,9	35,0	31,2	35,7
Exports to EC/imports from EC	%	151,6	192,6	179,4	190,5
Exports/GDP	%	43,3	42,2	42,2	40,5
Financial indicators					
Overall balance of payments	Mio SDR	− 19,1	− 19,1	− 5,4	9,1
International reserves	Mio USD	135,1	126,9	115,8	117,4
External public debt	Mio USD	341,0	362,6	343,7	324,0
Debt service/exports	%	12,7	16,4	19,4	22,6
Official development assistance					
Total net ODA	Mio USD	40,5	35,4	32,7	31,3
Bilateral net ODA	Mio USD	30,3	30,0	22,3	23,5
Net ODA: EC/bilateral	%	33,3	20,4	20,7	18,1
Multilateral net ODA	Mio USD	10,2	5,4	10,5	7,8
Multilateral: EDF/multilateral	%	66,2	43,2	61,3	55,3
Food aid					
Cereals	000 t	6660	30	0,0	1 570
Dairy products	000 t	290	150	140	0,0
Total	Mio USD	1 513	299	135	425
Origin of GDP					
Agriculture, forestry, fisheries	%	20,0	19,8	18,5	21,6
Industry	%	21,1	23,5	20,8	:
Services	%	58,9	56,8	:	:
Index of price changes	75 = 100	226,0	235,7	241,6	267,4

FIJI

Production and exports	Units	1981	1982	1983	1984
Main products					
Cereals, total	000 t	18	21	18	24
Rice, paddy	000 t	17	20	16	22
Tubers and roots	000 t	31	35	51	75
Copra	000 t	21	22	24	25
Centrifugal sugar	000 t	470	487	276	480
Bananas	000 t	5	5	6	6
Coconuts	000 t	210	217	234	234
Cow milk	000 t	50	40	35	30
Beef and buffalo meat	000 t	3	3	3	3
Roundwood	000 m3	224	181	213	213
Sawn wood	000 m3	93	72	80	80
Fishing	000 t	24	28	29	31
Gold ore	kg	960	1 423	1 200	1 200
Canned fish	000 t	7	6	8	6
Main exports					
SITC 031.1 Fish, fresh or frozen	Mio USD	3.2	0.7	0.5	0.7
	%	1,1	0,3	0,2	0,3
SITC 032.01 Prepared or pres. fish	Mio USD	19,2	10,0	14,5	13,2
	%	6,5	3,7	6,5	5,6
SITC 061.1 Sugar	Mio USD	152,3	133,7	109,5	100,5
	%	51,2	49,6	49,1	42,3
SITC 061.5 Molasses	Mio USD	11,1	5,4	3,1	6,1
	%	3,7	2,0	1,4	2,6
SITC 332.1 Petroleum spirit	Mio USD	7,6	7,1	7,3	6,6
	%	2,6	2,6	3,3	2,8
SITC 332. Lamp oil	Mio USD	33,4	32,0	24,6	28,4
	%	11,2	11,9	11,0	12,0
SITC 332.4 Residual fuel oil	Mio USD	18,9	17,4	13,6	11,7
	%	6,3	6,5	6,1	4,9
SITC 422.3 Copra and coconut oil	Mio USD	7,4	6,6	10,4	16,9
	%	2,5	2,4	4,6	7,1

Population 1985:	1 150 000	→ Taux de croissance 1970-85:		5,7 %
PNB 1985:	3 330,0 Mio USD	→ Taux de croissance 1970-85:		9,3 %
PNB/h 1985:	3 340,0 USD	→ Taux de croissance 1970-81:		1,6 %

Exportations 1984:	1 801,3 Mio USD	Importations 1984:	726,6 Mio USD
Exportations vers la CE 1983:	805,2 Mio USD	Importations de la CE 1983:	511,2 Mio USD
Élèves: enseign. primaire 1982:	165 559	Élèves: enseign. secondaire 1982:	32 692
Personnes/lit d'hôpital 1982:	129	Personnes/médecin 1982:	2 560

	Unités	1981	1982	1983	1984
Commerce extérieur					
Exportations	75 = 100	180,5	166,2	156,6	191,2
Importations	75 = 100	187,0	178,9	153,6	162,8
Balance commerciale	Mio USD	865,4	767,0	789,8	1 074,8
Exportations/importations	%	203,7	196,1	215,2	247,9
Balance commerciale avec la CE	Mio USD	240,9	217,0	294,0	
Export. vers la CE/import. de la CE	%	140,3	139,4	157,5	
Exportations/PIB	%				
Indicateurs financiers					
Balance des paiements	Mio DTS	99,9	132,7	− 83,6	10,9
Réserves internationales	Mio USD	198,8	311,9	186,9	199,4
Dette extérieure publique	Mio USD	1 208,3	1 595,1	1 282,3	1 083,8
Service de la dette/exportations	%	17,0	14,7	11,2	12,8
Aide publique au développement					
APD net total	Mio USD	43,5	62,3	63,7	75,4
APD net bilatéral	Mio USD	39,2	58,6	57,7	69,7
APD net CE/bilatéral	%	87,6	95,3	96,4	93,4
APD net multilatéral	Mio USD	4,3	3,7	6,0	5,7
APD net FED/multilatéral	%	19,4	21,3	54,4	45,4
Origine du PIB					
Agriculture, forêts, pêche	%	6,4	6,3	6,0	5,7
Industrie	%	61,9	62,0	:	:
Services	%	31,7	31,7	:	:
Indice d'évolution des prix	75 = 100	185,4	223,0	252,1	280,5

GABON

Productions et exportations	Unités	1981	1982	1983	1984
Principales productions					
Céréales, total	000 t	10	11	11	11
Maïs	000 t	10	10	10	10
Tubercules et racines	000 t	373	393	404	396
Arachides non décortiquées	000 t	7	7	8	8
Sucre centrifugé brut	000 t	15	15	17	15
Bananes	000 t	8	8	8	8
Bois rond	000 m³	2 464	2 482	2 525	2 706
Bois scié	000 m³	108	108	108	108
Panneaux à base de bois	000 m³	167	201	201	201
Pêche	000 t	44	53	53	53
Minerai de manganèse	000 t	787	757	947	1 081
Minerai d'uranium	t	1 022	976	1 007	917
Minerai d'or	kg	20	30	17	17
Pétrole brut	000 t	7 652	7 748	7 468	8 346
Gaz naturel	térajoule	6 000	6 000	5 796	6 000
Principales exportations					
CTCI 242.31 Bois brut	Mio USD	94,4	96,1	97,6	
	%	5,6	6,1	6,6	
CTCI 243.31 Bois scié	Mio USD	20,7	1,2	7,4	
	%	1,2	0,1	0,5	
CTCI 283.7 Minerai de manganèse	Mio USD	89,8	79,9	103,1	
	%	5,3	5,1	7,0	
CTCI 331.1 Huile brute de pétrole	Mio USD	1 307,7	1 275,2	1 122,2	
	%	76,9	81,5	76,1	
CTCI 332.1 Essence de pétrole	Mio USD	20,4	7,5	10,5	
	%	1,2	0,5	0,7	
CTCI 332.3 Gasoils, fueloils légers domestiques	Mio USD	25,6	8,8	8,2	
	%	1,5	0,6	0,6	
CTCI 232.4 Huiles lourdes	Mio USD	40,3	33,2	31,5	
	%	2,4	2,1	2,1	

GAMBIA

Population 1985:	640 000	→	Rate of growth 1970-85:	2,2 %
GNP 1985:	170,0 Mio USD	→	Rate of growth 1970-85:	6,6 %
GNP/capita 1985:	230,0 USD	→	Rate of growth 1970-81:	1,7 %

Total exports 1984:	52,7 Mio USD	Total imports 1984:	116,7 Mio USD
Exports to EC 1983:	19,0 Mio USD	Imports from EC 1983:	44,1 Mio USD
Pupils: primary school 1983:	60 529	Pupils: secondary school 1983:	14 430
Pers. by hospital bed 1982:	815	Pers. by doctor 1982:	11 632

	Units	1981	1982	1983	1984
External trade					
Total exports	75 = 100	43,5	58,8	91,9	107,6
Total imports	75 = 100	192,2	168,3	163,0	239,5
Balance of trade	Mio USD	− 72,4	− 53,2	− 34,4	− 64,1
Exports/imports	%	22,7	35,1	56,6	45,1
Balance of trade with EC	Mio USD	− 40,6	− 3,9	− 25,1	
Exports to EC/imports from EC	%	22,7	79,6	43,1	
Exports/GDP	%	37,5	30,7		
Financial indicators					
Overall balance of payments	Mio SDR	7,0	− 21,6	− 7,8	
International reserves	Mio USD	3,9	8,4	2,9	2,3
External public debt	Mio USD	211,9	233,3	247,3	263,4
Debt service/exports	%	8,1	22,9	14,0	
Official development assistance					
Total net ODA	Mio USD	68,2	47,6	42,1	53,5
Bilateral net ODA	Mio USD	40,2	27,1	22,3	33,1
Net ODA: EC/bilateral	%	33,1	47,6	58,0	53,3
Multilateral net ODA	Mio USD	27,9	20,5	19,7	20,4
Multilateral: EDF/multilateral	%	49,2	32,6	10,2	19,8
Food aid					
Cereals	000 t	9,5	8,3	3,6	9,9
Dairy products	000 t	0,8	0,5	0,7	0,5
Total	Mio USD	5,7	4,0	2,8	4,1
Origin of GDP					
Agriculture, forestry, fisheries	%	22,9	27,4	:	:
Industry	%	15,7	14,1	:	:
Services	%	61,5	58,5	:	:
Index of price changes	75 = 100	165,2	172,3	214,4	235,9

GAMBIA

Production and exports	Units	1981	1982	1983	1984
Main products					
Cereals, total	000 t	99	109	60	78
Millet	000 t	42	49	29	33
Rice, paddy	000 t	39	37	19	27
Unshelled groundnuts	000 t	109	151	106	114
Palm oil	000 t	3	3	3	3
Roundwood	000 m³	904	681	771	777
Fishing	000 t	13	10	11	13
Salted fish	000 t	3	4	3	3
Main exports					
SITC 031 Fish	Mio USD	0,7	1,0	1,0	
	%	3,3	3,5	2,2	
SITC 081.3 Oil seed cake	Mio USD	3,3	1,0	1,0	
	%	15,5	3,5	2,2	
SITC 221 Oil seeds	Mio USD	7,5	14,2	21,6	
	%	35,2	49,3	48,0	
SITC 421.4 Groundnut oil	Mio USD	6,4	5,3	7,6	
	%	30,0	18,4	16,9	

GHANA

Population 1985:	13 590 000 →	Rate of growth 1970-85:		3,1 %
GNP 1985:	4 960,0 Mio USD →	Rate of growth 1970-85:		5,5 %
GNP/capita 1985:	390,0 USD →	Rate of growth 1970-81:		− 2,7 %

Total exports 1984:	571,0 Mio USD	Total imports 1984:	591,0 Mio USD
Exports to EC 1983:	197,5 Mio USD	Imports from EC 1983:	230,1 Mio USD
Pupils: primary school 1983:	1 653 455	Pupils: secondary school 1983:	753 665
Pers. by hospital bed 1982:	665	Pers. by doctor 1982:	7 245

	Units	1981	1982	1983	1984
External trade					
Total exports	75 = 100	118,4	123,1	69,5	77,5
Total imports	75 = 100	161,6	66,8	71,1	75,0
Balance of trade	Mio USD	− 400,4	380,8	− 47,4	− 20,0
Exports/imports	%	68,6	172,4	91,5	96,6
Balance of trade with EC	Mio USD	− 120,1	− 124,0	− 32,6	
Exports to EC/imports from EC	%	73,9	62,3	85,9	
Exports/GDP	%	3,2	3,0	5,1	6,8
Financial indicators					
Overall balance of payments	Mio SDR	− 30,7	− 1,2	− 243,7	− 66,6
International reserves	Mio USD	145,6	138,9	144,8	301,6
External public debt	Mio USD	1 499,1	1 495,1	1 471,2	1 466,5
Debt service/exports	%	10,3	12,5	25,0	14,7
Official development assistance					
Total net ODA	Mio USD	147,7	141,2	109,9	215,9
Bilateral net ODA	Mio USD	104,1	68,4	56,4	90,7
Net ODA: EC/bilateral	%	48,7	58,2	64,3	22,8
Multilateral net ODA	Mio USD	43,6	72,7	53,6	125,2
Multilateral: EDF/multilateral	%	37,7	54,2	25,7	37,1
Food aid					
Cereals	000 t	72,5	51,4	29,4	90,1
Dairy products	000 t	2,9	0,0	3,1	6,4
Total	Mio USD	36,4	12,7	11,5	32,8
Origin of GDP					
Agriculture, forestry, fisheries	%	54,2	57,8	56,3	51,6
Industry	%	9,0	6,3	5,6	8,5
Services	%	38,5	38,0	39,4	41,3

GHANA

Production and exports	Units	1981	1982	1983	1984
Main products					
Cereals, total	000 t	725	544	308	902
Sorghum	000 t	131	86	56	156
Millet	000 t	119	76	40	106
Maize	000 t	378	346	172	574
Rice, paddy	000 t	97	36	40	66
Tomatoes	000 t	140	200	250	300
Tubers and roots	000 t	2 874	3 192	3 315	5 693
Unshelled groundnuts	000 t	126	111	91	90
Palm kernels	000 t	30	30	30	30
Palm oil	000 t	21	23	20	30
Cocoa beans	000 t	247	203	168	173
Pineapples	000 t	6	7	6	5
Coconuts	000 t	160	160	140	120
Oranges	000 t	30	35	35	35
Natural rubber	000 t	10	9	9	6
Roundwood	000 m³	8 215	8 075	8 075	8 075
Sawn wood	000 m³	255	215	215	239
Wood-band panels	000 m³	91	68	68	68
Fishing	000 t	230	237	243	238
Manganese ore	000 t	223	160	197	248
Bauxite ore	000 t	181	63	70	52
Gold ore	kg	10 500	10 300	9 700	8 900
Diamonds	000 ca.	836	684	369	
Salted fish	000 t	58	55	57	55
Canned fish	000 t	2	1	1	1
Aluminium (684.1)	000 t	191	174	43	
Main exports					
SITC 031.1 Fish, fresh or frozen	Mio USD	8,4	22,1	26,2	
	%	1.0	2.4	5.1	
SITC 032 Prep. or preserved fish and crustacea	Mio USD	3,7	:	:	
	%	0.4	:	:	
SITC 072.1 Cocoa beans	Mio USD	398,8	382,4	239,8	
	%	45,7	42,2	46,8	
SITC 072.32 Cocoa butter	Mio USD	17,7	35,1	24,1	
	%	2,0	3,9	4,7	
SITC 242 Wood, rough	Mio USD	10,9	9,0	8,1	
	%	1,2	1,0	1,6	
SITC 243 Wood, shaped	Mio USD	22,0	15,7	13,8	
	%	2,5	1,7	2,7	
SITC 332 Petroleum products	Mio USD	57,2	:	:	
	%	6,5	:	:	
SITC 684.1 Aluminium unwrought	Mio USD	232,4	339,1	108,8	
	%	26,6	37,4	21,2	

GRENADA

Population 1985:	110 000	→ Rate of growth 1970-85:	1,3 %
GNP 1985:	90,0 Mio USD	→ Rate of growth 1970-85:	5,9 %
GNP/capita 1985:	970,0 USD	→ Rate of growth 1970-81:	0,1 %

Total exports 1983:	21,4 Mio USD	Total imports 1983:	29,6 Mio USD
Exports to EC 1983:	11,9 Mio USD	Imports from EC 1983:	13,0 Mio USD
Pupils: primary school 1982:	17 704	Pupils: secondary school 1977:	5 938
Pers. by hospital bed 1980:	188	Pers. by doctor 1978:	4 400

	Units	1981	1982	1983	1984
External trade					
Total exports	75 = 100	230,3	151,0	179,7	
Total imports	75 = 100	134,6	127,4	127,0	
Balance of trade	Mio USD	− 3,9	− 11,7	− 8,2	
Exports/imports	%	87,5	60,5	72,3	
Balance of trade with EC	Mio USD	11,2	2,0	− 1,1	
Exports to EC/imports from EC	%	224,1	122,4	91,7	
Exports/GDP	%	49,8	46,7	46,5	45,1
Financial indicators					
Overall balance of payments	Mio SDR	− 3,2	− 5,2	3,6	0,5
International reserves	Mio USD	16,1	13,0	14,1	14,2
External public debt	Mio USD	29,5	50,5	46,8	41,0
Debt service/exports	%	7,7	9,9	24,2	24,2
Official development assistance					
Total net ODA	Mio USD	6,1	6,7	8,0	27,5
Bilateral net ODA	Mio USD	0,3	1,9	2,2	22,8
Net ODA: EC/bilateral	%	32,1	5,3	2,2	3,7
Multilateral net ODA	Mio USD	5,8	4,8	5,7	4,7
Multilateral: EDF/multilateral	%	34,1	11,5	44,9	54,5
Food aid					
Dairy products	t	630	0,0	380	250
Total	000 USD	840	0,0	360	390
Index of price changes	75 = 100	213,7	225,1	244,4	248,3
Main products					
Tubers and roots	000 t	3	4	4	4
Cocoa beans	000 t	3	2	2	3
Bananas	000 t	15	14	14	14
Main exports					
SITC 051.3 Bananas	Mio USD	6,6	5,7	6,2	
	%	24,0	31,6	28,9	
SITC 072.1 Cocoa beans	Mio USD	6,6	3,7	3,8	
	%	24,0	20,5	17,7	
SITC 075.24 Nutmeg	Mio USD	2,4	2,6	3,1	
	%	8,7	14,4	14,5	

GUINEA-BISSAU

Population 1985:	890 000	→	Rate of growth 1970-85:	4,1 %
GNP 1985:	150,0 Mio USD	→	Rate of growth 1970-85:	7,2 %
GNP/capita 1985:	170,0 USD	→	Rate of growth:	– %

Total exports 1983:	11,7 Mio USD	Total imports 1983:	79,6 Mio USD
Exports to EC 1983:	1,1 Mio USD	Imports from EC 1983:	19,6 Mio USD
Pupils: primary school 1982:	74 359	Pupils: secondary school 1982:	8 432
Pers. by hospital bed 1982:	529	Pers. by doctor 1982:	7 306

	Units	1981	1982	1983	1984
External trade					
Total exports	75 = 100	341,8	150,9	189,0	
Total imports	75 = 100	208,1	254,4	214,5	
Balance of trade	Mio USD	– 56,0	– 85,0	– 67,9	
Exports/imports	%	27,5	9,9	14,7	
Balance of trade with EC	Mio USD	– 7,1	– 18,8	– 18,5	
Exports to EC/imports from EC	%	52,6	7,2	5,8	
Exports/GDP	%	11,2	7,8	5,7	
Financial indicators					
Overall balance of payments	Mio SDR	:	– 14,4	– 12,3	– 6,1
International reserves	Mio USD				
External public debt	Mio USD	158,9	177,6	250,8	269,2
Debt service/exports	%	:	29,8	24,5	19,4
Official development assistance					
Total net ODA	Mio USD	65,2	65,2	64,2	55,2
Bilateral net ODA	Mio USD	41,4	38,5	38,3	32,8
Net ODA: EC/bilateral	%	47,2	42,9	49,3	49,6
Multilateral net ODA	Mio USD	23,8	26,7	25,9	22,4
Net ODA: EDF/multilateral	%	25,4	39,5	17,0	39,7
Food aid					
Cereals	000 t	18,5	27,5	21,6	36,4
Dairy products	t	254,0	579,0	475,0	333,0
Total	Mio USD	10,5	7,2	9,7	13,0
Origin of GDP					
Agriculture, forestry, fisheries	%	49,3	46,8	43,2	
Industry	%	15,9	14,4	:	
Services	%	34,8	38,8	:	
Index of price changes	75 = 100	131,7	150,9	192,3	

GUINEA-BISSAU

Production and exports	Units	1981	1982	1983	1984
Main products					
Cereals, total	000 t	132	160	139	163
Sorghum	000 t	20	26	23	21
Millet	000 t	14	16	16	20
Maize	000 t	13	10	10	10
Rice, paddy	000 t	80	103	85	105
Unshelled groundnuts	000 t	30	35	22	30
Palm kernels	000 t	9	10	6	11
Coconuts	000 t	25	25	25	25
Roundwood	000 m³	553	555	557	558
Fishing	000 t	3	4	3	3
Main exports					
SITC 221.2 Copra	Mio USD	2,4	1,8	3,9	
	%	11,3	19,2	33,3	

Population 1985:	6 070 000 →	Taux de croissance 1970-85:		3,0 %
PNB 1985:	1 950,0 Mio USD →	Taux de croissance 1970-85:		8,3 %
PNB/h 1985:	320,0 USD →	Taux de croissance 1970-81:		− 0,3 %

Exportations 1983:	420,5 Mio USD	Importations 1983:	252,6 Mio USD
Exportations vers la CE 1982:	128,8 Mio USD	Importations de la CE 1983:	124,1 Mio USD
Élèves: enseign. primaire 1983:	284 386	Élèves : enseign. secondaire 1983:	97 719
Personnes/lit d'hôpital 1982:	592	Personnes/médecin 1982:	8 100

	Unités	1981	1982	1983	1984
Commerce extérieur					
Exportations	75 = 100	309,6	312,7	295,0	
Importations	75 = 100	215,5	192,0	163,7	
Balance commerciale	Mio USD	108,9	149,5	167,9	
Exportations/importations	%	132,7	150,5	166,5	
Balance commerciale avec la CE	Mio USD	− 0,8	5,6	:	
Export. vers la CE/import. de la CE	%	99,5	104,6	:	
Exportations/PIB	%	27,9	29,8	29,1	
Indicateurs financiers					
Balance des paiements	Mio DTS				
Réserves internationales	Mio USD				
Dette extérieure publique	Mio USD	1 692,9	1 567,4	1 582,1	1 571,9
Service de la dette/Exportations	%				
Aide publique au développement					
APD net total	Mio USD	106,6	90,1	67,5	123,2
APD net bilatéral	Mio USD	55,9	55,3	25,9	71,9
APD net CE/bilatéral	%	32,3	34,0	67,7	34,8
APD net multilatéral	Mio USD	50,7	34,8	41,6	51,3
APD net FED/multilatéral	%	42,3	22,9	29,7	27,0
Aide alimentaire					
Céréales	000 t	32,2	35,8	19,6	36,1
Produits laitiers	t	402	3	5	4
Total	Mio USD	13,1	9,9	6,6	9,1
Origine du PIB					
Agriculture, forêts, pêche	%	42,7	41,1	38,4	:
Industrie	%	23,0	23,3	23,0	:
Services	%	:	:	:	:
Indices d'évolution des prix	75 = 100	126,3	131,9	147,0	159,7

GUINÉE

Productions et exportations	Unités	1981	1982	1983	1984
Principales productions					
Céréales, total	000 t	607	613	508	520
Maïs	000 t	48	49	39	42
Riz, paddy	000 t	485	490	396	403
Haricots, pois, lentilles	000 t	45	45	45	45
Tubercules et racines	000 t	642	648	654	658
Arachides non décortiquées	000 t	84	85	77	82
Palmistes	000 t	40	40	40	40
Huile de palme	000 t	42	45	45	45
Sucre centrifugé brut	000 t	20	22	20	20
Bananes	000 t	101	102	103	104
Lait de vache	000 t	42	43	44	43
Viande de bovins	000 t	18	19	19	19
Bois rond	000 m³	3 610	3 618	3 626	3 635
Bois scié	000 m³	90	90	90	90
Pêche	000 t	18	18	18	18
Minerai de bauxite	000 t	12 822	11 827	12 986	12 986
Diamants	000 carats	37	38	40	47
Principales exportations					
CTCI 283.3 Bauxite	Mio USD	409,7	385,7	399,3	
	%	92,8	86,5	94,9	
CTCI 667.2 Diamants	Mio USD	1,1	9,9	0,5	
	%	0,2	2,2	0,1	

Population 1985:	390 000	→ Taux de croissance 1970-85:			2,0%
PNB 1978:	118 Mio USD	→ Taux de croissance 1970-78:			3,7%
PNB/h 1978:	341 USD	→ Taux de croissance 1970-78:			−4,5%

Exportations 1983:	25,4 Mio USD	Importations 1983		15,8 Mio USD
Exportations vers la CE 1983	17,3 Mio USD	Importations de la CE 1983		5,7 Mio USD
Élèves: Enseign. primaire 1975:	36 000	Élèves: enseign. secondaire 1975:		4 523
Personnes/lit d'hôpital 1982:	95	Personnes/médecin 1982:		62 000

	Unités	1981	1982	1983	1984
Commerce extérieur					
Exportations	75 = 100	123,0	113,3	106,8	
Importations	75 = 100	231,9	208,7	84,7	
Balance commerciale	Mio USD	− 14,0	− 12,0	9,6	
Exportations/Importations	%	67,7	69,2	160,8	
Balance commerciale avec la CE	Mio USD	4,2	4,3	11,6	
Export. vers la CE/Import. de la CE	%	134,2	143,7	303,6	
Exportations/PIB	%				
Indicateurs financiers					
Balance des paiements	Mio DTS				
Réserves internationales	Mio USD				
Dette extérieure publique	Mio USD	133,8	146,2	141,8	146,0
Service de la dette/Exportations	%				
Aide publique au développement					
APD net total	Mio USD	10,2	14,0	11,1	15,0
APD net bilatéral	Mio USD	4,3	5,1	4,0	8,0
APD net CE/bilatéral	%	73,2	89,0	71,5	79,3
APD net multilatéral	Mio USD	6,0	8,9	7,1	7,1
APD net FED/multilatéral	%	35,8	37,2	14,7	11,2
Aide alimentaire					
Céréales	t	645	2 500	2 300	7 100
Produits laitiers	t	0,0	0,0	0,0	500
Total	000 USD	260	970	1 033	2 375
Principales productions					
Tubercules et racines	000 t	87	87	88	89
Palmistes	000 t	3	3	3	3
Huile de palme	000 t	5	5	5	5
Fèves de cacao	000 t	8	9	9	8
Café vert	000 t	7	7	7	7
Bananes	000 t	16	16	17	18
Noix de coco	000 t	7	7	8	8
Bois rond	000 m³	453	498	567	587
Bois scié	000 m³	13	13	23	24
Pêche	000 t	3	2	2	4
Principales exportations					
CTCI 072.1 Fèves de cocao	Mio USD	16,5	11,4	13,6	
	%	56,5	42,4	53,6	

GUYANA

Population 1985:	970 000	→	Rate of growth 1970-85:		0,7 %
GNP 1985:	460,0 Mio USD	→	Rate of growth 1970-85:		4,9 %
GNP/capita 1985:	570,0 USD	→	Rate of growth 1970-81:		0,7 %

Total exports 1985:	207,0 Mio USD	Total imports 1983:		152,4 Mio USD
Exports to EC 1983:	94,0 Mio USD	Imports from EC 1983:		27,3 Mio USD
Pupils: primary school 1981:	130 003	Pupils: secondary school 1976:		73 285
Pers. by hospital bed 1981:	200	Pers. by doctor 1981:		7 350

	Units	1981	1982	1983	1984
External trade					
Total exports	75 = 100	125,9	119,5	86,4	58,9
Total imports	75 = 100	103,7	71,2	44,5	
Balance of trade	Mio USD	94,5	182,7	155,7	
Exports/imports	%	126,6	175,0	202,1	
Balance of trade with EC	Mio USD	70,1	81,1	66,7	
Exports to EC/imports from EC	%	191,0	299,8	344,0	
Exports/GDP	%	65,7	54,8	46,4	51,9
Financial indicators					
Overall balance of payments	Mio SDR	− 91,7	− 45,7	− 22,1	23,3
International reserves	Mio USD	6,9	10,6	6,5	5,8
External public debt	Mio USD	890,6	856,5	828,1	828,3
Debt service/exports	%	31,3	23,8	26,2	14,4
Official development assistance					
Total net ODA	Mio USD	64,7	39,0	30,7	23,1
Bilateral net ODA	Mio USD	16,1	13,7	10,5	6,4
Net ODA: EC/bilateral	%	29,6	34,2	31,2	24,4
Multilateral net ODA	Mio USD	48,6	25,2	20,2	16,7
Multilateral: EDF/Multilateral	%	12,2	29,1	17,1	10,9
Food aid					
Cereals	t	1 070,0	1 300,0	3 200,0	0,0
Dairy products	t	600,0	700,0	120,0	350,0
Total	Mio USD	1 070,0	1 050,0	684,0	1 080,0
Origin of GDP					
Agriculture, forestry, fisheries	%	22,2	23,4	24,2	24,6
Industry	%	30,5	29,0	:	:
Services	%	47,3	47,7	53,0	50,7
Index of price changes	75 = 100	219,3	231,3	247,0	314,6

GUYANA

Production and exports	Units	1981	1982	1983	1984
Main products					
Cereals, total	000 t	277	303	247	313
Rice, paddy	000 t	276	303	246	312
Tubers and roots	000 t	15	16	17	17
Centrifugal sugar	000 t	306	292	248	237
Coconuts	000 t	34	38	43	40
Roundwood	000 m³	200	200	200	201
Sawn wood	000 m³	70	70	70	70
Fishing	000 t	23	26	28	32
Bauxite ore	000 t	2 396	1 783	1 087	1 704
Gold ore	kg	599	269	143	346
Main exports					
SITC 042 Rice	Mio USD	41,2	26,0	21,7	
	%	9,2	6,1	7,0	
SITC 061.1 Sugar	Mio USD	93,5	83,8	70,3	
	%	20,8	19,7	22,8	
SITC 283.3 Bauxite	Mio USD	180,2	143,1	120,7	
	%	40,1	33,6	39,2	

JAMAICA

Population 1985:	2 340 000	→	Rate of growth 1970-85:	1,5 %
GNP 1985:	2 090,0 Mio USD	→	Rate of growth 1970-85:	3,0 %
GNP/capita 1985:	940,0 USD	→	Rate of growth 1970-81:	− 2,2 %

Total exports 1985:	564,0 Mio USD	Total imports 1985:	1 110,0 Mio USD
Exports to EC 1983:	151,5 Mio USD	Imports from EC 1983:	129,9 Mio USD
Pupils: primary school 1983:	341 748	Pupils: secondary school 1983:	233 354
Pers. by hospital bed 1980:	258	Pers. by doctor 1980:	2 848

	Units	1981	1982	1983	1984
External trade					
Total exports	75 = 100	125,7	94,3	96,6	94,2
Total imports	75 = 100	132,5	122,3	84,7	104,4
Balance of trade	Mio USD	− 501,6	− 634,1	− 193,7	− 432,6
Exports/imports	%	66,3	53,8	79,6	63,1
Balance of trade with EC	Mio USD	20,8	− 24,3	21,6	
Exports to EC/imports from EC	%	112,1	86,9	116,6	
Exports/GDP	%	47,7	38,3	38,0	55,0
Financial indicators					
Overall balance of payments	Mio SDR	− 290,6	− 158,9	− 162,7	20,5
International reserves	Mio USD	85,2	109,0	63,2	96,9
External public debt	Mio USD	1 966,9	2 281,7	2 538,7	2 925,9
Debt service/exports	%	56,0	41,1	33,8	40,9
Official development assistance					
Total net ODA	Mio USD	154,7	180,3	180,7	170,3
Bilateral net ODA	Mio USD	110,1	151,2	156,2	156,0
Net ODA: EC/bilateral	%	28,9	15,0	13,1	14,2
Multilateral net ODA	Mio USD	44,6	29,1	24,5	14,3
Multilateral: EDF/multilateral	%	27,8	11,6	12,6	35,6
Food aid					
Cereals	000 t	55,5	105,3	98,5	132,9
Dairy products	000 t	3,1	1,7	0,1	6,6
Total	Mio USD	24,5	20,4	19,4	36,3
Origin of GDP					
Agriculture, forestry, fisheries	%	7,6	6,8	6,5	5,6
Industry	%	35,3	33,4	35,1	38,9
Services	%	61,1	64,1	63,0	59,0
Index of price changes	75 = 100	264,8	286,2	322,8	410,6

JAMAICA

Production and exports	Units	1981	1982	1983	1984
Main products					
Rum	000 hl	176	150	150	150
Tomatoes	000 t	23	17	19	30
Tubers and roots	000 t	223	183	205	248
Centrifugal sugar	000 t	200	196	198	193
Bananas	000 t	150	160	160	150
Coconuts	000 t	161	116	112	120
Oranges	000 t	33	33	32	32
Cow milk	000 t	48	48	49	49
Beef and buffalo meat	000 t	12	12	14	15
Roundwood	000 m³	55	43	102	117
Sawn wood	000 m³	25	25	23	31
Fishing	000 t	8	8	9	10
Bauxite ore	000 t	11 607	8 158	7 682	8 735
Motor spirit	000 t	155	191	160	150
Light oils	000 t	136	217	201	200
Heavy oils	000 t	315	294	504	400
Alumina	000 t	1 253	879		
Main exports					
SITC 051.3 Bananas	Mio USD	4,3	7,6	13,1	
	%	0,4	1,0	1,9	
SITC 061.1 Sugar	Mio USD	46,5	47,6	57,3	48,6
	%	4,7	6,4	8,4	6,5
SITC 112.4 Alcoholic beverages	Mio USD	20,5	20,1	18,9	38,0
	%	2,1	2,7	2,8	5,1
SITC 122.1 Cigars	Mio USD	9,3	8,6		
	%	0,9	1,2		
SITC 283.3 Bauxite	Mio USD	172,1	129,5	109,2	
	%	17,5	17,5	15,9	
SITC 332 Petroleum products	Mio USD	27,8	26,4		
	%	2,8	3,6		
SITC 513.65 Alumina	Mio USD	588,1	348,4	314,6	
	%	59,7	47,1	45,9	

KENYA

Population 1985:	20 330 000 →	Rate of growth 1970-85:	4,0 %
GNP 1985:	5 960,0 Mio USD →	Rate of growth 1970-85:	9,3 %
GNP/capita 1985:	290,0 USD →	Rate of growth 1970-81:	3,3 %

Total exports 1985:	958,0 Mio USD	Total imports 1985:	1 437,0 Mio USD
Exports to EC 1983:	388,2 Mio USD	Imports from EC 1983:	463,1 Mio USD
Pupils: primary school 1983:	4 323 822	Pupils: secondary school 1983:	517 033
Pers. by hospital bed 1982:	601	Pers. by doctor 1982:	10 136

	Units	1981	1982	1983	1984
External trade					
Total exports	75 = 100	262,9	214,3	214,0	237,5
Total imports	75 = 100	228,5	176,0	151,4	169,8
Balance of trade	Mio USD	− 882,2	− 625,9	− 403,1	− 464,0
Exports/imports	%	57,6	61,0	70,8	70,0
Balance of trade with EC	Mio USD	− 333,1	− 196,3	− 74,9	
Exports to EC/imports from EC	%	54,9	63,8	83,8	
Exports/GDP	%	25,6	25,1	25,2	26,3
Financial indicators					
Overall balance of payments	Mio SDR	− 295,1	− 105,8	95,0	72,7
International reserves	Mio USD	231,1	211,7	376,0	389,8
External public debt	Mio USD	3 569,6	3 828,0	3 612,0	3 877,3
Debt service/exports	%	36,5	42,8	36,8	33,0
Official development assistance					
Total net ODA	Mio USD	449,3	484,9	400,3	410,9
Bilateral net ODA	Mio USD	364,8	338,9	342,3	325,5
Net ODA: EC/bilateral	%	48,3	49,9	39,7	41,8
Multilateral net ODA	Mio USD	84,5	146,0	58,0	85,5
Multilateral: EDF/multilateral	%	54,4	19,7	28,6	19,4
Food aid					
Cereals	000 t	200,0	137,1	121,8	126,8
Dairy products	000 t	8,4	2,9	3,9	3,0
Total	Mio USD	62,6	31,3	33,8	25,4
Origin of GDP					
Agriculture, forestry, fisheries	%	32,4	33,0	32,8	31,0
Industry	%	21,7	21,1	21,0	20,7
Services	%	48,7	48,8	49,6	51,7
Index of price changes	75 = 100	186,7	205,3	227,0	249,4

KENYA

Production and exports	Units	1981	1982	1983	1984
Main products					
Cereals, total	000 t	2 231	2 943	2 587	1 768
Wheat	000 t	214	248	251	144
Sorghum	000 t	94	56	35	98
Maize	000 t	1 768	2 502	2 178	1 422
Pulses, total	000 t	200	288	270	68
Tubers and roots	000 t	1 386	1 560	1 365	1 525
Centrifugal sugar	000 t	399	335	353	404
Raw coffee	000 t	91	88	95	119
Tea	000 t	91	96	119	116
Bananas	000 t	136	138	140	142
Pineapples	000 t	190	202	137	168
Coconuts	000 t	80	34	55	70
Sisal	000 t	41	50	50	51
Cow milk	000 t	882	1 101	1 001	701
Beef and buffalo meat	000 t	166	186	156	109
Roundwood	000 m³	27 436	28 557	29 788	31 115
Sawn wood	000 m³	181	181	181	181
Fishing	000 t	57	81	97	90
Salted fish	000 t	6	11	13	9
Motor spirit	000 t	369	322	301	319
Light oils	000 t	535	464	448	182
Heavy oils	000 t	648	735	605	619
Main exports					
SITC 053.9 Fruits and nuts pres.	Mio USD	26,8	25,0	31,4	
	%	2,2	2,6	3,2	
SITC 061.1 Sugar	Mio USD	37,0	4,8	1,5	
	%	3,1	0,5	0,2	
SITC 071.1 Coffee	Mio USD	244,7	248,6	240,6	
	%	20,4	25,4	24,6	
SITC 074.1 Tea	Mio USD	148,9	143,9	192,6	
	%	12,4	14,7	19,7	
SITC 265.4 Sisal	Mio USD	19,6	18,7	18,2	
	%	1,6	1,9	1,9	
SITC 332.1 Petroleum spirit	Mio USD	49,6	41,0	40,4	
	%	4,1	4,2	4,1	
SITC 332.2 Lamp oil	Mio USD	98,8	83,9	53,2	
	%	8,2	8,6	5,4	
SITC 332.3 Distillate fuel oil	Mio USD	62,2	49,6	43,2	
	%	5,2	5,1	4,4	
SITC 332.4 Residual fuel oil	Mio USD	152,8	71,0	43,4	
	%	12,7	7,3	4,4	

Population 1985 Kiribati:	60 000 →	Rate of growth:			– %
GNP 1985:	30,0 Mio USD →	Rate of growth 1970-85:			3,1 %
GNP/capita 1985:	450,0 USD →	Rate of growth:			– %

Total exports 1983	4,5 Mio USD	Total imports 1983:			20,8 Mio USD
Exports to EC 1979:	3,4 Mio USD	Imports from EC 1983:			1,9 Mio USD
Pupils: primary school 1984:	13 194	Pupils: secondary school 1984:			2 074
Pers. by hospital bed 1982:	223	Pers. by doctor 1982:			3 158

	Units	1981	1982	1983	1984
External trade: Kiribati					
Total exports	75 = 100	69,4	55,6	12,4	
Total imports	75 = 100	180,7	172,2	172,8	
Balance of trade	Mio USD	3,3	– 0,7	– 16,3	
Exports/imports	%	115,1	96,6	21,4	
Balance of trade with EC	Mio USD				
Exports to EC/imports from EC	%				
Exports/GDP	%				
Official development assistance: Kiribati					
Total net ODA	Mio USD	15,3	15,1	16,8	11,9
Bilateral net ODA	Mio USD	13,7	14,4	14,4	10,4
Net ODA: EC/bilateral	%	69,5	64,9	62,4	50,8
Multilateral net ODA	Mio USD	1,6	0,7	2,4	1,6
Multilateral: EDF/multilateral	%	63,1	32,4	63,0	57,3
Official development assistance: Tuvalu					
Total net ODA	Mio USD	5,3	6,2	4,2	5,5
Bilateral net ODA	Mio USD	4,5	5,5	3,8	5,2
Net ODA: EC/bilateral	%	59,2	61,5	60,4	67,2
Multilateral net ODA	Mio USD	0,9	0,7	0,4	0,3
Multilateral: EDF/multilateral	%	47,7	61,3	37,5	53,6
Main products: Kiribati					
Copra	000 t	13	12	10	13
Bananas	000 t	4	4	4	4
Coconuts	000 t	96	90	77	90
Fishing	000 t	20	20	24	26
Main products: Tuvalu					
Coconuts	t	4 582	2 350	2 000	2 700
Fishing	t	180	436	793	793
Salted fish	t	100	100	100	100
Canned fish	t	100	100	200	
Main exports:Tuvalu					
SITC 221.2 Copra	000 USD	34,0	27,0	55,0	
	%	81,0	73,0	78,6	

LESOTHO

	Units	1981	1982	1983	1984
Population 1985: 1 530 000 → Rate of growth 1970-85: 2,5 %					

Population 1985: 1 530 000 → Rate of growth 1970-85: 2,5 %
GNP 1985: 730,0 Mio USD → Rate of growth 1970-85: 12,1 %
GNP/capita 1985: 480,0 USD → Rate of growth 1970-81: 6,9 %

Total exports 1982: 40,0 Mio USD   Total imports 1982: 530,0 Mio USD
Exports to EC 1976: 3,6 Mio USD   Imports from EC 1976: 1,9 Mio USD
Pupils: primary school 1982: 277 945   Pupils: secondary school 1982: 28 717
Pers. by hospital bed 1980: 487   Pers. by doctor 1980: 18 642

	Units	1981	1982	1983	1984
External trade					
Total exports	75 = 100	408,2	320,1		
Total imports	75 = 100	335,5	334,2		
Balance of trade	Mio USD	− 481,0	− 490,0		
Exports/imports	%				
Balance of trade with EC	Mio USD	9,6	7,5		
Exports to EC/imports from EC	%				
Exports/GDP	%	16,2	14,4		
Financial indicators					
Overall balance of payments	Mio SDR	1,6	5,5	25,9	9,9
International reserves	Mio USD	43,4	47,5	66,7	48,6
External public debt	Mio USD	207,8	219,6	229,1	257,5
Debt service/exports	%	12,0	30,4	76,2	74,9
Official development assistance					
Total net ODA	Mio USD	101,0	89,6	104,3	97,3
Bilateral net ODA	Mio USD	59,4	53,4	63,9	65,8
Net ODA: EC/bilateral	%	46,7	38,2	43,0	34,5
Multilateral net ODA	Mio USD	41,6	36,2	40,4	31,5
Multilateral EDF/multilateral	%	16,7	18,6	13,6	23,8
Food aid					
Cereals	000 t	40,0	9,5	42,7	49,6
Dairy products	000 t	2,0	3,5	3,2	3,6
Total	Mio USD	14,6	7,3	14,7	15,3
Origin of GDP					
Agriculture, forestry, fisheries	%	26,0	22,7		
Industry	%	24,4	22,1	:	:
Services	%	48,9	54,9		
Index of price changes	75 = 100	374,8	420,1	482,8	540,5
Main products					
Cereals, total	000 t	172	125	123	132
Wheat	000 t	17	14	15	17
Sorghum	000 t	48	26	31	34
Maize	000 t	106	83	76	79
Roundwood	000 m³	293	293	293	293
Diamonds	000 ca	53	42		

LIBERIA

Population 1985:	2 190 000	→ Rate of growth 1970-85:			3,3 %
GNP 1985:	1 040,0 Mio USD	→ Rate of growth 1970-85:			7,4 %
GNP/capita 1985:	470,0 USD	→ Rate of growth 1970-81:			− 0,7 %

Total exports 1985:	436,0 Mio USD	Total imports 1985:		284,0 Mio USD
Exports to EC 1984:	316,5 Mio USD	Imports from EC 1984:		145,3 Mio USD
Pupils: primary school 1980:	227 431	Pupils: secondary school 1980:		54 623
Pers. by hospital bed 1982:	652	Pers. by doctor 1982:		9 235

	Units	1981	1982	1983	1984
External trade					
Total exports	75 = 100	132,9	120,0	107,3	114,0
Total imports	75 = 100	144,1	129,3	124,3	109,7
Balance of trade	Mio USD	46,2	44,2	11,0	85,9
Exports/imports	%	109,7	110,3	102,7	123,6
Balance of trade with EC	Mio USD	204,9	234,2	164,8	171,2
Exports to EC/imports from EC	%	240,0	294,6	209,3	217,8
Exports/GDP	%	49,8	45,6	39,8	
Financial indicators					
Overall balance of payments	Mio SDR	− 46,3	− 62,8	− 34,5	− 32,4
International reserves	Mio USD	8,3	6,5	20,4	3,5
External public debt	Mio USD	822,8	895,7	913,6	952,9
Debt service/exports	%	7,0	8,6	8,2	9,4
Official development assistance					
Total net ODA	Mio USD	108,5	108,9	118,4	133,2
Bilateral net ODA	Mio USD	88,7	86,4	88,4	107,6
Net ODA: EC/bilateral	%	22,0	17,6	31,4	18,1
Multilateral net ODA	Mio USD	19,8	22,4	30,0	25,6
Multilateral: EDF/multilateral	%	20,3	13,9	12,7	7,3
Food aid					
Cereals	000 t	35,9	39,5	51,9	128,6
Dairy products	t	0,0	100		
Total	Mio USD	20,3	13,0	15,8	24,4
Origin of GDP					
Agriculture, forestry, fisheries	%	34,3	36,3	36,1	:
Industry	%	25,7	28,1	25,7	:
Services	%	38,6	40,8	39,0	:
Index of price changes	75 = 100	137,8	141,6	145,9	148,3

LIBERIA

Production and exports	Units	1981	1982	1983	1984
Main products					
Cereals, total	000 t	260	250	290	298
Rice, paddy	000 t	260	250	290	298
Tubers and roots	000 t	361	367	370	371
Palm kernels	000 t	8	8	8	8
Palm oil	000 t	25	30	30	34
Centrifugal sugar	000 t	5	5	5	5
Cocoa beans	000 t	7	5	6	6
Raw coffee	000 t	8	12	8	12
Bananas	000 t	75	77	78	79
Pineapples	000 t	7	7	7	7
Coconuts	000 t	7	7	7	7
Oranges	000 t	7	7	7	7
Natural rubber	000 t	77	72	74	88
Roundwood	000 m³	4 308	4 400	4 023	4 174
Sawn wood	000 m³	199	172	161	153
Fishing	000 t	13	14	15	15
Iron ore	000 t	13 873	15 634	10 159	9 359
Diamonds	000 ca	301	413	330	239
Motor spirit	000 t	70	75	73	75
Light oils	000 t	125	135	137	136
Heavy oils	000 t	345	350	348	350
Main exports					
SITC 071.1 Coffee	Mio USD	19,4	22,8	18,2	13,7
	%	3,7	4,8	4,3	3,1
SITC 072.1 Cocoa beans	Mio USD	13,8	8,8	11,5	15,3
	%	2,6	1,9	2,7	3,4
SITC 231.1 Natural rubber	Mio USD	86,7	53,4	73,1	
	%	16,6	11,3	17,3	
SITC 242.3 Sawn and veneered logs	Mio USD	32,3	29,2	22,2	
	%	6,2	6,2	5,3	
SITC 275.1 Industrial diamonds	Mio USD	23,4	26,3	17,2	
	%	4,5	5,6	4,1	
SITC 281.3 Iron ore	Mio USD	325,4	309,9	267,4	
	%	62,1	65,6	63,3	

Population 1985:	9 980 000	→ Taux de croissance 1970-85:	2,6 %
PNB 1985:	2 510,0 Mio USD	→ Taux de croissance 1970-85:	4,1 %
PNB/h 1985:	250,0 USD	→ Taux de croissance 1970-81:	− 2,3 %

Exportations 1985:	286,7 Mio USD	Importations 1985:	465,1 Mio USD
Exportations vers la CE 1983:	135,2 Mio USD	Importations de la CE 1983:	145,8 Mio USD
Élèves: enseign. primaire 1978:	1 311 000	Élèves: enseign. secondaire 1975:	131 836
Personnes/lit d'hôpital 1980:	405	Personnes/médecin 1981:	9 939

	Unités	1981	1982	1983	1984
Commerce extérieur					
Exportations	75 = 100	110,2	112,0	105,5	115,5
Importations	75 = 100	128,9	119,6	112,1	112,3
Balance commerciale	Mio USD	− 148,7	− 109,5	− 101,2	− 72,3
Exportations/importations	%	68,6	75,1	75,4	82,5
Balance commerciale avec la CE	Mio USD	− 184,7	− 82,5	− 10,5	
Export. vers la CE/import. de la CE	%	37,9	61,5	92,8	
Exportations/PIB	%	13,5	13,3		
Indicateurs financiers					
Balance des paiements	Mio DTS	− 116,0	− 77,0	− 154,0	199,0
Réserves internationales	Mio USD	26,5	20,0	29,2	58,9
Dette extérieure publique	Mio USD	2 086,9	2 169,1	2 239,0	2 129,1
Service de la dette/exportations	%	13,6	40,2	29,4	35,8
Aide publique au développement					
APD net total	Mio USD	234,3	241,7	179,1	150,6
APD net bilatéral	Mio USD	148,9	162,0	105,7	86,5
APD net CE/bilatéral	%	41,5	65,3	60,2	74,6
APD net multilatéral	Mio USD	85,4	79,7	73,4	64,1
APD net FED/multilatéral	%	30,3	27,0	28,1	31,3
Aide alimentaire					
Céréales	000 t	47,6	115,4	94,4	126,1
Produits laitiers	000 t	0,9	1,2	1,2	2,5
Total	Mio USD	13,4	38,5	32,8	31,5
Origine du PIB					
Agriculture, forêts, pêche	%	39,7	41,1	:	:
Industrie	%	15,9	15,0	:	:
Services	%	40,6	40,8	:	:
Indice d'évolution des prix	75 = 100	204,3	262,8	328,3	361,4

MADAGASCAR

Productions et exportations	Unités	1981	1982	1983	1984
Principales productions					
Céréales, total	000 t	2 134	2 085	2 281	2 274
Maïs	000 t	121	113	132	141
Riz, paddy	000 t	2 011	1 970	2 147	2 131
Haricots, pois, lentilles	000 t	50	55	58	57
Turbercules et racines	000 t	2 307	2 533	2 793	2 866
Arachides non décortiquées	000 t	33	32	31	32
Sucre centrifugé brut	000 t	112	87	103	80
Café vert	000 t	83	81	81	81
Bananes	000 t	280	281	286	224
Ananas	000 t	47	50	50	51
Noix de coco	000 t	75	76	77	78
Oranges	000 t	60	61	81	81
Sisal	000 t	15	18	19	20
Fibres de coton	000 t	11	10	10	12
Viande de bovins	000 t	134	135	136	136
Bois rond	000 m³	6262	6262	6262	6262
Bois scié	000 m³	234	234	234	234
Pêche	000 t	50	49	55	56
Minerai de chrome	000 t	100	100	100	100
Tissus de coton	Mio m²	89	87	91	
Poisson salé	000 t	1	1	2	2
Essence	000 t	64	56	28	30
Huiles légères	000 t	102	101	56	60
Huiles lourdes	000 t	144	155	85	90
Principales exportations					
CTCI 011.1 Viande bovine	Mio USD	4,6	2,9	2,0	3,8
	%	1,4	0,9	0,7	1,1
CTCI 031 Poissons	Mio USD	16,8	21,3	23,8	23,2
	%	5,2	6,5	7,7	6,8
CTCI 061.2 Sucre raffiné	Mio USD	1,5	1,6	12,1	5,6
	%	0,5	0,5	3,9	1,6
CTCI 071.1 Café	Mio USD	95,9	93,3	114,8	141,7
	%	29,6	28,3	37,0	41,7
CTCI 075.21 Vanille	Mio USD	27.4	47,4	61,7	51,1
	%	8,5	14,4	19,9	15,0
CTCI 075.23 Girofles	Mio USD	65,2	65,0	16,2	35,5
	%	20,1	19,7	5,2	10,5
CTCI 263.1 Coton Brut	Mio USD	7,6	7,3	0,1	0,1
	%	2,3	2,2	0,0	0,0
CTCI 265.4 Sisal	Mio USD	3,7	4,4	1,4	1,7
	%	1,2	1,3	0,5	0,5
CTCI 283.9 Minerais et conc.min.non ferreux	Mio USD	5,8	4,9	3,1	1,4
	%	1,8	1,5	1,0	0,4
CTCI 332.4 Huiles lourdes	Mio USD	15,5	14,9	11,6	1,0
	%	4,8	4,5	3,8	0,3
CTCI 652.1 Tissus de coton non mercerisés	Mio USD	7,2	9,4	16,8	17,8
	%	2,2	2,9	5,4	5,2

MALAWI

Population 1985:	7 060 000 →	Rate of growth 1970-85:			3,1 %
GNP 1985:	1 160,0 Mio USD →	Rate of growth 1970-85:			9,1 %
GNP/capita 1985:	170,0 USD →	Rate of growth 1970-77:			3,6 %

Total exports 1985:	252,0 Mio USD	Total imports 1985:	284,0 Mio USD
Exports to EC 1981:	114,7 Mio USD	Imports from EC 1981:	117,2 Mio USD
Pupils: primary school 1982:	868 849	Pupils: secondary school 1982:	21 646
Pers. by hospital bed 1981:	521	Pers. by doctor 1980:	48 198

	Units	1981	1982	1983	1984
External trade					
Total exports	75 = 100	196,8	179,8	138,0	225,0
Total imports	75 = 100	139,8	122,7	124,0	107,4
Balance of trade	Mio USD	− 76,3	− 57,1	− 118,7	44,0
Exports/imports	%	78,2	81,4	61,8	116,4
Balance of trade with EC	Mio USD	− 2,5			
Exports to EC/imports from EC	%	97,9			
Exports/GDP	%	25,3	21,6	18,9	
Financial indicators					
Overall balance of payments	Mio SDR	− 40,9	− 33,0		
International reserves	Mio USD	49,0	22,7	15,4	56,6
External public debt	Mio USD	869,8	861,0	918,1	925,8
Debt service/exports	%	42,3	31,1		
Official development assistance					
Total net ODA	Mio USD	137,6	121,2	116,7	158,5
Bilateral net ODA	Mio USD	82,1	65,1	56,2	51,7
Net ODA: EC/bilateral	%	70,6	74,4	64,4	70,3
Multilateral net ODA	Mio USD	55,5	56,1	60,5	106,8
Multilateral: EDF/multilateral	%	25,2	19,2	9,5	13,6
Food aid					
Cereals	000 t	14,8	0,6	2,2	2,9
Dairy products	t	300	0,0	259	8
Total	000 USD	3 760	122	1 900	669
Index of price changes	75 = 100	218,0	244,9	294,1	

MALAWI

Production and exports	Units	1981	1982	1983	1984
Main products					
Cereals, total	000 t	1 428	1 596	1 556	1 589
Maize	000 t	1 245	1 415	1 369	1 398
Rice, paddy	000 t	42	40	36	42
Pulses, total	000 t	207	212	218	224
Tubers and roots	000 t	563	566	414	531
Unshelled groundnuts	000 t	180	170	170	170
Centrifugal sugar	000 t	167	172	175	150
Unmanufactured tobacco	000 t	51	59	72	73
Tea	000 t	32	38	32	37
Cotton lint	000 t	9	8	8	8
Roundwood	000 m³	5 856	6 041	6 235	6 444
Fishing	000 t	51	58	67	64
Main exports					
SITC 061.1 Sugar	Mio USD	56,9	7,3	8,5	
	%	20,8	2,9	3,7	
SITC 061.2 Refined sugar	Mio USD	9,7	16,5	0,0	3,9
	%	3,6	6,6	0,0	1,3
SITC 074.1 Tea	Mio USD	33,9	43,3	47,2	79,9
	%	12,4	17,3	20,6	25,8
SITC 121 Tobacco	Mio USD	111,6	111,9	118,2	
	%	40,7	44,7	51,6	
SITC 221.1 Groundnuts	Mio USD	12,2	4,4	1,2	
	%	4,4	1,8	0,5	
SITC 263.1 Raw cotton	Mio USD	1,7	1,2	:	
	%	0,6	0,5	:	
SITC 541.7 Medicaments incl. veterinary	Mio USD	3,4	1,6	0,1	0,5
	%	1,2	0,7	0,1	0,2
SITC 652.1 Cotton fabrics not mercerized	Mio USD	4,6	3,1	5,7	5,1
	%	1,7	1,2	2,5	1,6
SITC 652.2 Cotton fabrics mercerized	Mio USD	6,1	0,0	0,1	
	%	2,2	0,0	0,0	

MALI

Population 1985: 8 210 000 → Taux de croissance 1970-85: 3,3 %
PNB 1985: 1 070,0 Mio USD → Taux de croissance 1970-85: 6,6 %
PNB/h 1985: 140,0 Mio USD → Taux de croissance 1970-81: 1,4 %

Exportations 1983: 98,2 Mio USD Importations 1984: 368,2 Mio USD
Exportations vers la CE 1983: 42,2 Mio USD Importations de la CE 1983: 134,2 Mio USD
Élèves: enseign. primaire 1982: 296 301 Élèves: enseign. secondaire 1982: 69 754
Personnes/lit d'hôpital 1982: 1 743 Personnes/médecin 1982: 26 447

	Unités	1981	1982	1983	1984
Commerce extérieur					
Exportations	75 = 100	327,7	250,0	268,8	
Importations	75 = 100	156,8	152,7	159,8	193,7
Balance commerciale	Mio USD	− 178,3	− 199,0	− 205,6	
Exportations/importations	%	40,2	31,5	32,3	
Balance commerciale avec la CE	Mio USD	− 52,4	− 93,0	− 92,0	
Export. vers la CE/import. de la CE	%	55,7	29,7	31,5	
Exportations/PIB	%	18,2	19,1	22,9	
Indicateurs financiers					
Balance des paiements	Mio DTS	− 5,7	− 23,4	− 11,8	
Réserves internationales	Mio USD	17,4	16,7	16,2	26,6
Dette extérieure publique	Mio USD	1 073,3	1 276,0	1 355,4	1 389,9
Service de la dette/exportations	%	7,1	6,1	8,1	9.3
Aide publique au développement					
APD net total	Mio USD	230,3	210,3	214,5	320,3
APD net bilatéral	Mio USD	140,2	136,1	128,6	232,4
APD net CE/bilatéral	%	67,2	46,1	45,1	77,6
APD net multilatéral	Mio USD	90,1	74,2	85,9	87,8
APD net FED/multilatéral	%	27,9	25,3	12,6	33,5
Aide alimentaire					
Céréales	000 t	32,2	53,3	75,2	113,4
Produits laitiers	t	1 019	1 125	839	1 912
Total	Mio USD	11,2	18,3	25,4	42,8
Origine du PIB					
Agriculture, forêts, pêche	%	41,9	43,1	45,9	:
Industrie	%	10,9	10,0	:	:
Services	%	47,2	46,9	43,2	:
Indice d'évolution des prix	75 = 100	175,6	191,2	207,0	239,1

Productions et exportations	Unités	1981	1982	1983	1984
Principales productions					
Céréales, total	000 t	1 197	1 324	1 509	1 113
Millet	000 t	950	1 057	1 097	876
Maïs	000 t	61	89	144	102
Riz, paddy	000 t	135	153	216	109
Haricots, pois, lentilles	000 t	47	51	55	50
Tubercules et racines	000 t	122	131	143	142
Arachides non décortiquées	000 t	128	94	75	54
Fibres de coton	000 t	40	37	50	54
Lait de vache	000 t	128	133	114	98
Viande de bovins	000 t	38	42	45	57
Bois rond	000 m³	4 365	4 489	4 613	4 751
Pêche	000 t	76	73	61	54
Poisson salé	000 t	6	6	4	2
Principales exportations					
CTCI 001.1 Bovins	Mio USD	4,8	5,9	12,0	
	%	4,0	6,4	12,2	
CTCI 221.1 Arachides	Mio USD	1,9	3,2	:	
	%	1,6	3,5	:	
CTCI 263.1 Coton brut	Mio USD	52,3	35,5	80,9	
	%	43,6	38,8	82,4	

Population 1985:	990 000	→ Taux de croissance 1970-85:	1,3 %
PNB 1985:	1 110,0 Mio USD	→ Taux de croissance 1970-85:	8,4 %
PNB/h 1985:	1 070,0 USD	→ Taux de croissance 1970-81:	3,7 %

Exportations 1985:	441,0 Mio USD	Importations 1985:	528,0 Mio USD
Exportations vers la CE 1983:	306,6 Mio USD	Importations de la CE 1983:	137,9 Mio USD
Élèves: enseign. primaire 1983:	138 790	Élèves: enseign. secondaire 1983:	77 838
Personnes/lit d'hôpital 1981:	321	Personnes/médecin 1980:	1 907

	Unités	1981	1982	1983	1984
Commerce extérieur					
Exportations	75 = 100	108,7	123,1	123,6	126,9
Importations	75 = 100	167,5	140,4	133,6	143,2
Balance commerciale	Mio USD	− 230,0	− 97,4	− 73,4	− 95,3
Exportations/importations	%	58,5	79,0	83,4	79,9
Balance commerciale avec la CE	Mio USD	132,1	173,0	168,7	
Export. vers la CE/import. de la CE	%	185,3	227,4	222,3	
Exportations/PIB	%	44,7	47,2	46,6	47,9
Indicateurs financiers					
Balance des paiements	Mio DTS	− 110,2	− 53,5	− 28,4	− 40,8
Réserves internationales	Mio USD	35,1	38,0	17,9	23,6
Dette extérieure publique	Mio USD	477,0	550,2	538,7	526,5
Service de la dette/exportations	%	20,3	20,5	25,2	20,2
Aide publique au développement					
APD net total	Mio USD	58,3	47,8	40,7	35,5
APD net bilatéral	Mio USD	48,7	32,6	27,2	27,5
APD net CE/bilatéral	%	88,5	53,8	69,7	64,7
APD net multilatéral	Mio USD	9,6	15,2	13,5	8,1
APD net FED/multilatéral	%	27,3	34,2	38,5	34,5
Aide alimentaire					
Céréales	000 t	20,0	32,6	22,0	8,4
Produits laitiers	t	612,0	513,0	309,0	605,0
Total	Mio USD	6,1	7,7	5,9	2,6
Origine du PIB					
Agriculture, forêts, pêche	%	14,3	15,3	13,9	13,7
Industrie	%	24,7	24,5	24,6	25,3
Services	%	60,9	60,3	61,5	61,0
Indice d'évolution des prix	75 = 100	199,3	216,6	235,5	253,9

MAURITANIE

Productions et exportations	Unités	1981	1982	1983	1984
Principales productions					
Céréales, total	000 t	83	59	38	34
Millet	000 t	66	40	20	15
Riz, paddy	000 t	11	15	14	17
Haricots, pois, lentilles	000 t	32	26	14	20
Dattes	000 t	12	10	11	10
Lait de vache	000 t	86	86	88	91
Lait de brebis	000 t	57	54	55	66
Lait de chèvre	000 t	70	72	73	74
Viande de bovins	000 t	16	15	14	13
Bois rond	000 m³	11	11	11	12
Pêche	000 t	62	58	54	55
Minerai de fer	000 t	5 243	7 660	7 402	9 100
Poisson salé	000 t	1	1	1	1
Principales exportations					
CTCI 031.1 Poissons frais	Mio USD	89,8	83,0	143,9	136,2
	%	34,4	35,6	47,2	45,8
CTCI 031.3 Crustacés et mollusques	Mio USD	1,3	3,7	1,8	2,9
	%	0,5	1,6	0,6	1,0
CTCI 281.3 Minerai de fer	Mio USD	167,0	138,6	130,9	145,9
	%	63,9	59,4	42,9	49,1

MOZAMBIQUE

Population 1985: 13 960 000 →	Taux de croissance 1970-85: 3,7 %
PNB 1985: 5 270,0 Mio USD →	Taux de croissance 1970-85: 5,7 %
PNB/h 1985: 300,0 USD →	Taux de croissance 1970-81: −4,5 %

Exportations 1983: 239,8 Mio USD	Importations 1984: 487,0 Mio USD
Exportations vers la CE 1983: 48,5 Mio USD	Importations de la CE 1983: 177,6 Mio USD
Élèves: enseign. primaire 1983: 1 162 617	Élèves: enseign. secondaire 1983: 121 033
Personnes/lit d'hôpital 1981: 848	Personnes/médecin 1980: 33 883

	Unités	1981	1982	1983	1984
Commerce extérieur					
Exportations	75 = 100	177,9	151,4	118,8	
Importations	75 = 100	155,7	149,9	119,9	116,8
Balance commerciale	Mio USD	− 290,3	− 319,7	− 260,3	
Exportations/importations	%	55,3	48,9	47,9	
Balance commerciale avec la CE	Mio USD	− 162,3	− 110,2	− 129,1	
Export. vers la CE/import. de la CE	%	26,6	34,9	27,3	
Exportations/PIB	%	19,5	16,3	15,1	
Aide publique au développement					
APD net total	Mio USD	143,6	207,9	210,8	259,1
APD net bilatéral	Mio USD	110,0	166,9	161,6	193,0
APD net CE/bilatéral	%	46,7	44,0	44,6	50,1
APD net multilatéral	Mio USD	32,7	40,9	49,2	66,1
APD net FED/multilatéral	%	32,2	9,9	30,3	32,3
Aide alimentaire					
Céréales	000 t	103,8	144,4	213,2	225,0
Produits laitiers	000 t	0,9	1,8	0,1	6,8
Total	Mio USD	33,8	33,3	58,0	82,3
Indice d'évolution des prix	75 = 100	186,9	210,0	231,6	

NIGER

Productions et exportations	Unités	1981	1982	1983	1984
Principales productions					
Céréales, total	000 t	1 689	1 704	1 748	1 090
Sorgho	000 t	322	357	362	240
Millet	000 t	1 314	1 292	1 325	780
Riz, paddy	000 t	40	42	45	51
Haricots, pois, lentilles	000 t	283	286	284	210
Oignons secs	000 t	110	110	112	115
Tubercules et racines	000 t	205	220	211	201
Arachides non décortiquées	000 t	118	88	74	30
Lait de vache	000 t	103	105	106	106
Lait de chèvre	000 t	117	120	123	124
Viande de bovins	000 t	40	35	35	37
Bois rond	000 m³	3 498	3 597	3 700	3 807
Pêche	000 t	8	7	7	7
Minerai d'uranium	t	4 369	4 260	3 426	3 267
Poisson salé	000 t	2	2	2	2
Principales exportations					
CTCI 001.1 Bovins	Mio USD	39,0			
	%	8,6			
CTCI 001.2 Ovins et caprins	Mio USD	15,7			
	%	3,4			
CTCI 054 Légumes et tubercules	Mio USD	3,1			
	%	0,7			
CTCI 122 Tabacs manufacturés	Mio USD	14,8			
	%	3,3			
CTCI 211.4 Peaux de caprins	Mio USD	1,9			
	%	0,4			
CTCI 286.0 Minerai d'uranium	Mio USD	360,7			
	%	79,3			

NIGERIA

Population 1985:	95 200 000	→ Rate of growth 1970-85:			3,6 %
GNP 1985:	75 940,0 Mio USD	→ Rate of growth 1970-85:			8,6 %
GNP/capita 1985:	760,0 USD	→ Rate of growth 1970-81:			2,0 %

Total exports 1985:	12 345,0 Mio USD	Total imports 1985:	8 734,0 Mio USD
Exports to EC 1983:	6 449,8 Mio USD	Imports from EC 1983:	3 655,5 Mio USD
Pupils: primary school 1980:	13 787 736	Pupils: secondary school 1979:	1 826 629
Pers. by hospital bed 1982:	1 251	Pers. by doctor 1982:	9 591

	Units	1981	1982	1983	1984
External trade					
Total exports	75 = 100	238,1	199,9	154,9	176,7
Total imports	75 = 100	257,3	184,3	116,0	155,5
Balance of trade	Mio USD	3 487,7	4 842,9	5 373,4	4 732,0
Exports/imports	%	122,4	143,5	176,7	150,4
Balance of trade with EC	Mio USD	− 1 907,6	− 270,1	2 794,3	
Exports to EC/imports from EC	%	75,2	95,6	176,4	
Exports/GDP	%	23,8	17,9	15,9	16,3
Financial indicators					
Overall balance of payments	Mio SDR	− 4 077,0	− 1 870,0	− 787,0	73,0
International reserves	Mio USD	3 895,0	1 613,0	990,0	1 462,0
External public debt	Mio USD	14 549,2	16 431,1	19 237,7	16 935,6
Debt service/exports	%	7,1	14,6	22,3	26,7
Official development assistance					
Total net ODA	Mio USD	40,7	36,8	47,6	32,9
Bilateral net ODA	Mio USD	16,7	16,7	29,1	14,7
Net ODA: EC/bilateral	%	61,7	74,4	39,8	82,3
Multilateral net ODA	Mio USD	24,0	20,1	18,4	18,3
Multilateral: EDF/multilateral	%	7,3	5,9	6,0	9,1
Origin of GDP					
Agriculture, forestry, fisheries	%	21,0	25,1	26,0	27,0
Industry	%	41,2	37,0	34,3	
Services	%	37,9	37,9	39,7	
Index of price changes	75 = 100	285,1	300,6	347,2	461,2

PAPUA NEW GUINEA

Production and exports	Units	1981	1982	1983	1984
Main products					
Tubers and roots	000 t	1 119	1 133	1 146	1 157
Copra	000 t	145	148	137	140
Palm oil	000 t	74	77	78	108
Centrifugal sugar	000 t	0	13	37	37
Cocoa beans	000 t	32	29	29	28
Raw coffee	000 t	51	41	56	46
Bananas	000 t	932	949	900	920
Coconuts	000 t	802	822	780	785
Roundwood	000 m³	6 831	6 910	6 910	6 910
Sawn wood	000 m³	124	124	124	124
Fishing	000 t	27	1	1	6
Copper ore	000 t	165	170	183	163
Gold ore	kg	18 010	17 700	18 300	16 000
Main exports					
SITC 031.1 Fish, fresh or frozen	Mio USD	30,7	2,7	1,7	
	%	3,6	0,3	0,2	
SITC 071.1 Coffee	Mio USD	110,2	104,9	106,3	
	%	12,8	13,3	13,2	
SITC 072.1 Cocoa beans	Mio USD	51,0	43,3	61,5	
	%	5,9	5,5	7,6	
SITC 221.2 Copra	Mio USD	28,7	17,4	29,9	
	%	3,3	2,2	3,7	
SITC 242.3 Sawn and veneered logs	Mio USD	43,6	66,4	59,3	
	%	5,1	8,4	7,4	
SITC 283.11 Copper ore	Mio USD	433,9	402,7	388,9	
	%	50,2	50,9	48,3	
SITC 422.2 Palm oil	Mio USD	21,1	29,2	:	
	%	2,4	3,7		
SITC 422.3 Copra and coconut oil	Mio USD	18,6	16,3	21,8	
	%	2,1	2,1	2,7	

RÉPUBLIQUE CENTRAFRICAINE

Population 1985:	2 610 000 → Taux de croissance 1970-85:	2,5 %
PNB 1985:	700,0 Mio USD → Taux de croissance 1970-85:	5,4 %
PNB/h 1985:	270,0 Mio USD → Taux de croissance 1970-81:	− 1,0 %

Exportations 1983:	109,4 Mio USD	Importations 1983:	71,1 Mio USD
Importations vers la CE 1983:	51,0 Mio USD	Importations de la CE 1983:	44,1 Mio USD
Élèves: enseign. primaire 1983:	291 444	Élèves: enseign. secondaire 1982:	55 368
Personnes/lit d'hôpital 1982:	616	Personnes/médecin 1982:	22 434

	Unités	1981	1982	1983	1984
Commerce extérieur					
Exportations	75 = 100	260,2	224,9	232,0	
Importations	75 = 100	114,4	186,2	104,3	
Balance commerciale	Mio USD	44,7	− 20,9	38,3	
Exportations/importations	%	157,3	83,5	153,9	
Balance commerciale avec la CE	Mio USD	− 5,0	− 3,0	6,9	
Export. vers la CE/import. de la CE	%	89,7	93,7	115,5	
Exportations/PIB	%	25,7	23,1	25,2	25,1
Indicateurs financiers					
Balance des paiements	Mio DTS	0,7	− 11,7	− 25,3	− 12,9
Réserves internationales	Mio USD	69,3	46,3	46,8	52,7
Dette extérieure publique	Mio USD	226,9	288,2	342,4	317,5
Service de la dette/exportations	%	3,9	4,6	16,3	10,6
Aide publique au développement					
APD net total	Mio USD	101,6	89,7	92,9	113,9
APD net bilatéral	Mio USD	72,9	69,9	65,1	68,8
APD net CE/bilatéral	%	97,0	89,6	90,9	92,0
APD net multilatéral	Mio USD	28,7	19,8	27,8	45,1
APD net FED/multilatéral	%	48,9	40,6	42,3	26,6
Aide alimentaire					
Céréales	000 t	1,4	4,5	4,2	10,7
Produits laitiers	t	0,0	15	11	391
Total	Mio USD	0,3	2,3	2,3	3,9
Origine du PIB					
Agriculture, forêts, pêche	%	39,7	37,3	39,6	39,2
Industrie	%	18,9	20,3	20,0	20,3
Services	%	41,4	42,3	:	:
Indice d'évolution des prix	75 = 100	230,2	262,5	286,1	311,8

RWANDA

Productions et exportations	Unités	1981	1982	1983	1984
Principales productions					
Céréales, total	000 t	286	316	343	294
Sorgho	000 t	193	214	236	171
Maïs	000 t	85	92	97	111
Haricots, pois, lentilles	000 t	228	249	294	273
Turbercules et racines	000 t	1 786	1 925	2 018	1 345
Arachides non décortiquées	000 t	18	19	20	15
Café vert	000 t	31	23	27	33
Thé	000 t	7	7	7	9
Bois rond	000 m³	4 973	5 157	5 266	5 461
Minerai d'étain	t	1 284	1 236	1 100	1 104
Concentrés de tungstène	t	467	600	500	267
Gaz naturel	Térajoule	40	42	42	42
Principales exportations					
CTCI 071.1 Café	Mio USD	70,5	70,6	79,2	
	%	66,4	79,7	81,7	
CTCI 074.1 Thé	Mio USD	9,8	6,1	6,7	
	%	9,2	6,9	6,9	

ST KITTS AND NEVIS

Population 1985:	50 000 →	Rate of growth 1970-85:			− 1,2 %
GNP 1985:	70,0 Mio USD →	Rate of growth 1970-85:			9,5 %
GNP/capita 1985:	1 520,0 USD →	Rate of growth 1970-81:			2,4 %

Total exports 1983:	47,5 Mio USD	Total imports 1983:		209,5 Mio USD
Exports to EC:	− Mio USD	Imports from EC:		− Mio USD
Pupils: primary school 1983:	8 070	Pupils: secondary school 1983:		4 060
Pers. by hospital bed 1980:	177	Pers. by doctor 1980:		3 125

	Units	1981	1982	1983	1984
External trade					
Total exports	75 = 100	81,8	68,2	216,0	
Total imports	75 = 100	104,2	83,3	872,7	
Balance of trade	Mio USD	− 7,0	− 5,0	− 161,9	
Exports/imports	%	72,0	75,0	22,7	
Balance of trade with EC	Mio USD				
Exports to EC/imports from EC	%				
Exports/GDP	%	61,7			
Financial indicators					
Overall balance of payments	Mio SDR	0,1	− 1,5	− 0,l	
International reserves	Mio USD				
External public debt	Mio USD				
Debt service/exports	%				
Official development assistance					
Total net ODA	Mio USD				
Bilateral net ODA	Mio USD				
Net ODA: EC/bilateral	%				
Multilateral net ODA	Mio USD	1,6	1,4	1,4	2,0
Net ODA: EDF/multilateral	%				
Origin of GDP					
Agriculture, forestry, fisheries	%	11,5	14,7	12,3	12,6
Industry	%	:	:	:	:
Services	%	:	:	:	:
Index of price changes	75 = 100	168,3	181,0	182,5	186,5
Main products					
Tubers and roots	000 t	3	3	3	3
Centrifugal sugar	000 t	33	37	28	31
Coconuts	000 t	2	2	2	2
Fishing	000 t	2	2	1	1

ST LUCIA

Population 1985:	130 000	→	Rate of growth 1970-85:		1,8 %
GNP 1985:	160,0 Mio USD	→	Rate of growth 1970-85:		10,1 %
GNP/capita 1985:	1 210,0 USD	→	Rate of growth 1970-81:		1,9 %

Total exports 1984:	45,8 Mio USD	Total imports 1984:	118,5 Mio USD
Exports to EC 1983:	33,3 Mio USD	Imports from EC 1981:	26,9 Mio USD
Pupils: primary school 1983:	32 107	Pupils: secondary school 1983:	5 314
Pers. by hospital bed 1981:	204	Pers. by doctor 1981:	3 704

	Units	1981	1982	1983	1984
External trade					
Total exports	75 = 100	258,5	269,9	308,7	287,4
Total imports	75 = 100	278,0	254,1	229,8	254,9
Balance of trade	Mio USD	− 88,0	− 75,1	− 57,6	− 72,7
Exports/imports	%	31,9	36,4	46,1	38,7
Balance of trade with EC	Mio USD	− 11,3			
Exports to EC/imports from EC	%	58,1			
Exports/GDP	%	56,3	55,1	63,5	64,0
Financial indicators					
Overall balance of payments	Mio SDR	− 4,0	2,1	0,7	
International reserves	Mio USD	7,6	8,2	8,9	12,4
External public debt	Mio USD				
Debt service/exports	%				
Official development assistance					
Total net ODA	Mio USD				
Bilateral net ODA	Mio USD				
Net ODA: EC/bilateral	%				
Multilateral net ODA	Mio USD	7,7	5,3	2,9	2,8
Multilateral: EDF/multilateral	%				
Food aid					
Cereals	t	487,0	0,0	0,0	100,0
Dairy products	t	50,0	0,0	0,0	0,0
Total	Mio USD	210,0	0,0	0,0	12,0
Origin of GDP					
Agriculture, forestry, fisheries	%	9,8	11,6	12,7	13,8
Industry	%	:	:	:	:
Services	%	:	:	:	:
Index of price changes	75 = 100	192,4	197,7	202,2	204,4

ST LUCIA

Production and exports	Units	1981	1982	1983	1984
Main products					
Tubers and roots	000 t	10	10	10	11
Copra	000 t	4	5	6	5
Bananas	000 t	58	59	69	85
Coconuts	000 t	26	29	32	31
Fishing	000 t	2	2	3	3
Main exports					
SITC 051.3 Bananas	Mio USD	14,7	26,2	32,0	
	%	35,7	60,9	65,0	
SITC 091.4 Margarine	Mio USD	1,6	:	:	
	%	4,0	:	:	
SITC 112.2 Beer	Mio USD	1,7	2,0	2,5	
	%	4,2	4,6	5,1	
SITC 422.3 Copra and coconut oil	Mio USD	2,6	1,6	1,6	
	%	6,2	3,7	3,2	

ST VINCENT AND THE GRENADINES

Population 1985:	100 000	→ Rate of growth 1970-85:	0,7 %
GNP 1985:	100,0 Mio USD	→ Rate of growth 1970-85:	9,7 %
GNP/capita 1985:	840,0 USD	→ Rate of growth 1970-81:	0,5 %

Total exports 1983:	39,3 Mio USD	Total imports 1983:	24,6 Mio USD
Exports to EC 1983:	19,0 Mio USD	Imports from EC 1983:	8,4 Mio USD
Pupils: primary school 1981:	21 497	Pupils: secondary school 1981:	8 058
Pers. by hospital bed 1980:	200	Pers. by doctor 1980:	4 182

	Units	1981	1982	1983	1984
External trade					
Total exports	75 = 100	411,7	415,9	515,0	
Total imports	75 = 100	113,9	105,9	98,6	
Balance of trade	Mio USD	3,0	5,3	14,7	
Exports/imports	%	110,6	120,1	159,8	
Balance of trade with EC	Mio USD	11,6	12,6	10,6	
Exports to EC/imports from EC	%	242,4	285,7	226,7	
Exports/GDP	%	60,0	60,3	67,4	
Financial indicators					
Overall balance of payments	Mio SDR	0,2	− 3,6	1,1	
International reserves	Mio USD	9,0	4,8	5,7	12,8
External public debt	Mio USD	22,7	23,4	28,0	33,2
Debt service/exports	%	2,9	5,0	3,7	
Official development assistance					
Total net ODA	Mio USD				
Bilateral net ODA	Mio USD				
Net ODA: EC/bilateral	%				
Multilateral net ODA	Mio USD	5,7	5,0	3,8	2,9
Multilateral: EDF/multilateral	%				
Origin of GDP					
Agriculture, forestry, fisheries	%	16,7	17,0	17,4	17,4
Industry	%	:	:	:	:
Services	%	:	:	:	:
Index of price changes	75 = 100	191,3	206,5	213,4	221,6
Main products					
Tubers and roots	000 t	25	28	30	46
Copra	000 t	2	2	2	2
Bananas	000 t	33	32	28	33
Coconuts	000 t	19	20	19	21
Fishing	000 t	1	1	1	1
Main exports					
SITC 051.3 Bananas	Mio USD	18,2	17,6	18,1	
	%	57,9	55,4	46,0	
SITC 051.71 Coconuts, brazil nuts etc.	Mio USD	0,7	0,4	0,3	
	%	2,2	1,3	0,8	
SITC 054.81 Frozen vegetables	Mio USD	2,0	2,0	8,8	
	%	6,4	6,3	22,4	

SAO TOME AND PRINCIPE

Population 1985:	110 000 →	Rate of growth 1970-85:	3,1 %
GNP 1985:	30,0 Mio USD →	Rate of growth 1970-85:	3,9 %
GNP/capita 1985:	310,0 USD →	Rate of growth 1970-81:	− 0,3 %

Total exports 1983:	7,4 Mio USD	Total imports 1983:	7,8 Mio USD
Exports to EC 1983:	5,0 Mio USD	Imports from EC 1983:	4,3 Mio USD
Pupils: primary school 1984:	16 013	Pupils: secondary school 1983:	6 436
Pers. by hospital bed 1982:	120	Pers. by doctor 1982:	2 263

	Units	1981	1982	1983	1984
External trade					
Total exports	75 = 100	219,6	144,5	105,0	
Total imports	75 = 100	202,9	193,7	69,1	
Balance of trade	Mio USD	− 7,4	− 11,7	− 0,4	
Exports/imports	%	67,7	46,7	95,0	
Balance of trade with EC	Mio USD	6,9	0,8	0,7	
Exports to EC/imports from EC	%	230,1	110,8	116,0	
Exports/GDP	%	40,6	41,3		
Financial indicators					
Overall balance of payments	Mio SDR	− 6,0	− 3,8	− 3,0	− 10,2
International reserves	Mio USD				
External public debt	Mio USD				
Debt service/exports	%				
Official development assistance					
Total net ODA	Mio USD	6,1	9,8	11,6	11,3
Bilateral net ODA	Mio USD	1,8	3,8	3,4	4,0
Net ODA: EC/bilateral	%	61,7	44,4	94,7	52,1
Multilateral net ODA	Mio USD	4,3	6,0	8,2	7,3
Multilateral: EDF/multilateral	%	10,8	26,8	55,1	58,2
Food aid					
Cereals	000 t	1,3	1,5	5,4	10,4
Dairy products	000 t	0,0	200,0	242,0	365,0
Total	Mio USD	0,4	0,6	2,1	3,6
Origin of GDP					
Agriculture, forestry, fisheries	%	34,6	35,4	43,5	:
Industry	%	7,6	8,0	:	:
Services	%	42,3	45,9	:	:
Index of price changes	75 = 100	179,6	190,1	212,2	234,3
Main products					
Tubers and roots	000 t	15	15	15	15
Copra	000 t	3	4	5	4
Palm kernels	000 t	1	1	1	1
Cocoa beans	000 t	7	5	5	4
Bananas	000 t	3	3	3	3
Coconuts	000 t	30	37	42	35
Roundwood	000 m³	6	2	6	6
Fishing	000 t	2	3	4	4
Main exports					
SITC 072.1 Cocoa beans	Mio USD	13,5	8,1	5,1	141
	%	87,1	79,4	68,8	

Population 1985:	6 440 000 → Taux de croissance 1970-85:	2,8 %
PNB 1985:	2 400,0 Mio USD → Taux de croissance 1970-85:	5,5 %
PNB/h 1985:	370,0 USD → Taux de croissance 1970-81:	– 1,7 %

Exportations 1984:	534,0 Mio USD	Importations 1984: 1 010,0 Mio USD
Exportations vers la CE 1983:	336,1 Mio USD	Importations de la CE 1983: 462,9 Mio USD
Élèves: enseign. primaire 1983:	533 394	Élèves: enseign. secondaire 1983: 113 561
Personnes/lit d'hôpital 1982:	901	Personnes/médecin 1982: 12 942

	Unités	1981	1982	1983	1984
Commerce extérieur					
Exportations	75 = 100	121,3	89,3	95,3	115,5
Importations	75 = 100	185,3	149,5	135,9	173,7
Balance commerciale	Mio USD	– 516,6	– 456,5	– 349,4	– 476,0
Exportations/importations	%	52,0	47,5	55,8	52,9
Balance commerciale avec la CE	Mio USD	– 339,3	– 1 142,7	– 126,8	
Export. vers la CE/import. de la CE	%	35,2	22,2	72,6	
Exportations/PIB	%	27,6	30,8	28,4	29,2
Indicateurs financiers					
Balance des paiements	Mio DTS				
Réserves internationales	Mio USD	8,7	11,4	12,2	3,7
Dette extérieure publique	Mio USD	1 700,6	2 152,5	2 178,8	2 283,8
Service de la dette/exportations	%	20,7	8,7	10,7	17,3
Aide publique au développement					
APD net total	Mio USD	396,7	284,8	322,2	368,3
APD net bilatéral	Mio USD	267,7	205,2	260,2	304,7
APD net CE/bilatéral	%	56,3	63,7	47,8	44,1
APD net multilatéral	Mio USD	129,0	79,6	62,0	63,5
APD net FED/multilatéral	%	46,8	49,8	26,1	32,6
Aide alimentaire					
Céréales	000 t	103,5	83,5	105,1	152,2
Produirts laitiers	000 t	2,3	2,1	0,1	8,6
Total	Mio USD	34,6	22,1	23,3	45,7
Origine du PIB					
Agriculture, forêts, pêche	%	18,1	22,0	20,9	16,7
Industrie	%	26,4	24,3	25,5	28,0
Services	%	55,6	53,7	53,5	55,3
Indice d'évolution des prix	75 = 100	153,5	206,2	243,8	262,8

SÉNÉGAL

Productions et exportations	Unités	1981	1982	1983	1984
Principales productions					
Céréales, total	000 t	960	782	523	710
Millet	000 t	736	585	352	471
Maïs	000 t	95	76	61	98
Riz, paddy	000 t	127	119	109	136
Tomates	000 t	13	25	20	22
Tubercules et racines	000 t	50	49	35	35
Arachides non décortiquées	000 t	872	1 004	512	682
Sucre centrifugé brut	000 t	49	59	50	54
Oranges	000 t	20	20	20	19
Lait de vache	000 t	81	84	84	77
Bois rond	000 m³	3 744	3 849	3 945	4 049
Pêche	000 t	207	213	223	223
Phosphates naturels	000 t	1 792	1 179	1 337	2 481
Poisson salé	000 t	18	16	16	16
Poisson en conserve	000 t	15	16	20	20
Essence	000 t	135	87	56	66
Huiles légères	000 t	150	210	156	50
Huiles lourdes	000 t	265	350	155	152
Principales exportations					
CTCI 031.1 Poissons frais	Mio USD	32,9	53,2	48,8	
	%	7,4	12,9	11.1	
CTCI 031.3 Crustacés et mollusques	Mio USD	23,4	35,9	38,6	
	%	5,3	8,7	8,8	
CTCI 032.01 Cons. poissons	Mio USD	37,5	41,6	63,5	
	%	8,5	10,1	14,4	
CTCI 081.3 Tourteaux	Mio USD	7,2	32,4	40,4	
	%	1,6	7,8	9,2	
CTCI 271.3 Phosphates naturels	Mio USD	61,1	67,2	74,6	
	%	13,8	16,3	16,9	
CTCI 332 Produits pétroliers	Mio USD	108,0	:	:	
	%	24,4	:	:	
CTCI 421.4 Huile d'arachide	Mio USD	20,9	90,1	:	
	%	4,7	21,8	:	
CTCI 652,2 Tissus de coton mercerisés	Mio USD	21,3	13,8	15,7	
	%	4,8	3,3	3,6	

SEYCHELLES

Population 1985:	70 000	→	Rate of growth 1970-85:		2,3 %
GNP 1985:	140 0 Mio USD	→	Rate of growth 1970-85:		10,6 %
GNP/capita 1985:	2 429 0 USD	→	Rate of growth 1970-81:		2,7 %

Total exports 1984:	25,6 Mio USD	Total imports 1984:		87.3 Mio USD
Exports to EC 1984:	1,2 Mio USD	Imports from EC 1984:		25,4 Mio USD
Pupils: primary school 1985:	14 444	Pupils: secondary school 1985:		3 975
Pers. by hospital bed 1982:	170	Pers. by doctor 1983:		2 151

	Units	1981	1982	1983	1984
External trade					
Total exports	75 = 100	221,1	706,5	943,7	1 193,6
Total imports	75 = 100	293,6	308,0	275,9	274,2
Balance of trade	Mio USD	− 88,7	− 82,8	− 67,5	− 61,6
Exports/imports	%	5,1	15,5	23,1	29,4
Balance of trade with EC	Mio USD	− 26,6	− 32,4	− 29,1	− 24,2
Exports to EC/imports from EC	%	1,7	1,1	1,6	4,7
Exports/GDP	%				
Financial indicators					
Overall balance of payments	Mio SDR	− 4,1	− 0,1	− 2,3	− 1,3
International reserves	Mio USD	13,8	13,1	10,0	5,4
External public debt	Mio USD	58,2	60,8	71,8	73,7
Debt service/exports	%	10,6	32,1	59,1	76,1
Official development assistance					
Total net ODA	Mio USD	17,0	18,3	15,6	15,1
Bilateral net ODA	Mio USD	15,0	15,1	13,8	13,6
Net ODA: EC/bilateral	%	78,0	74,8	69,4	53,9
Multilateral net ODA	Mio USD	2,0	3,2	1,9	1,5
Multilateral: EDF/multilateral	%	29,5	44,4	28,0	32,0
Food aid					
Cereals	000 t	1,3	1,1	0,3	1,5
Dairy products	t	102,0	101,0	206,0	107,0
Total	Mio USD	1,1	0,7	0,4	0,7
Main products					
Copra	000 t	4	3	4	3
Bananas	000 t	1	1	2	2
Coconuts	000 t	22	18	21	17
Fishing	000 t	4	4	4	4
Main exports					
SITC 031.1 Fish, fresh or frozen	Mio USD	0,7	1,1	1,4	1,4
	%	14,4	7,3	6,7	5,6
SITC 221.2 Copra	Mio USD	2,7	1,3	1,7	1,2
	%	55,9	8,8	8,3	4,5
SITC 332 Petroleum products	Mio USD	0,0	10,9	14,7	20,2
	%	0,0	71,9	72,7	78,9

SIERRA LEONE

Population 1985:	3 600 000 →	Rate of growth 1970-85:	2,0 %
GNP 1985:	1 380,0 Mio USD →	Rate of growth 1970-85:	7,8 %
GNP/capita 1985:	370,0 USD →	Rate of grɔwth 1970-81:	− 0,9 %

Total exports 1985:	112,0 Mio USD	Total imports 1985:	156,0 Mio USD
Exports to EC 1983:	82,6 Mio USD	Imports from EC 1983:	67,4 Mio USD
Pupils: primary school 1980:	263 724	Pupils: secondary school 1979:	63 157
Pers. by hospital bed 1982:	884	Pers. by doctor 1982:	18 284

	Units	1981	1982	1983	1984
External trade					
Total exports	75 = 100	140,8	87,6	62,3	101,3
Total imports	75 = 100	125,4	101,1	104,0	104,5
Balance of trade	Mio USD	5,6	− 33,4	− 75,0	− 18,8
Exports/imports	%	102,8	79,3	54,8	88,7
Balance of trade with EC	Mio USD	21,0	− 31,6	15,2	
Exports to EC/imports from EC	%	118,6	62,9	122,6	
Exports/GDP	%	17,9	14,3	12,3	
Financial indicators					
Overall balance of payments	Mio SDR	− 79,9	− 12,0	− 6,7	− 25,0
International reserves	Mio USD	16,0	8,4	16,2	7,7
External public debt	Mio USD	482,9	484,9	470,0	471,6
Debt service/exports	%	38,3	11,8	10,1	12,3
Official development assistance					
Total net ODA	Mio USD	60,1	82,1	66,0	60,7
Bilateral net ODA	Mio USD	33,8	55,9	35,6	36,0
Net ODA: EC/bilateral	%	64,8	63,1	63,9	34,1
Multilateral net ODA	Mio USD	26,3	26,2	30,3	24,7
Multilateral: EDF/multilateral	%	42,4	24,9	43,5	23,1
Food aid					
Cereals	000 t	13,5	35,3	19,1	28,4
Dairy products	000 t	2,6	1,6	1,5	2,0
Total	Mio USD	12,4	14,4	7,9	8,4
Origin of GDP					
Agriculture, forestry, fisheries	%	33,4	32,0	31,7	
Industry	%	20,1	19,6	20,0	
Services	%	46,9	48,8	48,8	
Index of price changes	75 = 100	247,5	313,5	526,8	

SIERRA LEONE

Production and exports	Units	1981	1982	1983	1984
Main products					
Cereals, total	000 t	540	626	652	520
Rice, paddy	000 t	500	583	609	460
Tubers and roots	000 t	130	134	139	134
Palm kernels	000 t	30	30	30	30
Palm oil	000 t	48	48	46	37
Cocoa beans	000 t	7	9	9	11
Raw coffee	000 t	9	9	5	2
Roundwood	000 m³	7 267	7 371	7 497	7 632
Fishing	000 t	51	53	51	53
Iron ore	000 t	0	42	192	224
Bauxite ore	000 t	606	632	785	924
Diamonds	000 ca	305	290	345	105
Salted fish	000 t	17	18	18	19
Motor spirit	000 t	23	24	20	28
Light oils	000 t	93	82	70	95
Heavy oils	000 t	56	57	58	65
Main exports					
SITC 071.1 Coffee	Mio USD	17,2	18,4	4,6	13,6
	%	12,8	21,1	5,1	9,3
SITC 072.1 Cocoa beans	Mio USD	13,8	9,4	17,6	23,1
	%	10,3	10,8	19,4	15,7
SITC 283.3 Bauxite	Mio USD	10,9	7,9	7,6	18,9
	%	8,1	9,1	8,4	12,8
SITC 667.2 Diamonds	Mio USD	64,6	28,4	21,4	45,0
	%	48,1	32,5	23,6	30,6

SOLOMON ISLANDS

Population 1985:	270 000	→	Rate of growth 1970-85:		3,5 %
GNP 1985:	140 Mio USD	→	Rate of growth 1970-85:		8,7 %
GNP/capita 1985:	510,0 USD	→	Rate of growth 1970/81:		1,9 %

Total exports 1985:	70,0 Mio USD	Total imports 1985:	69,0 Mio USD
Exports to EC 1983:	13,7 Mio USD	Imports from EC 1983:	3,2 Mio USD
Pupils: primary school 1981:	30 246	Pupils: secondary school 1980:	4 030
Pers. by hospital bed 1981:	175	Pers. by doctor 1980:	7 500

	Units	1981	1982	1983	1984
External trade					
Total exports	75 = 100	421,9	373,7	434,8	602,5
Total imports	75 = 100	264,4	207,3	245,2	230,0
Balance of trade	Mio USD	− 10,5	− 1,6	− 3,0	27,3
Exports/imports	%	86,2	97,3	95,8	141,4
Balance of trade with EC	Mio USD	12,1	8,9	10,5	
Exports to EC/imports from EC	%	258,3	320,6	428,2	
Exports/GDP	%	46,3	42,4		
Financial indicators					
Overall balance of payments	Mio SDR	− 5,8	19,9	13,7	18,2
International reserves	Mio USD	21,6	37,2	47,3	60,6
External public debt	Mio USD	27,2	39,5	48,8	55,4
Debt service/exports	%	0,2	0,2	0,1	0,5
Official development assistance					
Total net ODA	Mio USD	31,1	28,4	27,5	19,4
Bilateral net ODA	Mio USD	24,3	22,0	18,2	13,9
Net ODA: EC/bilateral	%	61,1	50,8	46,6	34,3
Multilateral net ODA	Mio USD	6,8	6,4	9,3	5,4
Multilateral: EDF/multilateral	%	22,9	41,0	47,6	48,3
Index of price changes	75 = 100	189,7	207,5	223,9	
Main products					
Tubers and roots	000 t	82	86	87	90
Copra	000 t	34	32	28	43
Palm oil	000 t	18	19	20	20
Coconuts	000 t	245	235	230	303
Roundwood	000 m³	512	512	512	512
Fishing	000 t	38	33	48	49
Canned fish	000 t	1	2	2	2
Main exports					
SITC 031.1 Fish, fresh or frozen	Mio USD	21,8	10,2	21,1	19,7
	%	33,4	17,6	34,2	21,3
SITC 221.2 Copra	Mio USD	9,2	8,3	7,2	25,2
	%	14,1	14,4	11,8	27,3
SITC 242 Wood, rough	Mio USD	16,9	22,0	:	:
	%	25,8	38,1	:	:
SITC 422.2 Palm oil	Mio USD	8,1	7,0	6,7	13,4
	%	12,4	12,1	10,9	14,5

SOMALIE

Population 1985:	4 650 000	→ Taux de croissance 1970-85:			3,5 %
PNB 1985:	1 450,0 Mio USD	→ Taux de croissance 1970-85:			9,0 %
PNB/h 1985:	270,0 USD	→ Taux de croissance 1970-81:			0,7 %

Exportations 1985:	91,0 Mio USD	Importations 1983:	112,0 Mio USD
Exportations vers la CE 1983:	26,6 Mio USD	Importations de la CE 1983:	150,4 Mio USD
Élèves: enseign. primaire 1983:	220 680	Élèves: enseign. secondaire 1983:	63 255
Personnes/lit d'hôpital 1982:	569	Personnes/médecin 1982:	12 191

	Unités	1981	1982	1983	1984
Commerce extérieur					
Exportations	75 = 100	171,6	166,6	169,2	50,8
Importations	75 = 100	331,6	269,1	227,7	70,5
Balance commerciale	Mio USD	− 360,9	− 268,7	− 202,4	− 64,0
Exportations/importations	%	29,6	35,5	42,5	41,3
Balance commerciale avec la CE	Mio USD	− 328,9	− 184,6	− 123,8	
Export. vers la CE/import. de la CE	%	2,8	11,0	17,7	
Exportations/PIB	%	7,0	9,9		
Indicateurs financiers					
Balance des paiements	Mio DTS	− 17,7	32,7	− 72,4	− 17,5
Réserves internationales	Mio USD	30,7	6,5	9,2	1,0
Dette extérieure publique	Mio USD	1 507,2	1 536,1	1 590,8	1 570,3
Service de la dette/exportations	%	36,9	13,5	28,6	48,8
Aide publique au développement					
APD net total	Mio USD	374,6	462,1	326,6	363,0
APD net bilatéral	Mio USD	186,5	302,1	174,2	212,9
APD net CE/bilatéral	%	35,1	28,0	53,2	61,9
APD net multilatéral	Mio USD	188,1	160,1	152,4	150,1
APD net FED/multilatéral	%	21,6	24,4	12,9	12,8
Aide alimentaire					
Céréales	000 t	217,9	136,5	80,2	213,8
Produits laitiers	000 t	8,6	10,7	7,0	7,3
Total	Mio USD	86,9	61,5	37,4	60,9
Origine du PIB					
Agriculture, forêts, pêche	%	50,7	50,0	:	:
Industrie	%	11,4	11,2	:	:
Services	%	31,2	31,1	:	:
Indice d'évolution des prix	75 = 100	333,1	372,7	474,9	522,3

Productions et exportations	Unités	1981	1982	1983	1984
Principales productions					
Céréales, total	000 t	373	406	359	497
Sorgho	000 t	207	235	120	221
Maïs	000 t	157	150	235	270
Tubercules et racines	000 t	37	38	39	40
Sucre centrifugé brut	000 t	27	34	31	35
Bananes	000 t	59	79	99	62
Lait de vache	000 t	159	161	140	140
Lait de brebis	000 t	98	98	98	97
Lait de chèvre	000 t	286	288	287	286
Viande de bovins	000 t	46	46	44	42
Bois rond	000 m³	4 642	4 848	5 023	5 168
Pêche	000 t	15	15	16	15
Poisson salé	000 t	1	1	1	1
Essence	000 t	80	85	80	85
Huiles légères	000 t	188	192	175	180
Huiles lourdes	000 t	6	5	5	6
Principales exportations					
CTCI 001.1 Bovins	Mio USD	27,1	36,5	36,4	
	%	17,8	24,7	24,3	
CTCI 001.2 Ovins et caprins	Mio USD	103,4	31,1	31,1	
	%	68,0	21,1	20,8	
CTCI 013.8 Viande en conserve	Mio USD	2,2	:	:	:
	%	1,4	:	:	:
CTCI 031.3 Crustacés et mollusques	Mio USD	1,8	:	:	:
	%	1,2	:	:	:
CTCI 051.3 Bananes fraîches	Mio USD	9,0	13,0	19,3	
	%	5,9	8,8	12,9	
CTCI 292.2 Gomme laque	Mio USD	1,4	:	:	:
	%	0,9	:	:	:

SUDAN

Population 1985:	21 550 000 →	Rate of growth 1970-85: 2,9 %
GNP 1985:	7 350,0 Mio USD →	Rate of growth 1970-85: 7,3 %
GNP/capita 1985:	330,0 USD →	Rate of growth 1970-81: − 0,2 %

Total exports 1985:	367,0 Mio USD	Total imports 1985:	757,0 Mio USD
Exports to EC 1983:	129,7 Mio USD	Imports from EC 1983:	505,1 Mio USD
Pupils: primary school 1982:	1 579 286	Pupils: secondary school 1982:	455 969
Pers. by hospital bed 1982:	1 196	Pers. by doctor 1982:	9 969

	Units	1981	1982	1983	1984
External trade					
Total exports	75 = 100	118,7	130,8	140,0	146,4
Total imports	75 = 100	158,7	181,4	148,8	119,8
Balance of trade	Mio USD	− 1 009,0	− 1 174,3	− 822,9	− 517,9
Exports/imports	%	33,6	32,4	42,2	54,8
Balance of trade with EC	Mio USD	− 475,6	− 304,1	− 375,4	
Exports to EC/imports from EC	%	25,2	31,8	25,7	
Exports/GDP	%	8,1	8,6	11,2	9,9
Financial indicators					
Overall balance of payments	Mio SDR	− 176,5	− 65,5	− 158,7	− 13,5
International reserves	Mio USD	17,0	20,5	16,6	17,2
External public debt	Mio USD	5 381,0	5 924,6	6 351,3	6 202,2
Debt service/exports	%	25,0	34,9	18,8	20,7
Official development assistance					
Total net ODA	Mio USD	630,6	739,9	956,3	616,3
Bilateral net ODA	Mio USD	408,2	522,8	790,3	420,8
Net ODA: EC/bilateral	%	47,5	34,5	27,0	31,4
Multilateral net ODA	Mio USD	222,5	217,1	166,0	195,5
Multilateral: EDF/multilateral	%	20,5	18,8	22,1	14,3
Food aid					
Cereals	000 t	220,9	206,8	369,0	392,8
Dairy products	000 t	4,0	0,9	2,5	2,4
Total	Mio USD	57,1	41,4	69,2	64,9
Origin of GDP					
Agriculture, forestry, fisheries	%	35,6	36,1	34,4	33,0
Industry	%	13,8	13,9	14,8	:
Services	%	50,6	50,0	50,8	:
Index of price changes	75 = 100	411,4	538,8	688,6	552,2

SUDAN

Production and exports	Units	1981	1982	1983	1984
Main products					
Cereals, total	000 t	4 179	2 473	2 312	1 446
Wheat	000 t	218	163	141	169
Sorghum	000 t	3 345	1 938	1 829	1 097
Millet	000 t	573	339	314	158
Tomatoes	000 t	92	116	120	80
Tubers and roots	000 t	298	291	298	287
Unshelled groundnuts	000 t	721	497	413	386
Centrifugal sugar	000 t	226	260	391	454
Bananas	000 t	52	53	55	50
Dates	000 t	134	118	119	115
Oranges	000 t	12	12	13	12
Cotton lint	000 t	97	154	201	219
Seed cotton	000 t	284	451	592	640
Cow milk	000 t	1 557	1 652	1 753	1 753
Sheep milk	000 t	554	569	585	600
Goat milk	000 t	510	531	552	550
Beef and buffalo meat	000 t	280	288	300	297
Roundwood	000 m³	17 431	17 935	18 449	18 973
Fishing	000 t	29	30	30	30
Chromium ore	000 t	26	25	25	25
Salted fish	000 t	2	2	2	2
Motor spirit	000 t	145	150	147	148
Light oils	000 t	510	530	490	510
Heavy oils	000 t	280	310	295	298
Main exports					
SITC 001.2 Sheep, lambs and goats	Mio USD	40,8	61,3	100,0	
	%	8,0	12,3	16,6	
SITC 081.3 Oil seed cake	Mio USD	16,0	15,0	24,8	
	%	3,1	3,0	4,1	
SITC 221.1 Groundnuts	Mio USD	94,5	34,3	9,7	
	%	18,5	6,9	1,6	
SITC 221.8 Oil seeds	Mio USD	52,6	53,6	21,8	
	%	10,3	10,7	3,6	
SITC 263.1 Raw cotton	Mio USD	118,6	123,5	185,3	
	%	23,3	24,7	30,8	
SITC 292.2 Natural gums, lacs	Mio USD	45,1	41,4	60,0	
	%	8,9	8,3	10,0	
SITC 421.4 Groundnut oil	Mio USD	12,0	8,3	3,6	
	%	2,4	1,7	0,6	

SURINAME

Population 1985:	370 000	→ Rate of growth 1970-85:			− 0,4 %
GNP 1985:	1 010,0 Mio USD	→ Rate of growth 1970-85:			8,5 %
GNP/capita 1984:	2 570,5 Mio USD	→ Rate of growth 1970-81:			5,4 %

Total exports 1984:	356,0 Mio USD	Total imports 1984:		346,0 Mio USD
Exports to EC 1983:	212,4 Mio USD	Imports from EC 1983:		67,1 Mio USD
Pupils: primary school 1979:	80 844	Pupils: secondary school 1979:		35 742
Pers. by hospital bed 1980:	123	Pers. by doctor 1980:		1 748

	Units	1981	1982	1983	1984
External trade					
Total exports	75 = 100	203,5	158,4	157,0	139,4
Total imports	75 = 100	179,1	163,4	130,8	137,2
Balance of trade	Mio USD	67,9	− 7,6	71,1	10,0
Exports/imports	%	115,0	98,2	121,5	102,9
Balance of trade with EC	Mio USD	72,5	100,6	145,2	
Exports to EC/imports from EC	%	183,4	210,6	316,3	
Exports/GDP	%	49,1	40,9	33,7	
Financial indicators					
Overall balance of payments	Mio SDR	10,9	− 39,8	− 101,9	− 50,4
International reserves	Mio USD	207,1	175,8	59,1	24,9
External public debt	Mio USD				
Debt service/exports	%				
Official development assistance					
Total net ODA	Mio USD	96,8	101,5	3,9	5,1
Bilateral net ODA	Mio USD	94,0	98,4	2,3	1,5
Net ODA: EC/bilateral	%	100,4	99,9	171,6	102,0
Multilateral net ODA	Mio USD	2,8	3,1	1,6	3,6
Multilateral: EDF/multilateral	%	38,4	53,4	46,5	85,5
Origin of GDP					
Agricuture, forestry, fisheries	%	11,1	10,7	9,9	:
Industry	%	31,3	28,2	26,6	:
Services	%	57,6	61,0	63,6	:
Index of price changes	75 = 100	215,2	228,0	239,5	252,4
Main products					
Cereals, total	000 t	281	301	268	302
Rice, paddy	000 t	281	301	268	302
Centrifugal sugar	000 t	8	7	6	7
Bananas	000 t	45	42	37	41
Oranges	000 t	9	8	9	9
Roundwood	000 m³	303	260	260	260
Sawn wood	000 m³	63	61	61	61
Fishing	000 t	3	3	4	4
Bauxite ore	000 t	4 006	3 276	2 978	3 375
Aluminium	000 t	41	43	29	23
Main exports					
SITC 032 Prep. or pres. fish and crustacea	Mio USD	25,4	23,4	16,9	
	%	4,9	5,8	4,2	
SITC 042 Rice	Mio USD	63,4	69,1	78,9	
	%	12,2	17,1	19,7	
SITC 051.3 Bananas	Mio USD	14,4	14,0	16,7	
	%	2,8	3,5	4,2	
SITC 684 Aluminium	Mio USD	45,5	58,1	50,3	
	%	8,8	14,4	12,5	

SWAZILAND

Population 1985:	650 000 → Rate of growth 1970-85:	3,0 %
GNP 1985:	490,0 Mio USD → Rate of growth 1970-85:	10,1 %
GNP/capita 1985:	650,0 USD → Rate of growth 1970-81:	3,2 %

Total exports 1982:	370,0 Mio USD	Total imports 1982: 450,0 Mio USD
Exports to EC 1976:	79,8 Mio USD	Imports from EC 1976: 2,4 Mio USD
Pupils: primary school 1983:	129 767	Pupils: secondary school 1980: 23 665
Pers. by hospital bed 1980:	289	Pers. by doctor 1980: 7 000

	Units	1981	1982	1983	1984
External trade					
Total exports	75 = 100	208,1	187,8		
Total imports	75 = 100	309,1	252,9		
Balance of trade	Mio USD	− 140.0	− 80,0		
Exports/imports	%	74,5	82,2		
Balance of trade with EC	Mio USD				
Exports to EC/imports from EC	%				
Exports/GDP	%	63,7			
Financial indicators					
Overall balance of payments	Mio SDR	− 32,9	− 4,7	16,0	22,5
International reserves	Mio USD	96,4	76,1	92,5	80,1
External public debt	Mio USD	239,5	245,4	245,4	262,0
Debt service/exports	%	5,5	6,5	6,8	8,0
Official development assistance					
Total net ODA	Mio USD	36,6	28,1	33,4	17,9
Bilateral net ODA	Mio USD	23,6	18,7	20,5	5,8
Net ODA: EC/bilateral	%	44,2	44,9	33,7	78,8
Multilateral net ODA	Mio USD	13,0	9,3	12,9	12,1
Multilateral EDF/multilateral	%	19,8	21,3	35,1	50,9
Food aid					
Cereals	t	500,0	0,0	600,0	5 200,0
Dairy products	t	300,0	10,0	737,0	308,0
Total	000 USD	900,0	45,0	1 196,0	1 367,0
Index of price changes	75 = 100	270,5	312,7	348,8	

SWAZILAND

Production and exports	Units	1981	1982	1983	1984
Main products					
Cereals, total	000 t	99	56	54	115
Maize	000 t	94	52	51	110
Tubers and roots	000 t	8	7	7	8
Centrifugal sugar	000 t	368	402	403	429
Pineapples	000 t	29	35	37	44
Oranges	000 t	50	54	48	47
Cotton lint	000 t	11	11	11	11
Seed cotton	000 t	32	32	32	32
Cow milk	000 t	37	37	38	38
Beef and buffalo meat	000 t	14	15	16	13
Roundwood	000 m³	2 223	2 223	2 223	2 223
Sawn wood	000 m³	136	136	136	136
Wood pulp	000 t	157	157	175	178
Main exports					
SITC 061.1 Sugar	Mio USD	144,3			
	%	39,6			
SITC 051.2 Citrus fruit	Mio USD	10,5			
	%	2,9			
SITC 251 Wood pulp	Mio USD	53,2			
	%	14,6			
SITC 661.83 Asbestos	Mio USD	20,4			
	%	5,6			

TANZANIA

Population 1985:	21 730 000 →	Rate of growth 1970-85:			3,3 %
GNP 1985:	5 840,0 Mio USD →	Rate of growth 1970-85:			8,9 %
GNP/capita 1985:	270,0 USD →	Rate of growth 1970-81:			0,5 %

Total exports 1983:	425 Mio USD	Total imports 1983:		537,6 Mio USD
Exports to EC 1983:	224,7 Mio USD	Imports from EC 1983:		214,8 Mio USD
Pupils: primary school 1983:	3 552 923	Pupils: secondary school 1982:		81 787
Pers. by hospital bed 1980:	619	Pers. by doctor 1980:		16 282

	Units	1981	1982	1983	1984
External trade					
Total exports	75 = 100	161,9	115,0	121,9	
Total imports	75 = 100	120,8	110,6	74,9	
Balance of trade	Mio USD	− 302,9	− 393,0	− 112,6	
Exports/imports	%	65,1	50,5	79,0	
Balance of trade with EC	Mio USD	− 111,8	− 11,8	9,9	
Exports to EC/imports from EC	%	69,7	95,7	104,6	
Exports/GDP	%	14,1	10,9		
Financial indicators					
Overall balance of payments	Mio SDR	1,6			
International reserves	Mio USD	18,8	4,8	19,4	26,9
External public debt	Mio USD	3 133,9	3 234,5	3 380,9	3 186,4
Debt service/exports	%	14,6			
Official development assistance					
Total net ODA	Mio USD	701,8	682,5	591,8	555,6
Bilateral net ODA	Mio USD	528,6	495,0	442,2	415,2
Net ODA: EC/bilateral	%	45,2	43,8	41,4	47,7
Multilateral net ODA	Mio USD	173,2	187,5	149,6	140,4
Multilateral: EDF/multilateral	%	23,4	16,0	18,1	22,7
Food aid					
Cereals	000 t	221,1	210,7	86,5	65,8
Dairy products	000 t	7,6	4,7	1,7	5,4
Total	MIO USD	68,7	63,8	32,5	34,7
Origin of GDP					
Agriculture, forestry, fisheries	%	51,5	51,6	:	
Industry	%	15,8	15,0	:	
Services	%	41,2	42,7	:	
Index of price changes	75 = 100	189,9	208,0	227,8	

Production and exports	Units	1981	1982	1983	1984
Main products					
Cereals, total	000 t	2 948	2 945	2 846	3 287
Sorghum	000 t	500	554	793	493
Millet	000 t	350	373	206	267
Maize	000 t	1 600	1 549	1 363	1 939
Rice, paddy	000 t	423	379	409	511
Pulses, total	000 t	316	322	355	'355
Tubers and roots	000 t	6 748	5 738	6 139	6 309
Unshelled groundnuts	000 t	56	58	58	59
Centrifugal sugar	000 t	114	124	102	132
Unmanufactured tobacco	000 t	14	11	14	16
Raw coffee	000 t	67	51	51	53
Tea	000 t	16	16	16	16
Bananas	000 t	1 000	1 000	1 000	1 000
Pineapples	000 t	48	49	50	50
Coconuts	000 t	320	320	320	320
Sisal	000 t	74	61	46	38
Cotton lint	000 t	59	45	44	48
Cow milk	000 t	403	397	403	418
Beef and buffalo meat	000 t	131	140	146	150
Roundwood	000 m³	19 994	20 759	21 260	22 024
Fishing	000 t	231	244	239	263
Diamonds	000 Car	227	220	250	:
Woven cotton fabrics	Mio m²	96	86		
Salted fish	000 t	38	35	33	41
Motor spirit	000 t	85	75	80	82
Light oils	000 t	130	140	140	138
Heavy oils	000 t	230	235	230	232
Main exports					
SITC 051.71 Coconuts, brazil nuts, etc.	Mio USD	60,4	19,9	20,2	
	%	10,7	5,0	4,8	
SITC 071.1 Coffee	Mio USD	151,7	140,6	151,0	
	%	26,9	35,1	35,5	
SITC 074.1 Tea	Mio USD	19,8	17,9	22,4	
	%	3,5	4,5	5,3	
SITC 075.23 Cloves	Mio USD	50,3	45,0	20,0	
	%	8,9	11,2	4,7	
SITC 121.0 Unmanufactured and scrap tobacco	Mio USD	18,1	:	:	
	%	3,2	:	:	
SITC 263.1 Raw cotton	Mio USD	77,4	41,9	45,6	
	%	13,7	10,4	10,7	
SITC 265.4 Sisal	Mio USD	32,5	22,9	11,6	
	%	5,8	5,7	2,7	
275.1 Industrial diamonds	Mio USD	22,5	:	:	
	%	4,0	:	:	
SITC 655.61 Twine, ropes	Mio USD	10,9	:	:	
	%	1,9	:	:	
SITC 667.2 Diamonds	Mio USD	30,6	:	:	
	%	5,4	:	:	

TCHAD

Population 1985:	5 020 000	→	Taux de croissance 1970-85:		2,2 %
PNB 1985:	410,0 Mio USD	→	Taux de croissance 1970-85:		1,1 %
PNB/h 1985:	80,0 USD	→	Taux de croissance 1970-81:		−5,6 %

Exportations 1983:	131,6 Mio USD	Importations 1983:	70,6 Mio USD
Exportations vers la CE 1983:	25,9 Mio USD	Importations de la CE 1983:	41,6 Mio USD
Élèves: enseign. primaire 1984:	288 478	Élèves: enseign. secondaire 1984:	45 612
Personnes/lit d'hôpital 1982:	1 278	Personnes/médecin 1982:	47 889

	Unités	1981	1982	1983	1984
Commerce extérieur					
Exportations	75 = 100	173,4	109,0	328,7	
Importations	75 = 100	46,5	60,4	64,2	
Balance commerciale	Mio USD	18,3	− 22,8	61,0	
Exportations/importations	%	135,7	65,7	186,4	
Balance commerciale avec la CE	Mio USD	− 0,4	− 19,0	− 15,7	
Export. vers la CE/import. de la CE	%	98,7	41,4	62,3	
Exportations/PIB	%	34,9			
Indicateurs financiers					
Balance des paiements	Mio DTS	− 0,8	2,3	15,4	18,7
Réserves internationales	Mio USD	7,3	12,4	28,0	44,2
Dette extérieure publique	Mio USD	261,8	225,7	219,0	208,3
Service de la dette/exportations	%	4,5	0,4	0,8	2,3
Aide publique au développement					
APD net total	Mio USD	59,7	64,7	95,3	115,2
APD net bilatéral	Mio USD	31,3	39,1	51,6	59,2
APD net CE/bilatéral	%	91,4	71,9	79,7	73,1
APD net multilatéral	Mio USD	28,4	25,6	43,6	56,0
APD net FED/multilatéral	%	41,5	40,1	36,1	39,2
Aide alimentaire					
Céréales	000 t	0,1	18,5	28,6	84,3
Produits laitiers	000 t	0,0	0,8	0,7	1,1
Total	Mio USD	0,4	4,0	8,7	27,9
Origine du PIB					
Agriculture, forêts, pêche	%	64,4	39,7		
Industrie	%	6,8	4,3		
Services	%	28,8	:		
Indice d'évolution des prix	75 = 100	156,8	187,2		

TCHAD

Productions et exportations	Unités	1981	1982	1983	1984
Principales productions					
Céréales, total	000 t	401	393	462	315
Millet	000 t	257	280	331	254
Maïs	000 t	35	30	29	22
Riz, paddy	000 t	44	23	18	2
Haricots, pois, lentilles	000 t	58	58	59	57
Tubercules et racines	000 t	455	485	500	539
Arachides non décortiquées	000 t	100	100	80	90
Sucre centrifugé brut	000 t	20	19	22	24
Dattes	000 t	30	31	32	30
Fibres de coton	000 t	26	38	60	36
Coton à graines	000 t	68	102	140	115
Lait de vache	000 t	117	122	126	105
Viande de bovins	000 t	30	31	31	28
Bois rond	000 m³	3 254	3 329	3 405	3 482
Pêche	000 t	115	115	110	110
Poisson salé	000 t	20	20	19	19
Principales exportations					
CTCI 263 Coton	Mio USD	55,0	30,6	18,7	
	%	79,3	70,0	14,2	

		1981	1982	1983	1984

Population 1985: 2 960 000 → Taux de croissance 1970-85: 2,8 %
PNB 1985: 750,0 Mio USD → Taux de croissance 1970-85: 5,3 %
PNB/h 1985: 250,0 USD → Taux de croissance 1970-81: 0,4 %

Exportations 1983: 225,6 Mio USD Importations 1983: 479,9 Mio USD
Exportations vers la CE 1983: 91,2 Mio USD Importations de la CE 1983: 279,6 Mio USD
Élèves: enseign. primaire 1983: 457 376 Élèves: enseign. secondaire 1983: 101 989
Personnes/lit d'hôpital 1982: 739 Personnes/médecin 1982: 19 417

	Unités	1981	1982	1983	1984
Commerce extérieur					
Exportations	75 = 100	165,4	201,5	180,7	
Importations	75 = 100	250,6	259,4	276,0	
Balance commerciale	Mio USD	− 229,3	− 199,5	− 254,3	
Exportations/importations	%	47,4	55,8	47,0	
Balance commerciale avec la CE	Mio USD	− 161,1	− 127,6	− 188,4	
Export. vers la CE/import. de la CE	%	43,8	46,3	32,6	
Exportations/PIB	%	23,5	27,7	31,0	
Indicateurs financiers					
Balance des paiements	Mio DTS	72,0	37,7	16,9	41,7
Réserves internationales	Mio USD	151,5	167,7	172,8	203,3
Dette extérieure publique	Mio USD	1 021,5	932,5	983,9	826,4
Service de la dette/exportations	%	14,9	12,3	17,4	28,5
Aide publique au développement					
APD net total	Mio USD	62,9	77,2	112,0	109,9
APD net bilatéral	Mio USD	37,4	54,2	51,6	55,0
APD net CE/bilatéral	%	83,4	78,5	73,1	74,8
APD net multilatéral	Mio USD	25,5	23,0	60,4	54,9
APD net FED/multilatéral	%	29,2	13,9	27,8	37,1
Aide alimentaire					
Céréales	000 t	5,0	2,4	5,0	9,0
Produits laitiers	000 t	0,7	0,9	1,9	1,5
Total	Mio USD	2,8	1,5	4,6	4,4
Origine du PIB					
Agriculture, forêts, pêche	%	22,4	22,6	21,5	
Industrie	%	25,6	28,3	28,1	
Services	%	45,8	46,8	:	
Indice d'évolution des prix	75 = 100	239,3	257,2	259,9	255,0

Productions et exportations	Unités	1981	1982	1983	1984
Principales productions					
Céréales, total	000 t	291	306	290	440
Millet	000 t	40	52	51	76
Maïs	000 t	151	151	145	222
Haricots, pois, lentilles	000 t	23	28	35	41
Tubercules et racines	000 t	963	874	820	814
Arachides non décortiquées	000 t	28	18	16	23
Palmistes	000 t	23	13	15	15
Huile de palme	000 t	20	20	14	14
Fèves de cacao	000 t	11	10	16	10
Café vert	000 t	9	9	6	3
Bananes	000 t	15	15	16	15
Coton à graines	000 t	24	21	27	24
Bois rond	000 m³	676	695	715	735
Pêche	000 t	10	15	15	15
Phosphates naturels	000 t	2 244	2 800	2 008	2 696
Poisson salé	000 t	3	4	4	3
Essence	000 t	75	78	75	75
Huiles légères	000 t	185	180	180	180
Huiles lourdes	000 t	155	165	160	160
Principales exportations					
CTCI 071.1 Café	Mio USD	17,9	18,8	12,8	
	%	8,7	10,6	7,9	
CTCI 072.1 Fèves de cacao	Mio USD	29,1	17,1	14,5	
	%	14,1	9,6	8,9	
CTCI 221.3 Noix et amandes de palmistes	Mio USD	3,0	:	:	:
	%	1,5	:	:	
CTCI 263.1 Coton brut	Mio USD	12,8	15,3	17,4	
	%	6,2	8,6	10,7	
CTCI 271.3 Phosphates naturels	Mio USD	104,2	77,9	68,2	
	%	50,5	44,0	42,0	
CTCI 661.2 Ciments hydr. même colorés	Mio USD	22,0	29,8	34,7	
	%	10,6	16,8	21,4	

TONGA

Population 1985:	100 000	→ Rate of growth 1970-85:			0,7 %
GNP 1985:	70 Mio USD	→ Rate of growth 1970-85:			8,0 %
GNP/capita 1985:	730 USD	→ Rate of growth 1970-81:			− 0,5 %

Total exports 1984:	9,0 Mio USD	Total imports 1984:		41,0 Mio USD
Exports to EC 1982:	0,1 Mio USD	Imports from EC 1982:		1,4 Mio USD
Pupils: primary school 1983:	16 329	Pupils: secondary school 1982:		17 085
Pers. by hospital bed 1982:	301	Pers. by doctor 1982:		2 463

	Units	1981	1982	1983	1984
External trade					
Total exports	75 = 100	153,7	74,9	94,8	155,2
Total imports	75 = 100	236,0	244,2	183,7	240,5
Balance of trade	Mio USD	− 31,3	− 37,3	− 25,8	− 32,0
Exports/imports	%	22,1	10,4	17,6	22,0
Balance of trade with EC	Mio USD	− 0,1	− 1,3		
Exports to EC/imports from EC	%	91,4	6,1		
Exports/GDP	%				
Official development assistance					
Total net ODA	Mio USD	18,0	17,4	17,9	15,7
Bilateral net ODA	Mio USD	14,5	12,4	13,3	12,4
Net ODA: EC/bilateral	%	26,5	17,6	14,6	7,9
Multilateral net ODA	Mio USD	3,5	4,9	4,7	3,3
Multilateral: EDF/multilateral	%	31,0	49,3	53,9	43,8
Food aid					
Cereals	000 t	0,0	3,4		
Dairy products	000 t	0,0	0,0	0,3	
Total	Mio USD	0,0	0,8	0,3	
Origin of GDP					
Agriculture, forestry, fisheries	%	50,7	49,0	46,7	
Industry	%	10,6	10,6	11,0	
Services	%	:	:	:	
Main products					
Tubers and roots	000 t	94	96	97	98
Unshelled groundnuts	000 t	2	2	2	2
Copra	000 t	14	7	4	5
Bananas	000 t	3	3	4	3
Coconuts	000 t	109	60	42	46
Oranges	000 t	3	3	3	3
Fishing	000 t	2	2	2	2
Main exports					
SITC 051.3 Bananas	Mio USD	0,5	0,1	0,4	
	%	5,3	2,1	6,7	
SITC 075.21 Vanilla	Mio USD	0,3	0,6	0,6	
	%	3,4	13,8	10,0	
SITC 221.2 Copra	Mio USD	2,8	:	:	
	%	31,9	:	:	
SITC 422.3 Copra and coconut oil	Mio USD	1,3	1,3	1,8	
	%	15,1	30,1	30,0	

TRINIDAD AND TOBAGO

Population 1985:	1 180 000	→ Rate of growth 1970-85:	0,9 %
GNP 1985:	7 140,0 Mio USD	→ Rate of growth 1970-85:	9,3 %
GNP/capita 1985:	6 010,0 Mio USD	→ Rate of growth 1970-81:	3,5 %

Total exports 1985:	2 164,0 Mio USD	Total imports 1985:	1 525,0 Mio USD
Exports to EC 1983:	291,9 Mio USD	Imports from EC 1983:	509,7 Mio USD
Pupils: primary school 1982:	169 853	Pupils: secondary school 1982:	90 815
Pers. by hospital bed 1980:	257	Pers. by doctor 1980:	1 130

	Units	1981	1982	1983	1984
External trade					
Total exports	75 = 100	212,1	174,1	132,7	122,6
Total imports	75 = 100	209,9	248,4	173,5	128,9
Balance of trade	Mio USD	636,2	− 612,6	− 229,3	254,0
Exports/imports	%	120,4	83,4	91,1	113,2
Balance of trade with EC	Mio USD	104,7	− 41,0	− 217,8	
Exports to EC/imports from EC	%	123,1	92,8	57,3	
Exports/GDP	%	44,7	36,0		
Financial indicators					
Overall balance of payments	Mio SDR	482,0	− 187,5	− 816,6	− 676,3
International reserves	Mio USD	3 347,5	3 080,5	2 104,5	1 356,7
External public debt	Mio USD	806,4	937,8	1 020,6	1 059,3
Debt service/exports	%	4,6	4,7	12,4	3,2
Official development assistance					
Total net ODA	Mio USD	− 1,4	5,7	5,5	4,6
Bilateral net ODA	Mio USD	− 5,9	1,4	1,7	1,5
Net ODA: EC/bilateral	%	114,6	35,5	52,9	60,8
Multilateral net ODA	Mio USD	4,5	4,3	3,8	3,1
Multilateral: EDF/multilateral	%	8,2	12,6	27,3	17,5
Origin of GDP					
Agriculture, forestry, fisheries	%	2,4	2,5		
Industry	%	52,2	11,5		
Services	%	45,5	:		
Index of price changes	75 = 100	322,3	361,1	409,1	

TRINIDAD AND TOBAGO

Production and exports	Units	1981	1982	1983	1984
Main products					
Cereals, total	000 t	6	6	6	6
Rice, paddy	000 t	3	3	3	3
Tubers and roots	000 t	20	18	19	20
Centrifugal sugar	000 t	94	79	77	70
Coconuts	000 t	48	54	58	52
Roundwood	000 m³	91	78	61	57
Sawn wood	000 m³	33	28	22	21
Fishing	000 t	4	5	4	4
Crude petroleum	000 t	9 780	9 143	8 256	8 760
Natural gas (Mio tera cal.)	teraj	124 525	124 525	119 600	115 104
Motor spirit	000 t	1 575	1 306	884	701
Light oils	000 t	1 423	1 277	617	587
Heavy oils	000 t	4 467	4 099	1 997	2 210
Nitrogenous fertilizers	000 t	23	30	23	67
Main exports					
SITC 061.1 Sugar	Mio USD	27,0	21,8	25,1	
	%	0,7	0,7	1,1	
SITC 331.01 Crude petroleum	Mio USD	1 612,4	1 116,4	1 099,4	
	%	42,9	36,2	46,7	
SITC 332.1 Petroleum spirit	Mio USD	295,2	348,9	201,4	
	%	7,8	11,3	8,6	
SITC 332.2 Lamp oil	Mio USD	105,1	148,3	95,8	
	%	2,8	4,8	4,1	
SITC 332.3 Distillate fuel oil	Mio USD	353,9	331,8	144,8	
	%	9,4	10,8	6,2	
SITC 332.4 Residual fuel oil	Mio USD	933,7	701,9	399,1	
	%	24,8	22,7	17,0	

Population 1985:	15 480 000	→	Rate of growth 1970-85:		3,1 %
GNP 1985:	5 000,0 Mio USD	→	Rate of growth 1970-85:		6,3 %
GNP/capita 1985:	220,0 USD	→	Rate of growth 1970-77:		− 2,8 %

Total exports 1984:	399 Mio USD		Total imports 1983:	257,6 Mio USD
Exports to EC 1983:	151,3 Mio USD		Imports from EC 1983:	92,4 Mio USD
Pupils: primary school 1982:	1 616 791		Pupils: secondary school 1982:	145 389
Pers. by hospital bed 1982:	689		Pers. by doctor 1982:	22 291

	Units	1981	1982	1983	1984
External trade					
Total exports	75 = 100	105,1	147,6	136,6	151,4
Total imports	75 = 100	232,7	239,5	200,1	
Balance of trade	Mio USD	− 22,5	80,6	102,5	
Exports/imports	%	92,5	126,2	139,8	
Balance of trade with EC	Mio USD	− 3,6	12,2	58,9	
Exports to EC/imports from EC	%	96,7	110,5	163,7	
Exports/GDP	%	2,8	3,6	6,3	
Financial indicators					
Overall balance of payments	Mio SDR	− 134,2			
International reserves	Mio USD	3,0	11,1	0,9	
External public debt	Mio USD	817,2	1 022,5	1 077,2	1 244,4
Debt service/exports	%	37,7			
Official development assistance					
Total net ODA	Mio USD	135,7	132,8	136,7	163,9
Bilateral net ODA	Mio USD	78,7	53,9	47,6	45,8
Net ODA: EC/bilateral	%	70,6	58,8	56,0	59,5
Multilateral net ODA	Mio USD	57,0	78,9	89,1	118,1
Multilateral: EDF/multilateral	%	18,6	8,8	18,7	19,1
Food aid					
Cereals	000 t	60,0	16,2	15,7	18,9
Dairy products	000 t	0,6	0,1	0,5	0,3
Total	Mio USD	13,3	5,4	7,0	7,6
Origin of GDP					
Agriculture, forestry, fisheries	%	81,8	61,5		
Industry	%	4,4	3,0		
Services	%	15,0	:		

UGANDA

Production and exports	Units	1981	1982	1983	1984
Main products					
Cereals, total	000 t	1 165	1 350	1 399	679
Sorghum	000 t	320	400	407	148
Millet	000 t	480	528	545	223
Maize	000 t	342	393	413	281
Pulses, total	000 t	293	361	401	304
Tubers and roots	000 t	4 475	4 810	5 305	2 880
Unshelled groundnuts	000 t	80	90	99	100
Raw coffee	000 t	98	167	157	204
Tea	000 t	2	3	3	5
Bananas	000 t	370	400	410	420
Cotton lint	000 t	5	5	10	19
Seed cotton	000 t	16	48	33	62
Cow milk	000 t	357	350	350	357
Beef and buffalo meat	000 t	92	86	86	88
Roundwood	000 m³	11 017	11 400	11 809	12 230
Fishing	000 t	167	170	172	212
Main exports					
SITC 071.1 Coffee	Mio USD	255,2	370,8	336,9	
	%	92,1	95,3	93,6	
SITC 263.1 Raw cotton	Mio USD	4,9	4,8	10,3	
	%	1,8	1,2	2,9	

Population 1985:	140 000 →	Taux de croissance 1970-85:	3,8 %
PNB 1985:	90,0 Mio USD →	Taux de croissance 1970-85:	8,6 %
PNB/h 1985:	720,0 USD →	Taux de croissance 1970-81:	− 5,7 %

Exportations 1985:	31,0 Mio USD	Importations 1985:	71,0 Mio USD
Exportations vers la CE 1983:	13,6 Mio USD	Importations de la CE 1983:	7,3 Mio USD
Élèves: enseign. primaire 1983:	22 244	Élèves: enseign. secondaire 1982:	2 904
Personnes/lit d'hôpital 1982:	283	Personnes/médecin 1982:	4 379

	Unités	1981	1982	1983	1984
Commerce extérieur					
Exportations	75 = 100	158,2	105,4	176,4	433,7
Importations	75 = 100	130,6	141,5	151,9	204,8
Balance commerciale	Mio USD	− 27,9	− 37,0	− 33,3	− 25,0
Exportations/importations	%	36,5	22,4	35,0	63,8
Balance commerciale avec la CE	Mio USD	7,2	2,2	6,4	
Export. vers la CE/import. de la CE	%	207,9	134,3	187,4	
Exportations/PIB	%				
Indicateurs financiers					
Balance des paiements	Mio DTS	:	2,9	0,9	− 2,6
Réserves internationales	Mio USD	8,5	5,7	6,6	8,1
Dette extérieure publique	Mio USD	3,0	5,0	11,7	11,6
Service de la dette/exportations	%		5,5	3,7	1,8
Aide publique au développement					
APD net total	Mio USD	30,4	26,0	26,9	24,4
APD net bilatéral	Mio USD	24,4	23,3	24,3	22,2
APD net CE/bilatéral	%	82,5	72,6	69,9	79,1
APD net multilatéral	Mio USD	6,1	2,7	2,5	2,3
APD net FED/multilatéral	%	83,1	48,1	40,3	32,2
Principales productions					
Tubercules et racines	000 t	30	30	30	30
Coprah	000 t	46	34	38	48
Noix de coco	000 t	325	253	265	326
Bois rond	000 m³	35	33	38	38
Pêche	000 t	3	3	2	3
Principales exportations					
CTCI 011.1 Viande bovine	Mio USD	1,1	1,3	1,4	5,3
	%	7,1	12,1	7,9	12,1
CTCI 072.1 Fèves de cacao	Mio USD	1,3	0,6	1,8	0,2
	%	8,3	5,5	10,3	0,6
CTCI 221.2 Coprah	Mio USD	12,3	7,4	13,1	
	%	76,3	69,1	73,4	

WESTERN SAMOA

Population 1985:	160 000 →	Rate of growth 1970-85:		0,9 %
GNP 1985:	110,0 Mio USD →	Rate of growth 1970-85:		16,9 %
GNP/capita 1985:	660,0 USD →	Rate of growth 1970-81:		0,0 %

Total exports 1985:	15,0 Mio USD	Total imports 1985:		51,0 Mio USD
Exports to EC 1983:	2,2 Mio USD	Imports from EC 1983:		2,9 Mio USD
Pupils: primary school 1983:	31 457	Pupils: secondary school 1982:		21 643
Pers. by hospital bed 1981:	231	Pers. by doctor 1981:		1 492

	Units	1981	1982	1983	1984
External trade					
Total exports	75 = 100	157,2	188,6	261,9	279,6
Total imports	75 = 100	185,7	113,8	142,9	138,1
Balance of trade	Mio USD	− 57,2	− 28,5	− 33,9	− 30,9
Exports/imports	%	16,4	32,0	35,4	39,1
Balance of trade with EC	Mio USD	− 1,4	0,3	− 0,7	
Exports to EC/imports from EC	%	68,6	116,2	74,9	
Exports/GDP	%				
Financial indicators					
Overall balance of payments	Mio SDR	− 1,3	1,3	2,6	3,2
International reserves	Mio USD	3,3	3,5	7,2	10,6
External public debt	Mio USD	87,0	83,9	80,8	82,0
Debt service/exports	%	43,6	26,5	23,4	19,4
Official development assistance					
Total net ODA	Mio USD	25,0	22,8	26,7	20,2
Bilateral net ODA	Mio USD	14,2	15,3	16,6	11,0
Net ODA: EC/bilateral	%	19,2	12,1	7,3	13,2
Multilateral net ODA	Mio USD	10,8	7,4	10,1	9,3
Multilateral EDF/multilateral	%	20,8	33,4	44,4	38,3
Food aid					
Cereals	000 t	400	30		
Dairy products	000 t	5	110		
Total	000 USD	220	183		
Origin of GDP					
Agriculture, forestry, fisheries	%	46,6	50,9	50,6	
Industry	%	:	:	:	
Services	%	:	:	:	

WESTERN SAMOA

Production and exports	Units	1981	1982	1983	1984
Main products					
Tubers and roots	000 t	43	42	41	42
Copra	000 t	19	19	24	23
Cocoa beans	000 t	2	1	1	2
Bananas	000 t	22	22	22	22
Pineapples	000 t	5	5	6	6
Coconuts	000 t	200	200	200	200
Roundwood	000 m³	131	131	131	131
Sawn wood	000 m³	21	21	21	21
Fishing	000 t	3	4	4	4
Main exports					
SITC 054.81 Frozen vegetables	Mio USD	2,0	2,7	1,6	
	%	18,1	20,1	8,5	
SITC 072.1 Cocoa beans	Mio USD	1,4	1,4	2,9	
	%	12,5	10,4	15,4	
SITC 221.2 Copra	Mio USD	4,1	3,2	0,9	
	%	37,0	23,9	4,9	

Population 1985:	30 360 000	→ Taux de croissance 1970-85:	2,3 %
PNB 1985:	5 220,0 Mio USD	→ Taux de croissance 1970-85:	4,4 %
PNB/h 1985:	170,0 USD	→ Taux de croissance 1970-81:	− 2,2 %

Exportations 1984:	1 004,0 Mio USD	Importations 1985:	1 025,0 Mio USD
Exportations vers la CE 1983:	396,1 Mio USD	Importations de la CE 1983:	303,0 Mio USD
Élèves: enseign. primaire 1978:	3 919 395	Élèves: enseign. secondaire 1977:	704 332
Personnes/lit d'hôpital 1982:	322	Personnes/médecin 1982:	13 452

	Unités	1981	1982	1983	1984
Commerce extérieur					
Exportations	75 = 100	234,7	176,9	160,5	116,1
Importations	75 = 100	109,3	97,8	90,2	74,3
Balance commerciale	Mio USD	1 010,8	617,7	546,2	311,1
Exportations/importations	%	199,2	167,7	164,9	144,9
Balance commerciale avec la CE	Mio USD	78,5	28,6	93,0	
Export. vers la CE/import. de la CE	%	123,6	108,9	130,7	
Exportations/PIB	%	35,1	33,3		
Indicateurs financiers					
Balance des paiements	Mio DTS	− 475,0	− 318,0	− 904,1	− 202,0
Réserves internationales	Mio USD	151,5	38,9	101,6	137,4
Dette extérieure publique	Mio USD	4 771,3	4 704,1	4 955,5	4 525,2
Service de la dette/exportations	%	17,5	11,4	9,2	18,1
Aide publique au développement					
APD net total	Mio USD	393,6	348,2	314,5	312,5
APD net bilatéral	Mio USD	291,6	256,5	193,9	209,7
APD net CE/bilatéral	%	67,0	64,7	78,5	75,9
APD net multilatéral	Mio USD	102,0	91,8	120,6	102,8
APD net FED/multilatéral	%	43,6	20,1	42,0	33,3
Aide alimentaire					
Céréales	000 t	75,8	85,2	62,7	113,0
Produits latiers	000 t	2,2	0,6	0,6	0,1
Total	Mio USD	25,1	20,2	14,0	19,4
Origine du PIB					
Agriculture, forêts, pêche	%	31,7	35,7		
Industrie	%	23,4	19,8		
Services	%	41,0	41,2		

ZAÏRE

Productions et exportations	Unités	1981	1982	1983	1984
Principales productions					
Céréales, total	000 t	947	988	1 019	1 073
Maïs	000 t	639	666	673	704
Riz, paddy	000 t	245	251	271	286
Haricots, pois, lentilles	000 t	163	108	115	119
Tubercules et racines	000 t	13 793	14 825	15 258	15 704
Arachides non décortiquées	000 t	347	349	367	376
Huile de palme	000 t	165	155	145	153
Café vert	000 t	73	84	83	81
Bananes	000 t	320	320	325	325
Ananas	000 t	155	160	160	160
Oranges	000 t	142	143	144	145
Caoutchouc naturel	000 t	21	23	24	21
Fibres de coton	000 t	7	23	26	26
Bois rond	000 m³	29 803	30 725	31 660	32 597
Bois scié	000 m³	105	95	112	112
Pêche	000 t	103	101	102	101
Minerai de cuivre	000 t	506	505	502	501
Minerai d'étain	t	2 472	2 623	2 100	2 412
Minerai de manganèse	000 t	31	4	2	8
Minerai de zinc	000 t	76	82	75	72
Minerai d'or	kg	2 027	1 869	4 000	3 000
Diamants	000 carats	7 161	6 164	11 768	13 300
Pétrole brut	000 t	1 048	1 145	1 296	1 607
Houille	000 t	140	120	130	130
Cuivre de fonderie	000 t	471	469	466	465
Principales exportations					
CTCI 071.1 Café	Mio USD	176,8	159,7	161,1	
	%	8,7	10,4	11,6	
CTCI 283.11 Minerai de cuivre	Mio USD	49,2	36,1	48,4	
	%	2,4	2,4	3,5	
CTCI 331 Pétrole brut part. raffiné	Mio USD	252,3	290,8	251,4	
	%	12,4	19,0	18,1	
CTCI 667.2 Diamants	Mio USD	49,7	43,6	82,0	
	%	2,4	2,8	5,9	
CTCI 682 Cuivre	Mio USD	721,8	585,2	527,7	
	%	35,6	38,2	38,0	

ZAMBIA

Population 1985:	6 670 000 →	Rate of growth 1970-85:	3,1 %
GNP 1985:	2 620,0 Mio USD →	Rate of growth 1970-85:	3,4 %
GNP/capita 1985:	400,0 USD →	Rate of growth 1970-81:	− 2,8 %

Total exports 1985:	539,0 Mio USD	Total imports 1985:	698,0 Mio USD
Exports to EC 1983:	332,5 Mio USD	Imports from EC 1983:	155,5 Mio USD
Pupils: primary school 1982:	1 082 600	Pupils: secondary school 1982:	110 729
Pers. by hospital bed 1981:	289	Pers. by doctor 1981:	7 261

	Units	1981	1982	1983	1984
External trade					
Total exports	75 = 100	120,2	106,2	101,7	84,5
Total imports	75 = 100	114,3	90,4	60,4	65,5
Balance of trade	Mio USD	− 86,0	22,3	264,6	77,7
Exports/imports	%	91,9	102,7	147,2	112,8
Balance of trade with EC	Mio USD	− 134,6	140,3	177,1	
Exports to EC/imports from EC	%	68,9	154,8	213,9	
Exports/GDP	%	28,6	27,6	30,6	36,5
Financial indicators					
Overall balance of payments	Mio SDR	− 352,0	14,0	− 53,0	− 100,0
International reserves	Mio USD	56,2	58,2	54,5	54,2
External public debt	Mio USD	3 016,5	3 259,4	3 379,2	3 503,8
Debt service/exports	%	40,4	22,7	12,1	12,7
Official development assistance					
Total net ODA	Mio USD	230,9	315,8	215,5	238,2
Bilateral net ODA	Mio USD	180,5	263,5	182,5	180,5
Net ODA: EC/bilateral	%	45,2	27,2	36,5	37,3
Multilateral net ODA	Mio USD	50,4	52,3	33,3	57,7
Multilateral EDF/multilateral	%	54,7	57,6	25,2	41,5
Food aid					
Cereals	000 t	101,7	59,2	73,3	118,1
Dairy products	t	2 232	21	14	3 255
Total	Mio USD	26,3	14,0	21,0	37,4
Origin of GDP					
Agriculture, forestry, fisheries	%	15,9	13,7	14,2	14,7
Industry	%	38,7	37,2	40,1	39,3
Services	%	42,9	46,6	44,6	44,0
Index of price changes	75 = 100	203,6	216,1	256,4	294,1

ZAMBIA

Production and exports	Units	1981	1982	1983	1984
Main products					
Cereals, total	000 t	1 066	798	992	921
Maize	000 t	1 007	750	935	872
Tubers and roots	000 t	213	224	235	235
Unshelled groundnuts	000 t	15	9	11	13
Centrifugal sugar	000 t	102	117	132	141
Cow milk	000 t	59	66	68	70
Beef and buffalo meat	000 t	31	33	30	33
Roundwood	000 m³	9 202	9 505	9 628	9 921
Sawn wood	000 m³	42	42	50	50
Fishing	000 t	39	56	67	65
Copper ore	000 t	587	530	578	633
Lead ore	000 t	16	24	15	9
Zinc ore	000 t	40	53	42	38
Gold ore	kg	310	306	300	300
Coal	000 t	507	604	452	468
Salted fish	000 t	2	4	4	4
Copper (smelter)	000 t	572	581	563	532
Copper (refined)	000 t	564	587	575	523
Motor spirit	000 t	170	160	160	150
Light oils	000 t	350	320	320	310
Heavy oils	000 t	177	150	160	155
Nitrogenous fertilizers	000 t	4	9	16	15
Main exports					
SITC 121 Tobacco	Mio USD	2,9	20,9	7,9	
	%	0,3	2,0	1,0	
SITC 121.0 Unmanufactured and scrap tobacco	Mio USD	4,6	1,7	:	
	%	0,4	0,2	:	
SITC 682 Copper	Mio USD	957,4	743,7	704,9	
	%	89,2	72,8	85,4	

ZIMBABWE

Population 1985:	8 380 000 →	Rate of growth 1970-85:	3,1 %
GNP 1985:	5 450,0 Mio USD →	Rate of growth 1970-85:	6,7 %
GNP/capita 1985:	650,0 USD →	Rate of growth 1970-81:	0,1 %

Total exports 1985:	1 053,0 Mio USD	Total imports 1985:	969,0 Mio USD
Exports to EC 1983:	338,1 Mio USD	Imports from EC 1983:	242,7 Mio USD
Pupils: primary school 1985:	2 229 396	Pupils: secondary school 1985:	497 766
Pers. by hospital bed 1980:	345	Pers. by doctor 1980:	6 411

	Units	1981	1982	1983	1984
External trade					
Total exports	75 = 100	143,2	118,1	133,8	119,0
Total imports	75 = 100	183,5	178,3	130,9	131,2
Balance of trade	Mio USD	− 265,4	− 434,9	78,1	− 49,0
Exports/imports	%	82,0	69,6	107,4	95,3
Balance of trade with EC	Mio USD	− 30,9	− 139,4	95,5	
Exports to EC/imports from EC	%	92,2	70,3	139,3	
Exports/GDP	%				
Financial indicators					
Overall balance of payments	Mio SDR	− 4,7	− 19,3	− 159,8	− 44,9
International reserves	Mio USD	169,5	140,4	75,4	45,4
External public debt	Mio USD	1 703,0	2 165,9	2 335,0	2 229,5
Debt service/exports	%	6,9	13,7	42,2	23,6
Official development assistance					
Total net ODA	Mio USD	212,3	215,8	208,2	297,5
Bilateral net ODA	Mio USD	144,9	186,0	185,5	244,2
Net ODA: EC/bilateral	%	53,1	48,6	44,5	41,3
Multilateral net ODA	Mio USD	67,4	29,8	22,8	53,3
Multilateral: EDF/multilateral	%	5,1	34,4	45,7	48,5
Food aid					
Cereals	000 t	3,0	0,0	15,3	105,3
Dairy products	000 t	0,0	3,0	4,8	4,3
Total	Mio USD	3,5	3,6	8,1	31,4
Origin of GDP					
Agriculture, forestry, fisheries	%	16,2	15,0	10,8	:
Industry	%	37,0	35,1	32,1	:
Services	%	50,1	54,3	61,1	:
Index of price changes	75 = 100	257,4	264,3	307,7	373,9

ZIMBABWE

Production and exports	Units	1981	1982	1983	1984
Main products					
Cereals, total	000 t	3 310	2 205	1 220	1 591
Wheat	000 t	183	192	124	99
Millet	000 t	138	98	100	120
Maize	000 t	2 833	1 808	910	1 283
Tubers and roots	000 t	71	85	94	104
Unshelled groundnuts	000 t	119	111	32	26
Centrifugal sugar	000 t	370	423	452	484
Unmanufactured tobacco	000 t	69	89	94	125
Cotton lint	000 t	58	46	50	84
Seed cotton	000 t	200	154	176	251
Cow milk	000 t	152	165	185	192
Beef and buffalo meat	000 t	66	77	77	76
Roundwood	000 m³	6 846	7 140	6 763	7 104
Sawn wood	000 m³	200	198	131	157
Paper and paperboard	000 t	62	67	65	64
Fishing	000 t	16	18	14	16
Iron ore	000 t	701	576	591	591
Copper ore	000 t	25	25	24	23
Phosphate rock production	000 t	125	122	133	134
Nickel ore	000 t	15	13	10	10
Chromium ore	000 t	536	432	431	476
Gold ore	kg	11 500	13 300	14 100	14 500
Coal	000 t	2 362	2 769	3 326	3 132
Salted fish	000 t	5	5	4	5
Copper (smelter)	000 t	30	31	31	30
Copper (refined)	000 t	17	26	25	24
Nitrogenous fertilizers	000 t	70	84	71	69
Phosphate fertilizers	000 t	40	38	45	40
Main exports					
SITC 061.1 Sugar	Mio USD	66,4	58,5	17,4	
	%	5,5	5,4	1,5	
SITC 121 Tobacco	Mio USD	315,7	253,1	171,6	
	%	26,2	23,3	15,2	
SITC 263.1 Raw cotton	Mio USD	88,5	69,4		
	%	7,3	7,0		
SITC 276.4 Asbestos, crude	Mio USD	109,9	80,1		
	%	9,1	8,0		
SITC 671.5 Other ferro-alloys	Mio USD	115,0	101,6		
	%	9,5	10,2		
SITC 672 Iron, steel primary forms	Mio USD	35,0	37,2		
	%	2,9	3,7		
SITC 673 Iron and steel shapes	Mio USD	25,5	17,1		
	%	2,1	1,7		
SITC 682.1 Copper	Mio USD	26,5	28,6		
	%	2,2	2,9		
SITC 683 Nickel	Mio USD	67,7	59,8		
	%	5,6	6,0		

**EDF and EIB interventions
under the Lomé III Convention**

**Les interventions du FED et de la BEI
au titre de la convention de Lomé III**

III

EDF and EIB interventions
under the Lomé III Convention

Les interventions de l'FED et de la BEI
au titre de la convention de Lomé III

Lomé I — Financing situation in 1985, by method of financing and by administrative body
Lomé I — Situation des financements fin 1985, par modes de financement et organismes gestionnaires

(Mio ECU)

	Total volume (Art. 95 of the Convention) Volume total (article 95 de la convention)		Commitments at end of 1985 Engagements pris fin 1985					
			Aid administered by Aide administrée par				Total	
			Commission		EIB/BEI			
	Amount Montant	%	Amount Montant	%	Amount Montant	%	Amount Montant	%
EDF resources / **Ressources du FED**	3 072,00	88,7	2 956,55	100	:	:	2 956,55	88,3
Grants / Subventions	2 150,00	62,1	2 047,73	69,3	:	:	2 047,73	61,2
of which: / *dont:*								
Interest-rate subsidies / Bonifications d'intérêt	:		60,13	2,0			60,13	1,8
Exceptional aid / Aides exceptionnelles	:		136,99	4,6			136,99	4,1
Special loans / Prêts spéciaux	446,00	12,9	434,26	14,7	:		434,26	13,0
Risk capital / Capitaux à risque	99,00	2,8	97,06	3,3			97,06	2,9
Stabex / Stabex	377,00	10,9	377,50	12,7			377,50	11,3
Special financing facility — Sysmin / Facilité de financement spécial — Sysmin	—				:		:	:
EIB resources / **Ressources de la BEI**	390,00	11,3			390,00	100,0	390,00	11,6
Loans from EIB resources / Prêts sur ressources propres								
Total / **Total**	3 462,00	100	2 956,55	100	390,00	100	3 346,55	100

Lomé II — Financing situation in 1985, by method of financing and by administrative body

Lomé II — Situation des financements fin 1985, par modes de financement et organismes gestionnaires

(Mio ECU)

	Total volume (Art. 95 of the Convention) / Volume total (article 95 de la convention)		Commitments at end of 1985 / Engagements pris fin 1985						
			Aid administered by / Aide administrée par				Total		
			Commission		EIB/BEI				
	Amount / Montant	%	Amount / Montant	%	Amount / Montant	%	Amount / Montant	%	
EDF resources	**4 724,00**	**87,3**	**3 615,14**	**100**			**3 615,14**	**85,7**	**Ressources du FED**
Grants	2 999,00	55,4	2 324,75	64,3			2 324,75	55,1	Subventions
of which:									*dont:*
Interest-rate subsidies	:		115,32	3,2			115,32	2,7	Bonifications d'intérêt
Exceptional aid	:		172,56	4,8			172,56	4,1	Aides exceptionnelles
Special loans	525,00	9,7	385,11	10,7			385,11	9,1	Prêts spéciaux
Risk capital	284,00	5,3	270,26	7,5			270,26	6,4	Capitaux à risque
Stabex	634,00	11,7	506,18	14,0			506,18	12,0	Stabex
Special financing facility — Sysmin			128,84	3,6			128,84	3,0	Facilité de financement spécial — Sysmin
EIB resources	282,00	5,2							Ressources de la BEI
Loans from EIB resources	685,00	12,7			602,50	100,0	602,50	14,3	Prêts sur ressources propres
Total	**5 409,00**	**100**	**3 615,14**	**100**	**602,50**	**100**	**4 217,64**	**100**	**Total**

Breakdown of commitments at end of 1985 by country and by sector (5th EDF and EIB ordinary loans)

Répartition des engagements pris fin 1985 par pays et par secteurs d'intervention (5e FED + prêts normaux BEI)

(Mio ECU)

| | dont/of which | | |
	Exceptional aid Aides exceptionnelles	Stabex	Total
Antigua and Barbuda	0,2		1,0
Bahamas			2,0
Barbados			5,6
Belize			1,0
Bénin	1,5	4,1	52,8
Botswana	0,2		26,0
Burkina Faso	0,5	1,1	83,1
Burundi	0,2	11,6	80,7
Cameroun	1,6	17,3	84,3
Cape Verde	1,2	0,5	17,0
Comores	0,4	6,6	17,0
Congo			36,2
Côte-d'Ivoire	0,8	54,5	102,0
Djibouti	0,3		7,2
Dominica	0,5	3,0	7,9
Ethiopia	48,3	10,8	210,3
Fiji	4,3	2,1	30,9
Gabon			25,0
Gambia		14,3	26,3
Ghana	4,4	63,9	124,1
Grenada		4,0	9,7
Guinea-Bissau		3,4	25,7
Guinée	1,1		66,4
Guinée équatoriale			6,8
Guyana			20,0
Jamaica		3,2	34,5
Kenya	2,4	31,1	106,0
Kiribati		1,6	5,8
Lesotho		1,3	35,7
Liberia			21,4
Madagascar	1,8	6,1	99,0
Malawi	0,4	4,7	88,6
Mali	14,1	10,0	105,0
Maurice	0,1		21,7
Mauritanie	4,4		47,9
Niger	13,6		92,6

	dont/of which		
	Exceptional aid Aides exceptionnelles	Stabex	Total
Nigeria	0,3		35,9
Papua New Guinea		41,9	67,6
Rép. Centrafricaine	0,5	4,2	56,3
Rwanda	2,0	7,7	77,9
St Kitts & Nevis			2,2
St Lucia	0,2	1,4	6,3
St Vincent	0,2		3,6
Solomon Islands		3,8	9,8
São Tome and Principe	0,1	7,0	11,2
Sénégal	2,1	64,9	130,1
Seychelles	0,2		7,8
Sierra Leone		13,6	40,2
Somalie	16,3	2,8	78,5
Sudan	17,5	32,2	145,7
Suriname			9,9
Swaziland	0,1	8,2	27,0
Tanzania	0,5	19,2	135,5
Tchad	11,7	6,1	72,5
Togo	0,6	28,8	67,2
Tonga	1,4	4,0	10,8
Trinidad and Tobago			12,1
Tuvalu		0,1	1,3
Vanuatu	0,2		7,7
Uganda	4,5		74,6
Western Samoa		5,1	14,7
Zaïre	2,8		149,0
Zambia	1,6		129,6
Zimbabwe	7,5		54,6
Non-alloc. projects			0,5
Regional projects			447,8
Total Blocked approps.			
Grand total	**172,6**	**506,2**	**3 615,1**

EDF commitments situation

Situation des engagements du FED

(Mio ECU — 31.12.1985)

Sector concerned	Secteurs d'intervention	Total	% of total I-VII / % sur total I-VII	% of total HV / % sur total HV
I. PRODUCTION DEVELOPMENT	I. DÉVELOPPEMENT DE LA PRODUCTION	1 712,1	47,3	58,2
1. Industrialization	**1. Industrialisation**	**755,2**		
10. General	10. Général	151,6		
11. Extractive industries	11. Industries extractives	206,0		
12. Metal industries	12. Industries métallurgiques	100,0		
13. Chemical industries	13. Industries chimiques	12,7		
14. Manufacturing industries	14. Industries manufacturières	76,9		
15. Agriculture and food industries	15. Industries agricoles et alimentaires	54,2		
16. Predominantly energy projects	16. Projets à dominance énergétique	241,3		
17. Infrastructure for industrial projects	17. Infrastr. intégr. à des projets industriels	10,1		
18. Craftwork	18. Artisanat	2,4		
19. Integrated industrial projects	19. Proj. intégr. à domin. industrielle	0,0		
2. Tourism	**2. Tourisme**	**23,2**		
3. Rural production	**3. Production rurale**	**933,7**		
30. General	30. Général	101,9		
31. Plantations	31. Plantations	267,2		
32. Irrigation schemes	32. Aménagements hydro-agricoles	68,3		
33. Agriculture	33. Agriculture	253,7		
35. Rearing	35. Élevage	96,5		
36. Fisheries	36. Pêche	36,4		
37. Forestry	37. Forêts	8,6		
38. Miscellaneous	38. Divers	67,5		
39. Integrated agricultural projects	39. Proj. intégrés à domin. agricole	117,9		
	Cooperatives credit-commerce	15,7		
II. ECONOMIC INFRASTRUCTURE	II. INFRASTRUCTURE ÉCONOMIQUE	637,6	17,6	21,7
4. Transport and communications	**4. Transports et communications**	**637,6**		
40. General	40. Général	13,0		
41. Roads and bridges	41. Routes et ponts	470,9		
42. Railways	42. Chemins de fer	55,8		
43. Ports and rivers	43. Ports et voies fluviales	37,3		

No. / English	No. / French	Detail	% I–IV	Total	% I–VII
44. Airports	44. Aéroports				
45. Telecommunications	45. Télécommunications	26,9			
46. Weather	46. Météo	33,7			
III. SOCIAL DEVELOPMENT	**III. DÉVELOPPEMENT SOCIAL**		18,4	541,8	15,0
5. Teaching and education	**5. Enseignement et formation**	249,3			—
50. General	50. Général	4,8			
51. Teaching infrastructure	51. Infrastructure d'enseignement	79,9			
52. Specific professional training projects	52. Projets spécifiques enseignement profession. et envoi instructeurs	33,2			
53. Grants	53. Bourses	130,2			
54. Apprenticeships	54. Stages	1,2			
6. Health	**6. Santé**	67,8			
60. General	60. Général	3,3			
61. Infrastructure	61. Infrastructure	51,3			
62. Campaigns and technical cooperation	62. Campagnes sanitaires et coopération technique	13,2			
7. Hydraulics, environment	**7. Hydrauliques, édilité, habitat**	224,7			
70. General	70. Général	65,8			
71. Village hydraulics	71. Hydraulique villageoise	89,0			
72. Urban water supplies	72. Adduction d'eau urbaine	49,5			
73. Urban improvement	73. Assainissement urbain	12,8			
74. Urban development	74. Aménagements urbanistiques	7,6			
IV. TRADE PROMOTION	**IV. PROMOTION COMMERCIALE**		1,7	49,6	1,4
8. Trade promotion	**8. Promotion commerciale**	49,6			
80. General	80. Général	21,6			
81. Commercial structure	81. Structures commerciales	3,1			
82. Fairs and exhibitions	82. Foires et expositions	10,6			
83. Commercial information	83. Information commerciale	3,9			
84. Marketing	84. Marketing	10,4			
TOTAL I TO IV	**TOTAL I A IV**		100,0	2 941,1	81,3
V. EXCEPTIONAL AID	V. AIDES EXCEPTIONNELLES			173,1	4,8
94. Disasters	94. Calamités	173,1			
VI. STABEX	VI. STABEX			466,7	12,9
VII. MISCELLANEOUS	VII. DIVERS			37,2	1,0
00. Information, documentation	00. Information, documentation	4,4			
01. Seminars	01. Colloque	4,8			
02. General technical cooperation	02. Program. et coop. techn. générale	23,1			
03. General studies	03. Etudes générales	1,9			
08. Control	08. Contrôle				
09. Administration and financial costs	09. Frais administratifs et financiers	3,0			
04. Multi-sector programmes	04. Programmes plurisectoriels				
Total I to VII	**Total I à VII**			3 618,1	100,0

Financements dans les États d'Afrique, des Caraïbes et du Pacifique (ACP) et les pays et territoires d'outre-mer (PTOM) de 1976 à 1985 (conventions de Lomé)

Répartition selon la localisation du projet d'investissement et l'origine des ressources

(Mio ECU)

	Prêts sur ressources propres			Opérations de capitaux à risque sur ressources budgétaires			Total des financements (¹)		
	Lomé I	Lomé II	Total	Lomé I	Lomé II	Total	Lomé I	Lomé II	Total
AFRIQUE	**338,5**	**479,0**	**817,5**	**94,26**	**222,13**	**316,39**	**432,76**	**701,13**	**1 133,89**
Occidentale	192,5	161,1	353,6	41,14	69,57	110,71	233,64	230,67	464,31
Bénin	—	13,5	13,5	0,35	4,50	4,85	0,35	18,00	18,35
Burkina Faso	8,0	—	8,0	7,83	7,00	14,93	15,93	7,00	22,93
Cap-Vert	—	—	—	3,58	1,80	5,38	3,58	1,80	5,38
Côte-d'Ivoire	47,4	56,2	103,6	2,93	2,43	5,36	50,33	58,63	108,96
Gambie	—	—	—	2,39	—	2,39	—	2,39	2,39
Ghana	16,0	—	16,0	2,25	16,03	18,28	18,25	16,03	34,28
Guinée	4,4	7,5	11,9	0,30	2,71	3,01	4,70	10,21	14,91
Guinée-Bissau	—	—	—	—	3,80	3,80	—	3,80	3,80
Liberia	7,4	3,5	10,9	0,29	2,20	2,49	7,69	5,70	13,39
Mali	—	—	—	6,36	3,40	9,76	6,36	3,40	9,76
Mauritanie	25,0	—	25,0	—	7,00	7,00	25,00	7,00	32,00
Niger	6,0	10,0	16,0	0,90	—	0,90	6,90	10,00	16,90
Nigeria	50,0	40,0	90,0	—	—	—	50,00	40,00	90,00
Sénégal	12,0	21,0	33,0	8,47	4,65	13,12	20,47	25,65	46,12
Togo	16,3	4,4	20,7	5,25	2,43	7,68	21,55	6,83	28,38
Regional	—	5,0	5,0	0,14	11,62	11,76	0,14	16,62	16,76
Centrale et équatoriale	32,6	158,4	191,0	24,96	44,22	69,18	57,56	202,62	260,18
Burundi	—	—	—	0,50	8,24	8,74	0,50	8,24	8,74
Cameroun	32,6	95,7	128,3	5,00	—	5,00	37,60	95,70	133,30
Rép. Centrafricaine	—	—	—	—	5,10	5,10	—	5,10	5,10
Congo	—	28,1	28,1	3,32	0,48	3,80	3,32	28,58	31,90
Gabon	—	32,0	32,0	—	2,50	2,50	—	34,50	34,50
Guinée équatoriale	—	—	—	—	2,00	2,00	—	2,00	2,00
Rwanda	—	—	—	3,00	2,70	5,70	3,00	2,70	5,70
São Tomé et Prince	—	—	—	7,50	2,00	9,50	7,50	2,00	9,50
Tchad	—	—	—	—	0,04	0,04	—	0,04	0,04
Zaïre	—	—	—	5,64	20,66	26,30	5,64	20,66	26,30
Regional	—	2,6	2,6	—	0,50	0,50	—	3,10	3,10
Orientale et australe	113,4	159,5	272,9	28,16	108,34	136,50	141,56	267,84	409,4
Botswana	6,5	29,0	35,5	1,75	—	1,75	8,25	29,00	37,25
Comores	—	—	—	0,02	0,16	0,18	0,02	0,16	0,18

Pays									
Djibouti	—	—	—	1,00	2,26	3,26	1,00	2,26	3,26
Éthiopie	—	—	—	—	12,5	12,5	—	12,5	12,5
Kenya	52,4	45,5	97,9	1,25	1,55	2,80	53,65	47,05	100,70
Lesotho	—	—	—	0,10	6,00	6,10	0,10	6,00	6,10
Madagascar	—	—	—	2,45	21,17	23,62	2,45	21,17	23,62
Malawi	14,5	7,5	22,0	1,55	11,50	13,05	16,05	19,00	35,05
Maurice	12,5	4,0	16,5	0,03	0,50	0,53	12,53	4,50	17,03
Ouganda	—	—	—	0,35	10,00	10,35	0,35	10,00	10,35
Seychelles	—	—	—	0,58	4,00	4,58	0,58	4,00	4,58
Somalie	—	—	—	0,25	9,56	9,81	0,25	9,56	9,81
Soudan	—	—	—	6,50	10,20	16,70	6,50	10,20	16,70
Swaziland	12,0	7,0	19,0	1,15	0,04	1,19	13,15	7,04	20,19
Tanzanie	5,0	—	5,0	7,75	11,00	18,75	12,75	11,00	23,75
Zambie	10,5	31,5	42,0	3,43	2,00	5,43	13,93	33,50	47,43
Zimbabwe	—	35,0	35,0	—	5,40	5,40	—	40,40	40,40
Régional	—	—	—	—	0,50	0,50	—	0,50	0,50
CARAÏBES	20,5	47,6	68,1	3,38	21,25	24,63	23,88	68,85	92,73
Barbade	7,5	9,6	17,1	—	—	—	7,50	9,60	17,10
Belize	—	2,0	2,0	—	0,60	0,60	—	2,60	2,60
Dominique	—	—	—	—	1,00	1,00	—	1,00	1,00
Grenade	—	—	—	—	1,00	1,00	—	2,40	2,40
Guyana	—	—	—	3,20	4,00	7,20	3,20	4,00	7,20
Jamaïque	—	—	—	3,20	4,00	7,20	—	9,00	9,00
Ste-Lucie	—	—	—	0,18	5,00	5,00	0,18	1,00	1,18
St-Vincent et les Grenadines	—	—	—	—	1,00	1,00	—	3,00	3,00
Surinam	—	32,0	32,0	—	3,00	3,00	—	4,25	4,25
Trinité et Tobago	10,0	—	42,0	—	4,25	4,25	10,00	32,00	42,00
Régional	3,0	—	3,0	—	—	—	3,00	—	3,00
PACIFIQUE	31,0	75,9	106,9	2,07	30,68	32,75	33,07	106,58	139,65
Fidji	24,0	28,0	52,0	0,17	7,80	7,97	24,17	35,80	59,97
Kiribati	—	—	—	—	0,20	0,20	—	0,20	0,20
Papouasie-N. Guinée	7,0	47,9	54,9	1,90	13,80	15,70	8,90	61,70	70,60
Salomon	—	—	—	—	0,10	0,10	—	0,10	0,10
Samoa occidentales	—	—	—	—	3,33	3,33	—	3,33	3,33
Tonga	—	—	—	—	2,32	2,32	—	2,32	2,32
Tuvalu	—	—	—	—	0,13	0,13	—	0,13	0,13
Vanuatu	—	—	—	—	3,00	3,00	—	3,00	3,00
États ACP Total	**390,0**	**602,5**	**992,5**	**99,71**	**274,06**	**373,77**	**489,71**	**876,56**	**1.366,27**
PTOM	**7,0**	**15,0**	**22,0**	**2,05**	**6,74**	**8,79**	**9,05**	**21,74**	**30,79**
Total général	**397,0**	**617,5**	**1.014,5**	**101,76**	**280,80**	**382,56**	**498,76**	**898,30**	**1.397,06**

(1) Non compris 146,1 millions sur ressources propres et 142 millions sur ressources du FED consentis de 1964 à 1976 dans le cadre des deux conventions de Yaoundé.

5th EDF: Aid by type and beneficiary country
Le 5e FED: Aides par nature et par pays bénéficiaire
(Situation de l'exécution financière au 31. 12. 1985)

(Mio ECU)

Pays bénéficiaire (1)	A. Aides non programmées — Décisions de financement — Bonifications d'intérêt (subventions) (2)	Capitaux à risque (3)	Aides exceptionnelles, aides d'urgence (subventions) (4)	Stabex (5)	Sysmin (6)	Total (7) = (2)+(3)+(4)+(5)+(6)	Paiements effectués (8)	B. Aides programmables — Décisions de financement — Dotations (9)	Subventions (10)	Prêts spéciaux (11)	Total (12) = (10)+(11)	Paiements effectués (13)	Total (A+B) Décisions de financement (14) = (7)+(12)	Paiements effectués (15) = (8)+(13)
I. Pays ACP	114,0	224,3	172,3	505,8	128,8	1 165,2	907,4	2 515,9	1 685,3	316,3	2 001,6	895,2	3 166,8	1 802,6
dont:														
Ethiopie	—	12,5	48,2	10,8	—	71,5	37,0	141,0	107,8	31,0	138,8	81,8	210,3	118,8
Tanzanie	—	11,0	0,5	19,2	—	30,7	28,3	120,7	93,2	11,6	104,8	45,5	135,5	73,8
Zaïre	—	18,2	2,8	—	40,0	61,0	45,1	104,0	71,4	16,6	88,0	40,0	149,0	86,1
Soudan	—	10,2	17,5	32,2	—	59,9	38,4	103,0	85,8	—	85,8	62,1	145,7	100,5
Ouganda	—	10,0	4,5	—	—	14,5	13,2	87,0	60,1	—	60,1	28,6	74,6	41,8
Mali	8,6	3,4	14,1	9,9	—	36,0	23,0	96,0	61,2	16,4	77,6	31,1	105,0	74,6
Kenya	—	21,2	2,4	31,1	—	54,7	41,4	88,0	51,4	11,0	62,4	26,7	106,0	54,1
Madagascar	3,6	—	1,8	6,1	—	29,1	14,7	78,0	60,1	9,8	69,9	28,2	99,0	68,1
Niger	—	7,0	13,6	—	—	17,2	17,4	80,5	67,4	8,0	75,4	29,5	92,6	45,6
Burkina Faso	—	13,5	0,5	—	—	14,0	14,7	84,5	67,6	7,0	74,6	37,3	83,1	44,2
Malawi	1,2	2,7	1,1	1,0	—	4,9	2,5	80,0	57,0	11,8	68,8	33,7	88,6	38,8
Guinée	1,1	9,6	1,1	4,7	—	9,6	9,6	80,0	54,5	7,0	61,5	36,4	66,4	28,9
Somalie	—	4,2	16,2	2,8	—	28,6	27,6	79,3	49,9	—	49,9	19,3	78,5	27,5
Sénégal	5,6	0,7	2,1	64,9	—	76,8	74,1	69,0	36,0	17,3	53,3	25,0	130,1	98,2
Rwanda	—	6,5	2,0	7,7	—	16,4	9,6	79,0	52,8	11,9	64,7	24,2	77,9	45,1
Burundi	—	—	1,6	11,6	—	13,2	16,4	77,0	50,7	11,9	62,6	35,5	84,3	34,3
Cameroun	20,9	2,0	1,7	11,6	2,8	31,2	31,6	69,0	44,5	—	44,5	17,9	72,5	36,9
Tchad	—	13,6	1,7	17,3	—	19,8	15,6	77,0	52,7	—	52,7	21,3	124,1	80,4
Ghana	8,5	1,5	4,4	63,9	—	81,9	21,3	62,0	35,2	7,0	42,2	14,0	129,6	72,6
Zambie	—	4,5	1,6	—	83,0	94,6	66,4	58,0	33,0	2,0	35,0	9,8	52,8	17,2
Bénin	8,5	1,5	1,5	4,1	—	10,1	5,5	55,0	36,3	6,4	42,7	11,7	124,1	83,0
Côte-d'Ivoire	10,6	—	0,8	54,5	—	65,9	58,8	54,0	17,8	18,3	36,1	24,2	102,0	83,0

Rép. Centrafricaine	1,5	5,1	0,5	4,2	9,8	9,2	49,0	41,8	4,7	46,5	27,7	56,3	36,9
Togo	—	7,0	0,4	28,8	30,9	30,9	43,0	29,4	6,9	36,3	23,7	67,2	54,6
Mauritanie	5,3	—	4,4	—	11,4	4,0	43,0	27,8	8,7	36,5	20,7	20,7	24,7
Sierra Leone	—	—	—	13,6	13,5	13,5	48,5	22,4	2,4	26,6	28,3	40,2	21,7
Congo	0,5	0,5	—	—	6,8	5,0	31,5	18,4	12,0	30,4	28,3	36,2	33,3
Liberia	0,7	0,7	0,1	—	1,2	1,2	31,0	15,5	4,7	20,2	—	21,4	5,6
Lesotho	6,3	6,0	—	1,3	7,4	3,8	29,0	19,5	8,8	28,3	—	35,7	16,4
Guinée-Bissau	—	3,8	—	3,4	7,2	4,9	25,0	18,5	—	18,5	—	25,7	13,4
Jamaïque	—	5,0	0,2	3,2	8,9	5,9	26,4	16,5	9,1	25,6	12,6	34,5	11,9
Botswana	—	—	—	—	6,5	5,0	23,0	17,2	2,3	19,5	8,5	26,0	10,1
Surinam	—	4,3	0,1	—	4,3	0,1	18,0	2,9	2,7	5,6	6,0	9,9	2,3
Maurice	2,1	0,5	—	—	7,0	0,2	20,5	12,7	7,7	13,0	5,1	21,7	6,4
Guyane	—	4,0	—	—	10,4	10,4	14,6	13,0	—	16,6	7,2	20,0	6,6
Swaziland	—	0,0	0,1	—	14,3	14,3	18,5	11,9	4,7	13,0	7,5	27,0	14,4
Gambie	—	—	0,0	3,0	14,3	—	14,0	12,0	—	16,6	4,0	26,3	18,4
Papouasie-Nouvelle Guinée	—	—	—	—	—	—	—	—	—	12,0	4,1	—	—
Fidji	13,8	13,8	4,3	41,8	57,0	53,9	23,0	6,2	4,4	10,6	3,0	67,6	56,9
Gabon	7,8	7,8	—	2,1	21,3	11,3	13,0	9,9	—	9,9	6,6	30,9	17,9
Iles Salomon	2,5	2,5	3,8	3,8	11,9	9,5	16,0	8,0	5,1	13,1	8,9	13,1	18,4
Nigeria	5,2	—	—	—	3,8	3,1	12,0	8,0	—	6,0	2,0	9,8	5,8
Zimbabwe	5,4	5,4	7,5	8,2	19,6	13,5	50,0	30,8	8,1	30,8	11,1	35,9	24,6
Autres pays ACP:				14,3			49,0	26,9		35,0		54,6	
Antigua et Barbuda	—	0,6	0,2	—	0,2	0,1	2,7	0,0	0,8	0,8	0,0	1,0	0,1
Bahamas	—	1,7	—	—	1,9	0,9	2,1	2,0	—	2,0	0,3	2,0	0,3
Barbade	1,9	0,2	1,2	0,5	0,9	0,9	3,7	3,7	—	3,7	2,6	5,6	2,2
Belize	0,3	2,3	0,4	6,6	3,4	3,4	5,5	0,1	—	0,1	1,3	1,0	1,0
Cap-Vert	—	2,4	0,5	—	7,2	7,2	16,0	13,6	—	13,6	1,0	17,0	5,9
Comores	—	2,0	—	3,0	2,6	2,4	14,5	9,8	—	9,8	2,5	17,0	11,0
Djibouti	0,6	0,0	3,0	4,0	4,5	4,5	5,4	4,6	—	4,6	3,8	7,2	4,6
Dominique	1,7	1,0	4,0	—	6,4	6,1	4,5	3,5	—	3,5	2,1	8,0	7,9
Grenade	0,2	—	—	1,6	2,0	1,8	3,5	3,3	—	3,3	2,7	9,7	1,0
Guinée équatoriale	2,3	—	1,6	7,0	1,8	7,1	3,5	4,8	—	4,8	1,8	5,8	2,4
Kiribati	2,4	—	7,0	—	7,1	2,1	8,5	4,0	—	4,0	0,6	9,7	9,7
São Tomé et Prince	2,0	—	—	1,3	2,5	8,5	4,0	4,1	—	4,1	0,6	5,8	—
St-Christophe et Nevis	0,0	1,0	1,4	—	8,5	4,2	4,0	1,7	—	2,2	—	11,2	4,0
Sainte-Lucie	—	3,3	0,2	5,1	4,2	7,3	2,2	3,7	0,5	3,7	1,9	2,2	3,0
Saint-Vincent	—	4,0	0,1	—	7,7	5,2	3,7	3,4	—	3,4	2,8	6,2	14,4
Samoa occidentales	—	2,3	1,4	4,0	5,2	0,2	6,2	6,2	—	3,6	6,2	3,6	3,4
Seychelles	0,1	0,1	—	—	0,2	0,8	7,3	3,6	—	3,6	2,7	7,8	8,0
Tonga	5,2	0,0	—	0,1	3,2	—	5,2	3,1	—	3,1	0,7	10,8	7,0
Trinité-et-Tobago	—	0,2	0,2	—	—	—	4,1	6,9	—	6,9	0,8	12,1	0,6
Tuvalu	0,1	—	—	—	—	—	10,5	1,1	—	1,1	0,4	—	3,0
Vanuatu	—	—	—	—	—	—	1,0	4,5	—	4,5	4,5	7,7	—
	(7,4)	(24,1)	(5,0)	(33,2)	(69,7)	(59,9)	(112,9)	(87,7)	(1,3)	(89,0)	(36,7)	(158,7)	(96,6)
II. Projets régionaux	1,3	25,9	—	—	27,2	5,9	631,5	352,3	66,8	421,1	204,2	448,3	210,1
Frais administratifs	—	—	—	—	—	—	5,9	3,0	—	3,0	2,5	3,0	2,5
Total ACP (I + II)	115,3	270,2	172,3	505,8	1 192,4	913,3	3 147,4	2 040,6	385,1	2 425,7	1 101,9	3 618,1	2 015,2
III. PTOM	2,9	6,7	0,9	9,8	20,3	16,8	50,6	20,1	3,8	23,9	9,0	44,2	25,8
Total 5e FED	118,2	276,9	173,2	515,6	1 212,7	930,1	3 196,0	2 060,7	388,9	2 449,6	1 110,9	3 662,3	2 041,0

Stabex 1975-85 — Aggregate balance-sheet by ACP State
Stabex 1975-85 — Bilan cumulatif par État ACP

	Total (in ECU) Montant total (en Écus)	
48. Belize	342 364	Belize
14. Benin	28 466 769	Bénin
27. Burkina Faso	8 308 636	Burkina Faso
21. Burundi	15 296 954	Burundi
11. Cameroon	33 655 272	Cameroun
43. Cape Verde	1 733 525	Cap-Vert
23. Central African Republic	13 026 301	République Centrafricaine
22. Chad	13 976 332	Tchad
24. Comoros	10 959 381	Comores
32. Congo	7 361 677	Congo
47. Djibouti	691 851	Djibouti
35. Dominica	6 427 781	Dominique
5. Ethiopia	53 807 619	Éthiopie
38. Fiji	5 379 813	Fidji
33. Gabon	6 703 311	Gabon
12. Gambia	30 411 215	Gambie
4. Ghana	90 647 339	Ghana
41. Grenada	3 963 333	Grenade
20. Guinea-Bissau	15 361 783	Guinée-Bissau
3. Cote d'Ivoire	113 324 801	Côte-d'Ivoire
40. Jamaica	4 295 408	Jamaïque
8. Kenya	44 865 565	Kenya
42. Kiribati	3 882 391	Kiribati
45. Lesotho	1 290 959	Lesotho
31. Liberia	7 586 943	Liberia
19. Madagascar	15 736 332	Madagascar
39. Malawi	4 934 458	Malawi
17. Mali	20 482 142	Mali
10. Mauritania	37 000 450	Mauritanie
29. Mozambique	8 947 277	Mozambique
13. Niger	28 527 573	Niger
6. Papua New Guinea	50 690 742	Papouasie-Nouvelle-Guinée
26. Rwanda	9 939 496	Rwanda
28. Sao Tome and Principe	9 230 664	São Tomé et Principe
1. Senegal	183 257 156	Sénégal
18. Sierra Leone	18 328 403	Sierra Leone
34. Solomon Islands	6 508 461	Iles Salomon
37. Somalia	5 512 701	Somalie
44. St Lucia	1 618 999	Sainte-Lucie
46. St Vincent	913 286	Saint-Vincent
2. Sudan	125 042 319	Soudan
15. Swaziland	21 414 187	Swaziland
7. Tanzania	50 473 947	Tanzanie
9. Togo	41 775 242	Togo
36. Tonga	5 830 836	Tonga
49. Tuvalu	316 364	Tuvalu
16. Uganda	20 595 453	Ouganda
25. Vanuatu	10 362 630	Vanuatu
27. Western Samoa	9 385 621	Samoa occidentales
Grand total	**1 208 592 066**	**Total général**

Stabex 1975-85 — Aggregate balance-sheet by product
Stabex 1975-85 — Bilan cumulatif par produit

	Total (in ECU) Montant total (en Écus)	
All groundnut products	333 780 778	Tous produits d'arachide
Coffee	282 196 654	Café
All cocoa products	161 299 447	Tous produits de cacao
All cotton products	81 330 854	Tous produits de coton
Iron ore	61 789 536	Minerai de fer
All wood products	45 349 687	Tous produits de bois
Oil cake	45 303 777	Tourteaux
All copra and coconut products	42 962 224	Tous produits de copra et de coco
Sisal	33 118 052	Sisal
Bananas	20 034 026	Bananes
All palm products	18 165 476	Tous produits de palme
Beans	17 838 522	Haricots
Tea	17 243 689	Thé
Cajou kernels	11 458 241	Amandes de cajou
Raw hides and skins	10 006 845	Peaux brutes et cuirs
Vanilla	8 173 099	Vanille
Sesame seeds	5 783 823	Graines de sésame
Cloves	5 212 874	Clous de girofle
Karite kernels	1 937 603	Amandes de karité
Essential oil	1 510 469	Huiles essentielles
Mohair	1 290 959	Mohair
Gum arabic	848 489	Gomme arabique
Prawns	710 289	Crevettes
Nutmeg	637 851	Noix de muscade
Pyrethrum	608 802	Pyrèthre
Grand total	**1 208 592 066**	**Total général**

EIB loans
Prêts de la BEI

(Mio ECU + %)

	Loans with interest rebate of 3 % from the EDF and from the own resources of the EIB in the ACP States under the Lomé II Convention. Situation of loans signed between 1. 1. 1981 and 31. 12. 1986 — Prêts assortis d'une bonification d'intérêt de 3 % du FED sur les ressources propres de la BEI dans les États ACP au titre de la convention de Lomé II. Situation des prêts signés du 1. 1. 1981 au 31. 12. 1986					Aid in the form of risk capital in the ACP States under the Lomé II Convention. Situation of contracts signed by 31. 12. 1986 — Concours sous forme de capitaux à risque dans les États ACP au titre de la convention de Lomé II. Situation des contrats signés au 31. 12. 1986					
Sector / Country — Secteurs / Pays	General Général	%	Energy Énergie	Industry Industrie	Other Autres infrastructures	General Général	%	Energy Énergie	Industry Industrie	Other Autres infrastructures	Tourism Tourisme
Benin / Bénin	13,50	2,24	13,50			4,500	1,61	4,50			
Burkina Faso						7,000	2,50		7,000		
Burundi	29,00	4,81	25,00	4,00		8,237	2,95	2,00	6,237		
Botswana											
Cameroon / Cameroun	95,70	15,88	47,00	24,10	24,60	1,800	0,64	1,80			
Cape Verde / Cap-Vert						5,100	1,82		5,100		
Central African Republic / République Centrafricaine											
Chad / Tchad						2,000	0,72		2,000		
Comoros / Comores						0,161	0,06		0,161		
Congo	28,10	4,66		22,00	6,10	0,480	0,17			0,480	
Djibouti											
Ethiopia / Éthiopie	32,00	5,31	7,00	15,00	10,00	2,260	0,81	1,80		0,460	
Gabon						13,000	4,65		12,500	0,500	
Gambia / Gambie						2,500	0,89			2,500	
Ghana	7,50	1,24		7,50		16,030	5,73		16,030		
Guinea / Guinée						2,705	0,97		2,705		
Guinea-Bissau / Guinée-Bissau						3,800	1,36		3,800		
Equatorial Guinea / Guinée équatoriale						2,000	0,72	2,00			
Côte-d'Ivoire	56,20	9,33	12,60	33,60	10,00	2,430	0,87		2,430		
Kenya	45,50	7,55	9,00	14,50	22,00	1,550	0,55		1,550		
Lesotho						6,000	2,15		6,000		
Liberia	3,50	0,58		3,50		2,200	0,79		2,200		
Madagascar						21,170	7,57		19,000	2,170	
Malawi	7,50	1,24		7,50		15,470	5,53	3,00	9,470		3,00
Mali						3,400	1,22			3,400	
Mauritius / Maurice	4,00	0,66		4,00		0,500	0,18		0,500		
Mauritania / Mauritanie						7,000	2,50			7,000	

	C1	C2	C3	C4	C5	C6	C7	C8	C9	C10	C11
Niger	50,00	8,30		40,00		2,00	2,700	0,97	0,700	0,040	
Nigeria			10,00				0,040	0,01			
Rwanda											
Sao Tome et Principe	21,00	3,49		21,00					2,300	0,500	1,85
Senegal							4,650	1,66	2,300		
Seychelles							4,000	1,43	4,000	0,200	
Somalie	7,00	1,16	7,00				9,560	3,42	2,560	0,037	
Soudan						7,00	10,200	3,65	4,000		
Swaziland	4,40	0,73			4,40	6,00	0,037	0,01	3,500		
Tanzanie						7,50	11,000	3,94	2,430		
Togo							2,430	0,87	10,000	0,500	
Ouganda						2,00	10,000	3,58	18,158	0,400	
Zaire							20,158	7,1	1,500	0,500	
Zambie	31,50	5,23	20,00	31,50	15,00		2,000	0,72	5,000	0,500	
Zimbabwe	35,00	5,81			2,60		5,400	1,93	0,500		
Regional – Afrique centrale	2,60	0,43					1,000	0,36			
Regional – Afrique de l'Est				5,00	5,00		0,500	0,18	0,500		
Regional – Afrique de l'Ouest	5,00	0,83					11,624	4,16	1,624	10,000	
Afrique	**479,00**	**79,48**	**151,10**	**233,20**	**94,70**	**39,60**	**226,592**	**81,07**	**153,455**	**28,687**	**4,85**
Bahamas	9,6	1,59		4,00	5,60		0,600	0,21	0,600		
Barbades								0,07	1,000		
Belize	2,00	0,33		2,00			1,000	0,36			
Dominique							1,000	0,86			
Grenade						2,40	2,400	1,43	4,000		
Guyane				4,00			4,000	1,79	5,000		
Jamaïque	4,00	0,66					5,000	0,36	1,000		
Ste-Lucie							1,000	0,36	1,000		
St-Christophe et Nevis						2,90	1,000	1,07	4,000	0,100	
St-Vincent							3,000	1,07		0,250	
Suriname											
Trinidad et Tobago	32,00	5,31	12,00	20,00			4,250	1,52	4,000	0,350	
Caraïbes	**47,60**	**7,89**	**12,00**	**30,00**	**5,60**	**5,30**	**22,250**	**7,96**	**16,600**	**0,350**	
Fidji	28,00	4,65		16,00			7,800	2,79	6,000	1,800	
Kiribati			12,00				0,000	0,07	0,200	0,200	
Papouasie-Nouvelle-Guinée	47,90	7,95		47,90			13,600	4,94	12,000	1,800	
Iles Salomon											
Tonga							0,100	0,04		0,100	
Tuvalu							2,325	0,83	2,000	0,325	
Vanuatu						3,00	0,125	0,04		0,125	
Samoa occidentales						3,00	3,000	1,07	3,000	0,325	
							3,325	1,19			
Pacifique	**75,90**	**12,60**	**12,00**	**63,90**		**3,00**	**30,675**	**10,97**	**23,000**	**4,675**	
Total	**602,50**	**100,00**	**175,10**	**327,10**	**100,30**	**47,90**	**279,517**	**100,00**	**193,055**	**33,712**	**4,85**

EIB loans
Prêts de la BEI

Country	Loans with interest rebate of 3 % from the EDF and from the own resources of the EIB in the ACP States under the Lomé III Convention. Situation of loans signed between 1.5.1986 and 31.12.1986 / Prêts assortis d'une bonification d'intérêt de 3 % du FED sur les ressources propres de la BEI dans les États ACP au titre de la convention de Lomé III. Situation des prêts signés du 1.5.1986 au 31.12.1986					Aid in the form of risk capital in the ACP States under the Lomé III Convention. Situation of contracts signed by 31.12.1986 / Concours sous forme de capitaux à risque au titre des États ACP au titre de la convention de Lomé III. Situation des contrats signés au 31.12.1986					Pays
	General Général	%	Energy Énergie	Industry Industrie	Other/ Autres infra-struc-tures	General Général	%	Energy Énergie	Industry Industrie	Other/ Autres infra-struc-tures	
Benin											Bénin
Burkina Faso	17,00	11,28									Burkina Faso
Burundi						3,00	5,53		3,00		Burundi
Botswana											Botswana
Cameroon	24,20	16,06	17,00	14,20							Cameroun
Cape Verde											Cap-Vert
Central African Republic											République Centrafricaine
Chad											Tchad
Comoros											Comores
Congo					10,00	10,00	18,43			10,00	Congo
Djibouti											Djibouti
Ethiopia											Éthiopie
Gabon											Gabon
Gambia											Gambie
Ghana											Ghana
Guinea											Guinée
Guinea-Bissau											Guinée-Bissau
Equatorial Guinea											Guinée équatoriale
Côte-d'Ivoire						4,00	7,37	4,00			Côte-d'Ivoire
Kenya						3,50	6,45			3,50	Kenya
Lesotho											Lesotho
Liberia											Liberia
Madagascar	2,50	1,66		2,50		3,25	5,99		3,25		Madagascar
Malawi						1,50	2,76		1,50		Malawi
Mali						3,50	6,45		3,50		Mali
Mauritius	15,00	9,95		15,00							Maurice

(Français)	C1	C2	C3	C4	C5	C6	C7	C8	C9	C10	(English)
Mauritanie											Mauritania
Niger											Niger
Nigeria											Nigeria
Rwanda											Rwanda
São Tomé et Principe											Sao Tome and Principe
Sénégal		13,30								50,00	Senegal
Seychelles											Seychelles
Somalie			9,00		9,00						Somalia
Soudan				24,88	15,59		13,50	9,00			Sudan
Suriname											Suriname
Swaziland											Swaziland
Tanzanie											Tanzania
Togo											Togo
Ouganda											Uganda
Zaïre										50,00	Zaire
Zambie									33,18		Zambia
Zimbabwe											Zimbabwe
Regional Afrique	**13,50**	**24,75**	**13,00**	**94,45**	**51,25**	**10,00**	**81,70**	**17,00**	**72,13**	**108,70**	**Regional Africa**
Bahamas						8,5					Bahamas
Barbades									5,64		Barbados
Belize								3,00			Belize
Dominique											Dominica
Grenade											Grenada
Guyane							10,00			10,00	Guyana
Jamaïque											Jamaica
Ste-Lucie									6,64	3,00	St Lucia
St-Vincent									1,99		St Vincent
Trinidad et Tobago											Trinidad and Tobago
Regional Caraïbes		**1,00**	**2,00**	**3,69**	**2,00**	**8,50**	**10,00**	**3,00**	**14,27**	**21,50**	**Regional Caribbean**
Fiji				1,84	1,00		3,50				Fiji
Kiribati									2,32	3,50	Kiribati
Papouasie-Nouvelle-Guinée								17,00	11,28	17,00	Papua New Guinea
Iles Salomon											Solomon Islands
Tonga											Tonga
Tuvalu											Tuvalu
Vanuatu											Vanuatu
Samoa occidentales											Western Samoa
Pacifique		**1,00**		**1,84**	**1,00**		**3,50**	**17,00**	**13,60**	**20,50**	**Pacific**
Total	**13,50**	**25,75**	**15,00**	**100,00**	**54,25**	**18,50**	**95,20**	**37,00**	**100,00**	**150,70**	**Total**

IV

Mediterranean countries

Pays méditerranéens

ALGÉRIE

Population 1985:	21 720 000	→	Taux de croissance 1970-85:		2,8 %
PNB 1985:	55 230,0 Mio USD	→	Taux de croissance 1970-85:		11,8 %
PNB/h 1985:	2 530,0 Mio USD	→	Taux de croissance 1970-81:		2,7 %

Exportations 1985:	10 149,1 Mio USD	Importations 1984:	9 813,4 Mio USD
Exportations vers la CE 1984:	8 238,8 Mio USD	Importations de la CE 1984:	6 242,6 Mio USD
Élèves: enseign. primaire 1983:	3 336 536	Élèves: enseign. secondaire 1983:	1 473 053
Personne/lit d'hôpital 1982:	406	Personne/médecin 1982:	2 780

	Unités	1981	1982	1983	1984
Commerce extérieur					
Exportations	75 = 100	309,9	267,5	260,1	277,0
Importations	75 = 100	189,2	178,8	172,9	171,8
Balance commerciale	Mio USD	1 993,9	796,5	826,5	1 622,5
Exportations/importations	%	117,6	107,5	108,0	115,8
Balance commerciale avec la CE	Mio USD	− 426,3	2 101,8	894,1	1 996,2
Export. vers la CE/import. de la CE	%	94,1	132,6	113,9	132,0
Exportations/PIB	%	34,6	31,7	27,5	25,7
Indicateurs financiers					
Balance des paiements	Mio DTS	101,0	− 969,0	− 392,0	− 324,0
Réserves internationales	Mio USD	3 695,3	2 422,0	1 880,4	1 464,2
Dette extérieure publique	Mio USD	22 605,9	20 308,6	18 858,5	17 500,5
Service de la dette/exportations	%	37,1	38,3	39,1	35,8
Aide publique au développement					
APD net total	Mio USD	167,5	136,5	144,6	121,5
APD net bilatéral	Mio USD	148,3	127,1	132,1	111,8
APD net CE/bilatéral	%	50,0	46,4	33,4	38,3
APD net multilatéral	Mio USD	19,2	9,4	12,5	9,7
APD net CCE/multilatéral	%	26,0	18,5	19,1	29,9
Aide alimentaire					
Céréales	t	4 736	200	0,0	0,0
Produits laitiers	t	733	36	4	124
Total	000 USD	2 755	224	20	404
Origine du PIB					
Agriculture, forêts, pêche	%	6,0	5,6	5,7	5,8
Industrie	%	56,4	55,7	53,9	:
Services	%	54,9	56,6	:	:
Indice d'évolution des prix	75 = 100	302,2	312,5	350,6	433,8

ALGÉRIE

Productions et exportations	Unités	1981	1982	1983	1984
Principales productions					
Céréales, total	000 t	2 126	1 524	1 291	1 861
Blé	000 t	1 218	977	790	1 200
Tomates	000 t	303	246	252	266
Tubercules et racines	000 t	528	415	491	521
Dattes	000 t	195	207	182	183
Oranges	000 t	230	201	162	183
Bois rond	000 m³	1 668	1 674	1 680	1 688
Minerai de fer	000 t	1 850	2 103	2 026	1 975
Phosphates naturels	000 t	916	946	893	1 000
Pétrole brut	000 t	36 943	33 542	31 588	28 296
Gaz naturel	térajoule	505 203	517 876	881 832	947 004
Principales exportations					
CTCI 331 Pétrole brut part. raffiné	Mio USD	9 992,4	5 861,7	5 393,2	4 434,0
	%	75,2	51,1	48,3	37,3
CTCI 332 Produits pétroliers	Mio USD	1 447,0	3 639,4	3 091,4	4 021,5
	%	10,9	31,7	27,7	33,8
CTCI 341.1 Gaz naturel	Mio USD	1 587,9	1 737,5	2 486,3	3 135,1
	%	11,9	15,1	22,3	26,4

CHYPRE

Population 1985:	670 000	→	Taux de croissance 1970-85:	0,7 %
PNB 1985:	2 650,0 Mio USD	→	Taux de croissance 1970-85:	11,1 %
PNB/h 1985:	3 790,0 USD	→	Taux de croissance 1970-81	6,1 %

Exportations 1985:	476,3 Mio USD	Importations 1985:	1 233,5 Mio USD
Exportations vers la CE 1985:	134,3 Mio USD	Importations de la CE 1985:	741,4 Mio USD
Élèves: enseign. primaire 1984:	45 146	Élèves: enseign. secondaire 1984:	48 518
Personne/lit d'hôpital 1982:	184	Personne/médecin 1982:	1 014

	Unités	1981	1982	1983	1984
Commerce extérieur					
Exportations	75 = 100	369,6	366,3	326,8	380,2
Importations	75 = 100	360,5	395,0	395,4	442,2
Balance commerciale	Mio USD	− 542,4	− 652,8	− 713,6	− 775,8
Exportations/importations	%	50,8	45,9	40,9	42,6
Balance commerciale avec la CE	Mio USD	− 397,8	− 431,4	− 485,5	− 593,6
Export. vers la CE/import. de la CE	%	29,1	28,5	22,0	21,3
Exportations/PIB	%	51,2	52,5	52,3	
Indicateurs financiers					
Balance des paiements	Mio DTS	72,7	127,1	38,2	93,8
Réserves internationales	Mio USD	426,4	523,2	519,1	540,5
Dette extérieure publique	Mio USD	658,1	844,6	837,2	925,8
Service de la dette/exportations	%	20,5	24,3	33,3	24,5
Aide publique au développement					
APD net total	Mio USD	43,3	30,7	17,8	17,4
APD net bilatéral	Mio USD	26,8	14,1	8,8	6,3
APD net CE/bilatéral	%	37,0	97,0	65,1	47,4
APD net multilatéral	Mio USD	16,5	16,6	9,0	11,1
APD net CCE/multilatéral	%	0,0	0,0	9,2	21,4
Origine du PIB					
Agriculture, forêts, pêche	%	10,1	10,5	9,7	10,4
Industrie	%	35,0	33,6	33,3	:
Services	%	59,0	60,0	61,3	:
Indice d'évolution des prix	75 = 100	195,7	216,2	231,1	239,0
Principales productions					
Tubercules et racines	000 t	222	218	235	234
Oranges	000 t	144	136	141	155

ÉGYPTE

Population 1985:	48 500 000	→ Taux de croissance 1970-85:			2,5 %
PNB 1985:	32 220,0 Mio USD	→ Taux de croissance 1970-85:			12,1 %
PNB/h 1985:	680,0 USD	→ Taux de croissance 1970-81:			5,2 %

Exportations 1985:	3 714,2 Mio USD	Importations 1985:	9 961,5 Mio USD
Exportations vers la CE 1985:	1 630,4 Mio USD	Importations de la CE 1985:	4 208,2 Mio USD
Élèves: enseign. primaire 1983:	5 349 579	Élèves: enseign. secondaire 1983:	3 201 703
Personnel/lit d'hôpital 1982:	509	Personne/médecin 1985:	568

	Unités	1981	1982	1983	1984
Commerce extérieur					
Exportations	75 = 100	230,6	222,6	229,3	224,0
Importations	75 = 100	224,7	230,8	261,2	273,7
Balance commerciale	Mio USD	− 5 607,3	− 5 957,8	− 7 060,6	− 7 625,9
Exportations/importations	%	36,6	34,4	31,3	29,2
Balance commerciale avec la CE	Mio USD	− 2 395,4	− 2 385,0	− 2 916,1	− 3 433,6
Export. vers la CE/import. de la CE	%	37,4	37,7	29,9	27,6
Exportations/PIB	%	32,0	29,1	28,8	27,7
Indicateurs financiers					
Balance des paiements	Mio DTS	44,0	− 221,0	77,0	− 159,0
Réserves internationales	Mio USD	716,0	698,0	771,0	736,0
Dette extérieure publique	Mio USD	18 448,8	19 212,0	19 793,7	19 925,2
Service de la dette/exportations	%	65,6	57,8	60,6	61,2
Aide publique au développement					
APD net total	Mio USD	1 292,3	1 416,5	1 437,9	1 768,0
APD net bilatéral	Mio USD	1 086,1	1 193,9	1 190,1	1 600,3
APD net CE/bilatéral	%	12,0	17,9	13,1	17,0
APD net multilatéral	Mio USD	206,2	222,6	247,9	167,7
APD net CCE/multilatéral	%	27,9	15,8	14,3	22,7
Aide alimentaire					
Céréales	000 t	1 801,9	2 016,1	1 586,4	1 904,5
Produits laitiers	000 t	25,4	24,3	25,3	25,4
Total	Mio USD	408,5	335,9	281,5	278,3
Origine du PIB					
Agriculture, forêts, pêche	%	19,6	19,8	19,8	19,9
Industrie	%	35,3	34,3	:	:
Services	%	:	:	:	:
Indice d'évolution des prix	75 = 100	219,6	238,2	267,6	301,5

Productions et exportations	Unités	1981	1982	1983	1984
Principales productions					
Céréales, total	000 t	8 239	8 522	8 701	7 927
Blé	000 t	1 938	2 017	1 996	1 815
Maïs	000 t	3 308	3 347	3 509	3 170
Riz, paddy	000 t	2 236	2 441	2 442	2 236
Tomates	000 t	2 454	2 657	2 862	2 780
Tubercules et racines	000 t	1 376	1 400	1 287	1 390
Sucre centrifugé brut	000 t	659	749	782	780
Bananes	000 t	137	165	169	147
Dattes	000 t	391	440	470	450
Oranges	000 t	895	1 201	1 243	1 182
Fibres de coton	000 t	499	460	400	400
Bois rond	000 m³	1 815	1 862	1 910	1 958
Minerai de fer	000 t	972	1 102	1 032	948
Phosphates naturels	000 t	720	708	647	1 043
Pétrole brut	000 t	29 405	32 772	35 957	41 100
Gaz naturel	térajoule	53 458	58 322	59 320	59 000
Filés de coton	000 t	245	238	230	244
Aluminium	000 t	142	141	140	158
Essence	000 t	2 055	2 150	2 200	2 300
Huiles légères	000 t	2 550	2 750	2 920	3 107
Huiles lourdes	000 t	7 358	8 336	8 911	9 475
Principales exportations					
CTCI 042 Riz	Mio USD	42,6	11,6	7,1	22,5
	%	1,3	0,4	0,2	0,7
CTCI 051.1 Oranges, clémentines, mandarines	Mio USD	47,3	52,8	73,8	76,4
	%	1,5	1,7	2,3	2,4
CTCI 263 Coton	Mio USD	477,4	419,5	454,4	493,5
	%	14,8	13,4	14,1	15,7
CTCI 331.01 Huile brute de pétrole	Mio USD	1 757,9	1 730,4	1 529,5	1 472,2
	%	54,4	55,5	47,6	46,9
CTCI 332 Produits pétroliers	Mio USD	324,3	335,2	473,4	335,0
	%	10,0	10,7	14,7	10,7
CTCI 651.3 Fils coton	Mio USD	155,1	123,8	195,9	220,5
	%	4,8	4,0	6,1	7,0
CTCI 652.1 Tissus de coton non mercerisés	Mio USD	33,6	22,6	20,0	34,1
	%	1,0	0,7	0,6	1,1
CTCI 684 Aluminium	Mio USD	132,2	115,6	95,7	132,5
	%	4,1	3,7	3,0	4,2

Population 1985:	4 230 000 →	Taux de croissance 1970-85:		2,4 %	
PNB 1985:	21 140,0 Mio USD →	Taux de croissance 1970-85:		8,9 %	
PNB/h 1985:	4 920,0 USD →	Taux de croissance 1970-81:		2,0 %	

Exportations 1985:	6 256,4 Mio USD	Importations 1985:	8 184,0 Mio USD	
Exportations vers la CE 1985:	1 917,2 Mio USD	Importations de la CE 1985:	3 591,2 Mio USD	
Élèves: enseign. primaire 1983:	685 714	Élèves: enseign. secondaire 1983:	229 146	
Personne/lit d'hôpital 1982:	205	Personne/médecin 1982:	376	

	Unités	1981	1982	1983	1984
Commerce extérieur					
Exportations	75 = 100	291,8	272,0	263,3	299,0
Importations	75 = 100	189,2	192,0	203,7	198,6
Balance commerciale	Mio USD	− 2 230,0	− 2 733,4	− 3 388,4	− 2 485,0
Exportations/importations	%	71,8	65,9	60,1	70,0
Balance commerciale avec la CE	Mio USD	− 765,9	− 1 195,6	− 1 692,8	− 1 533,6
Export. vers la CE/import. de la CE	%	71,9	59,5	50,9	55,2
Exportations/PIB	%	40,6	35,4	33,4	39,6
Indicateurs financiers					
Balance des paiements	Mio DTS	443,0	851,0	− 532,0	− 551,0
Réserves internationales	Mio USD	3 496,7	3 839,3	3 651,2	3 060,3
Dette extérieure publique	Mio USD	15 184,4	16 246,4	16 255,9	16 144,5
Service de la dette/exportations	%	48,0	46,0	39,6	30,6
Aide publique au développement					
APD net total	Mio USD	772,4	857,4	1 345,0	1 255,9
APD net bilatéral	Mio USD	772,1	857,4	1 345,0	1 255,9
APD net CE/bilatéral	%	− 0,1	9,2	3,9	4,5
APD net multilatéral	Mio USD	0,3			
APD net CCE/multilatéral	%				
Aide alimentaire					
Céréales	000 t	4,4	6,0	3,0	3,9
Produits laitiers	000 t	0,7	0,8	0,5	0,7
Total	Mio USD	3,1	2,2	1,5	1,8
Origine du PIB					
Agriculture, forêts, pêche	%	5,5	5,5	4,9	5,2
Industrie	%	:	:	:	:
Services	%	18,1	18,6	:	:

Productions et exportations	Unités	1981	1982	1983	1984
Principales productions					
Céréales, total	000 t	261	197	427	171
Tomates	000 t	283	310	370	351
Tubercules et racines	000 t	219	202	201	200
Bananes	000 t	66	73	67	68
Oranges	000 t	781	1 064	844	934
Fibres de coton	000 t	95	88	93	88
Lait de vache	000 t	702	742	776	821
Phosphates naturels	000 t	1 919	2 148	1 966	2 065
Filés de coton	000 t	14	17	17	17
Acide sulfurique	000 t	298	163	172	188
Engrais azotés	000 t	62	74	82	71
Engrais phosphatés	000 t	38	60	97	120
Engrais potassiques	000 t	885	940	956	1 166
Principales exportations					
CTCI 051 Fruits frais et	Mio USD	314,7	270,1	240,2	193,6
noix non ol.	%	5,6	5,1	4,7	3,3
CTCI 053.5 Jus de fruits	Mio USD	115,3	122,9	120,6	170,5
	%	2,0	2,3	2,4	2,9
CTCI 263.1 Coton brut	Mio USD	121,8	119,3	130,9	182,9
	%	2,2	2,3	2,6	3,2
CTCI 512 Produits chimiques	Mio USD	180,9	153,1	165,5	200,0
organiques	%	3,2	2,9	3,2	3,4
CTCI 561 Engrais manufacturés	Mio USD	166,7	133,4	141,6	170,6
	%	2,9	2,5	2,8	2,9
CTCI 599 Produits chimiques n.d.a.	Mio USD	281,6	235,9	212,9	221,5
	%	5,0	4,5	4,2	3,8
CTCI 667.2 Diamants	Mio USD	1 397,2	1 157,7	1 207,7	1 212,6
	%	24,7	21,9	23,6	20,9
CTCI 698.9 Ouvrages en étain	Mio USD	319,2	493,8	337,5	531,4
	%	5,6	9,4	6,6	9,2
CTCI 841 Vêtements	Mio USD	231,5	222,8	207,8	217,4
	%	4,1	4,2	4,1	3,7

JORDANIE

Population 1985:	3 510 000	→	Taux de croissance 1970-85:		2,9 %
PNB 1985:	4 010,0 Mio USD	→	Taux de croissance		–
PNB/h 1985:	1 560,0 USD	→	Taux de croissance		–

Exportations 1985:	780,8 Mio USD	Importations 1985:	2 593,2 Mio USD
Exportations vers la CE 1985:	48,3 Mio USD	Importations de la CE 1985:	792,9 Mio USD
Élèves: enseign. primaire 1983:	487 890	Élèves: enseign. secondaire 1983:	311 402
Personne/lit d'hôpital 1982:	717	Personne/médecin 1984:	1 123

	Unités	1981	1982	1983	1984
Commerce extérieur					
Exportations	75 = 100	477,7	482,3	363,6	492,6
Importations	75 = 100	430,5	440,2	412,7	367,9
Balance commerciale	Mio USD	– 2 414,5	– 2 478,6	– 2 459,3	– 1 934,0
Exportations/importations	%	23,3	23,0	18,5	28,1
Balance commerciale avec la CE	Mio USD	– 1 086,1	– 932,7	– 903,2	– 815,0
Export. vers la CE/import. de la CE	%	1,7	6,1	5,0	6,0
Exportations/PIB	%	53,3	49,7	43,0	
Indicateurs financiers					
Balance des paiements	Mio DTS	134,7	– 93,4	117,2	22,1
Réserves internationales	Mio USD	1 086,7	884,1	824,2	515,0
Dette extérieure publique	Mio USD	2 475,6	2 517,5	2 835,9	3 126,6
Service de la dette/exportations	%	37,0	31,3	40,8	36,6
Aide publique au développement					
APD net total	Mio USD	1 064,8	798,5	788,3	696,6
APD net bilatéral	Mio USD	1 031,6	765,4	766,5	675,4
APD net CE/bilatéral	%	4,2	2,8	4,6	3,2
APD net multilatéral	Mio USD	33,3	33,2	21,8	21,2
APD net CCE/multilatéral	%	12,3	22,2	27,8	17,2
Aide alimentaire					
Céréales	000 t	12,8	0,7	5,4	0,4
Produits laitiers	000 t	0,3	2,8	0,1	0,0
Total	Mio USD	4,7	5,1	0,9	0,1
Origine du PIB					
Agriculture, forêts, pêche	%	7,2	7,0	7,5	7,5
Industrie	%	32,1	31,4	31,3	:
Services	%	61,9	63,0	62,7	:
Indice d'évolution des prix	75 = 100	178,0	188,3	195,9	204,7

Productions et exportations	Unités	1981	1982	1983	1984
Principales productions					
Haricots, pois, lentilles	000 t	12	12	16	5
Tomates	000 t	205	195	212	209
Tubercules et racines	000 t	7	8	13	17
Bananes	000 t	7	7	7	14
Oranges	000 t	29	32	31	13
Bovins, effectifs	000 têtes	36	33	35	35
Phosphates naturels	000 t	4 244	4 890	4 749	6 213
Principales exportations					
CTCI 051 Fruits frais et	Mio USD	41,8	30,4	20,6	22,3
noix non oléag.	%	5,7	4,1	3,7	3,0
CTCI 054 Légumes et tubercules	Mio USD	73,3	54,3	46,6	45,8
	%	10,0	7,4	8,4	6,1
CTCI 075.24 Noix de muscade	Mio USD	27,4	20,5	5,8	:
	%	3,7	2,8	1,0	:
CTCI 271.3 Phosphates naturels	Mio USD	165,2	162,7	141,8	:
	%	22,6	22,0	25,5	:
CTCI 632 Articles manufacturés	Mio USD	20,6	14,5	8,7	20,8
en bois	%	2,8	2,0	1,6	2,8

Population 1985:	2 670 000	→	Taux de croissance 1970-85:		0,5 %
PNB	– Mio USD	→	Taux de croissance		–
PNB/h	– USD	→	Taux de croissance		–

Exportations 1984:	582,0 Mio USD	Importations 1983:	2 718,7 Mio USD
Exportations vers la CE 1983:	39,2 Mio USD	Importations de la CE 1983:	1 334,7 Mio USD
Élèves: enseign. primaire 1982:	382 500	Élèves: enseign. secondaire 1980:	287 310
Personne/lit d'hôpital 1980:	260	Personne/médecin 1980:	614

	Unités	1981	1982	1983	1984
Commerce extérieur					
Exportations	75 = 100	77,3	69,1	62,2	51,9
Importations	75 = 100	126,7	120,7	116,6	
Balance commerciale	Mio USD	– 2 085,9	– 2 037,7	– 2 021,1	
Exportations/importations	%	29,4	27,5	25,7	
Balance commerciale avec la CE	Mio USD	– 1 243,3	– 1 290,5	– 1 295,5	
Export. vers la CE/import. de la CE	%	3,2	4,5	2,9	
Exportations/PIB	%				
Indicateurs financiers					
Balance des paiements	Mio DTS				
Réserves internationales	Mio USD	1 516,4	2 608,1	1 902,5	671,6
Dette extérieure publique	Mio USD	386,0	332,1	286,2	238,0
Service de la dette/exportations	%				
Aide publique au développement					
APD net total	Mio USD	455,1	187,0	122,6	77,6
APD net bilatéral	Mio USD	430,0	147,3	83,2	55,3
APD net CCE/bilatéral	%	5,6	19,9	35,7	43,1
APD net multilatéral	Mio USD	25,1	39,8	39,5	22,4
APD net CCE/multilatéral	%	29,6	18,2	13,5	3,2
Aide alimentaire					
Céréales	000 t	19,2	24,5	12,0	1,3
Produits laitiers	000 t	2,8	2,9	1,0	0,1
Total	Mio USD	10,6	11,8	4,2	1,5
Principales productions					
Céréales, total	000 t	30	30	26	21
Tubercules et racines	000 t	141	127	151	181
Oranges	000 t	200	205	205	220
Bois rond	000 m³	474	466	469	470

Population 1985:	3 600 000	→ Taux de croissance 1970-85:	4,0 %
PNB 1985:	27 000,0 Mio USD	→ Taux de croissance 1970-85:	5,2 %
PNB/h 1985:	7 500,0 USD	→ Taux de croissance 1970-81:	− 4,1 %

Exportations 1985:	10 841,0 Mio USD	Importations 1983:	6 586,3 Mio USD
Exportations vers la CE 1983:	3 934,7 Mio USD	Importations de la CE 1983:	3 668,1 Mio USD
Élèves: enseign. primaire 1982:	721 710	Élèves: enseign. secondaire 1982:	340 703
Personne/lit d'hôpital 1982:	201	Personne/médecin 1982:	619

	Unités	1981	1982	1983	1984
Commerce extérieur					
Exportations	75 = 100	227,7	215,4	168,7	162,8
Importations	75 = 100	236,6	202,6	185,9	
Balance commerciale	Mio USD	7 193,9	7 554,0	4 954,3	
Exportations/importations	%	185,8	205,3	175,2	
Balance commerciale avec la CE	Mio USD	2 782,0	− 3 000,0	266,5	
Export. vers la CE/import. de la CE	%	151,2	26,1	107,3	
Exportations/PIB	%	54,3	46,9	43,1	
Indicateurs financiers					
Balance des paiements	Mio DTS	− 3 509,0	− 1 814,0	− 1 664,0	− 1 311,0
Réserves internationales	Mio USD	9 002,9	7 059,5	5 218,7	3 634,2
Dette extérieure publique	Mio USD				
Service de la dette/exportations	%				
Aide publique au développement					
APD net total	Mio USD	10,7	12,1	5,7	5,0
APD net bilatéral	Mio USD	2,0	2,4	2,4	2,2
APD net CE/bilatéral	%	85,4	84,4	92,2	94,2
APD net multilatéral	Mio USD	8,7	9,8	3,3	2,8
APD net CCE/multilatéral	%				
Origine du PIB					
Agriculture, forêts, pêche	%	1,9	2,1	2,3	2,4
Industrie	%	69,8	69,4	64,0	:
Services	%	20,1	10,2	:	:
Indice d'évolution des prix	75 = 100	185,5	200,9	202,4	203,1
Principales productions					
Tomates	000 t	168	182	195	195
Tubercules et racines	000 t	97	108	115	93
Pétrole brut	000 t	58 726	55 380	52 506	65 748
Essence	000 t	429	500	520	560
Huiles légères	000 t	1 015	1 060	1 170	1 280
Huiles lourdes	000 t	2 034	2 160	2 200	2 440
Principales exportations					
CTCI 331.01 Huile brute de	Mio USD	15 513,3	12 592,0	10 714,0	
pétrole	%	99,6	85,5	92,8	

Population 1985:	380 000	→ Taux de croissance 1970-85:			0,9 %
PNB 1985	1 190,0 Mio USD	→ Taux de croissance 1970-85:			11,9 %
PNB/h 1985	3 300,0 USD	→ Taux de croissance 1970-81:			8,8 %

Exportations 1985:	400,0 Mio USD	Importations 1985:	758,0 Mio USD
Exportations vers la CE 1984:	268,4 Mio USD	Importations de la CE 1984:	546,9 Mio USD
Élèves: enseign. primaire 1982:	33 208	Élèves: enseign. secondaire 1982:	27 257
Personne/lit d'hôpital 1982:	115	Personne/médecin 1982:	872

	Unités	1981	1982	1983	1984
Commerce extérieur					
Exportations	75 = 100	268,4	246,4	217,5	236,3
Importations	75 = 100	227,0	209,0	194,0	189,6
Balance commerciale	Mio USD	– 403,2	– 372,6	– 364,6	– 316,8
Exportations/importations	%	52,6	52,4	49,9	55,4
Balance commerciale avec la CE	Mio USD	– 294,5	– 275,7	– 261,3	– 278,6
Export. vers la CE/import. de la CE	%	51,6	51,9	49,7	49,1
Exportations/PIB	%	81,5	69,3	67,2	
Indicateurs financiers					
Balance des paiements	Mio DTS	125,6	47,2	97,3	31,1
Réserves internationales	Mio USD	1 073,8	1 083,6	1 112,3	990,2
Dette extérieure publique	Mio USD	134,5	136,5	133,7	113,7
Service de la dette/exportations	%	1,1	0,9	2,8	1,3
Aide publique au développement					
APD net total	Mio USD	49,6	25,0	44,1	11,5
APD net bilatéral	Mio USD	38,9	23,6	42,7	10,0
APD net CE/bilatéral	%	99,2	84,2	76,7	41,9
APD net multilatéral	Mio USD	10,6	1,4	1,4	1,5
APD net CCE/multilatéral	%	93,9	48,5	70,3	87,2
Aide alimentaire					
Céréales	000 t	8,3	5,3		
Produits laitiers	t	400	200	0,0	200
Total	Mio USD	2,0	0,8	0,0	0,2
Origine du PIB					
Agriculture, forêts, pêche	%	3,8	4,0	4,5	4,5
Industrie	%	41,5	40,8	39,5	:
Services	%	54,7	55,2	56,1	:
Indice d'évolution des prix	75 = 100	292,8	317,0	312,1	311,3
Principales productions					
Céréales, total	000 t	9	12	12	9
Tomates	000 t	18	17	18	16
Tubercules et racines	000 t	15	12	15	14
Lait de vache	000 t	26	26	28	28
Viande de bovins	000 t	2	2	2	2
Pêches	000 t	1	1	1	1

Population 1985: 21 940 000 → Taux de croissance 1970-85: 2,4 %
PNB 1985: 13 390,0 Mio USD → Taux de croissance 1970-85: 6,7 %
PNB/h 1985: 610,0 USD → Taux de croissance 1970-81: 1,7 %

Exportations 1985: 2 165,1 Mio USD   Importations 1985: 3 849,5 Mio USD
Exportations vers la CE 1984: 1 291,7 Mio USD   Importations de la CE 1984: 1 665,4 Mio USD
Élèves: enseign. primaire 1985: 2 279 887   Élèves: enseign. secondaire 1985: 1 200 383
Personne/lit d'hôpital 1982: 859   Personne/médecin 1982: 16 355

	Unités	1981	1982	1983	1984
Commerce extérieur					
Exportations	75 = 100	150,4	133,4	133,6	140,8
Importations	75 = 100	170,9	169,4	141,2	153,4
Balance commerciale	Mio USD	− 2 032,3	− 2 256,7	− 1 534,5	− 1 734,9
Exportations/importations	%	53,3	47,7	57,3	55,6
Balance commerciale avec la CE	Mio USD	− 775,4	− 888,0	− 415,2	− 373,7
Export. vers la CE/import. de la CE	%	63,1	59,0	75,0	77,6
Exportations/PIB	%	20,8	19,8	22,5	25,5
Indicateurs financiers					
Balance des paiements	Mio DTS	− 350,0	− 381,0	− 213,0	− 96,0
Réserves internationales	Mio USD	230,0	218,0	107,0	49,0
Dette extérieure publique	Mio USD	11 129,5	11 540,5	12 859,3	13 296,0
Service de la dette/exportations	%	75,9	79,6	61,1	52,8
Aide publique au développement					
APD net total	Mio USD	1 033,5	771,1	395,8	351,0
APD net bilatéral	Mio USD	968,0	708,5	309,0	319,7
APD net CE/bilatéral	%	17,0	21,6	41,4	44,4
APD net multilatéral	Mio USD	65,5	62,6	86,8	31,2
APD net CEE/multilatéral	%	44,1	30,9	47,1	12,3
Aide alimentaire					
Céréales	000 t	247,2	338,2	254,4	384,9
Produits laitiers	000 t	1,7	3,1	7,1	9,0
Total	Mio USD	54,4	59,3	52,4	70,4
Origine du PIB					
Agriculture, forêts, pêche	%	14,9	18,0	16,9	:
Industrie	%	33,6	31,6	31,9	:
Services	%	51,5	50,4	51,2	:
Indice d'évolution des prix	75 = 100	230,0	271,5	295,0	339,5

MAROC

Productions et exportations	Unités	1981	1982	1983	1984
Principales productions					
Céréales, total	000 t	2 128	4 914	3 579	3 755
Blé	000 t	892	2 183	1 970	1 989
Tubercules et racines	000 t	396	539	544	525
Sucre centrifugé brut	000 t	369	384	470	451
Oranges	000 t	690	695	691	746
Lait de vache	000 t	780	790	800	830
Bois rond	000 m³	1 585	1 652	1 685	1 717
Minerai de fer	000 t	29	132	176	163
Minerai de cuivre	000 t	8	22	24	18
Phosphates naturels	000 t	18 562	17 835	19 842	21 351
Minerai de plomb	000 t	116	105	97	144
Poisson en conserve	000 t	58	45	42	48
Acide sulfurique	000 t	768	665	727	758
Principales exportations					
CTCI 031 Poissons	Mio USD	93,4	87,8	109,0	137,4
	%	4,0	4,3	5,3	6,3
CTCI 032 Cons. poissons	Mio USD	89,9	66,2	55,1	63,0
et crustacés	%	3,9	3,2	2,7	2,9
CTCI 051.1 Oranges, clémentines,	Mio USD	206,6	179,0	196,3	119,8
mandarines	%	8,9	8,7	9,5	5,5
CTCI 054 Légumes	Mio USD	75,6	63,0	102,0	70,9
et tubercules	%	3,3	3,1	4,9	3,3
CTCI 271.3 Phosphates naturels	Mio USD	739,7	570,1	534,3	525,0
	%	31,9	27,7	25,9	24,2
CTCI 283 Minerai non ferreux	Mio USD	85,5	65,8	58,4	59,3
	%	3,7	3,2	2,8	2,7
CTCI 332,1 Essence de pétrole	Mio USD	59,1	56,4	0,0	71,0
	%	2,5	2,7	0,0	3,3
CTCI 513 Produits chimiques	Mio USD	259,4	262,5	172,2	399,6
inorganiques	%	11,2	12,8	8,4	18,4
CTCI 561.29 Aut. engrais	Mio USD	49,9	48,5	0,0	72,6
phosphatés	%	2,2	2,4	0,0	3,3
CTCI 657.5 Tapis points noués	Mio USD	58,3	48,6	0,0	43,5
	%	2,5	2,4	0,0	2,0
CTCI 841 Vêtements	Mio USD	124,7	139,2	161,5	175,2
	%	5,4	6,8	7,8	8,1

Population 1985:		10 270 000	→ Taux de croissance 1970-85:		3,4 %
PNB 1985:		17 060,0 Mio USD	→ Taux de croissance 1970-85:		13,0 %
PNB/h 1985:		1 630,0 USD	→ Taux de croissance 1970-81:		5,0 %

Exportations 1985:	1 627,0 Mio USD	Importations 1985:	3 844,0 Mio USD
Exportations vers la CE 1984:	728,9 Mio USD	Importations de la CE 1984:	1 160,7 Mio USD
Élèves: enseign. primaire 1983:	1 823 684	Élèves: enseign. secondaire 1983:	755 095
Personne/lit d'hôpital 1981:	904	Personne/médecin 1981:	2 236

	Unités	1981	1982	1983	1984
Commerce extérieur					
Exportations	75 = 100	226,1	217,9	206,8	199,3
Importations	75 = 100	301,9	240,5	272,1	246,6
Balance commerciale	Mio USD	− 2 936,9	− 1 987,7	− 2 619,4	− 2 262,1
Exportations/importations	%	41,7	50,5	42,3	45,0
Balance commerciale avec la CE	Mio USD	− 308,5	− 182,3	− 905,9	− 431,9
Export. vers la CE/import. de la CE	%	81,6	84,5	42,0	62,8
Exportations/PIB	%	14,6	13,4	13,1	12,6
Indicateurs financiers					
Balance des paiements	Mio DTS	16,0	87,0	− 124,0	− 14,0
Réserves internationales	Mio USD	291,0	198,0	52,0	268,0
Dette extérieure publique	Mio USD	3 856,4	3 782,1	3 940,1	3 765,1
Service de la dette/exportations	%	18,4	19,0	17,7	17,8
Aide publique au développement					
APD net total	Mio USD	1 500,3	961,5	997,8	862,9
APD net bilatéral	Mio USD	1 445,6	944,5	957,6	838,7
APD net CE/bilatéral	%	3,2	3,9	2,9	1,4
APD net multilatéral	Mio USD	54,7	17,0	40,2	24,1
APD net CCE/multilatéral	%	8,6	21,2	12,6	7,8
Aide alimentaire					
Céréales	000 t	10,3	7,5	6,6	6,5
Produits laitiers	000 t	3,2	0,1	0,1	0,0
Total	Mio USD	7,9	1,4	2,3	1,9
Origine du PIB					
Agriculture, forêts, pêche	%	19,2	19,6	21,4	19,9
Industrie	%	26,7	25,0	:	:
Services	%	54,1	55,4	56,1	56,5
Indice d'évolution des prix	75 = 100	285,9	338,2	356,9	381,6

SYRIE

Productions et exportations	Unités	1981	1982	1983	1984
Principales productions					
Céréales, total	000 t	3 559	2 283	2 696	1 445
Haricots, pois, lentilles	000 t	193	149	212	129
Oignons secs	000 t	175	187	159	136
Tomates	000 t	723	790	831	727
Tubercules et racines	000 t	311	279	315	322
Fibres de coton	000 t	131	158	194	158
Phosphates naturels	000 t	1 319	1 461	1 231	1 515
Pétrole brut	000 t	8 520	8 191	9 359	8 964
Filés de coton	000 t	35	42	52	34
Essence	000 t	442	380	474	490
Huiles légères	000 t	1 969	1 980	2 095	2 150
Huiles lourdes	000 t	4 680	4 900	4 800	4 900
Principales exportations					
CTCI 263.1 Coton brut	Mio USD	142,3	115,4	173,9	
	%	6,8	5,7	9,0	
CTCI 331 Pétrole brut part. raffiné	Mio USD	1 285,0	1 039,9	1 052,5	
	%	61,1	51,3	54,7	
CTCI 332 Produits pétroliers	Mio USD	376,5	473,9	271,1	
	%	17,9	23,4	14,1	

Population 1985: 7 260 000 → Taux de croissance 1970-85: 2,3 %
PNB 1985: 8 730,0 Mio USD → Taux de croissance 1970-85: 10,7 %
PNB/h 1985: 1 220,0 USD → Taux de croissance 1970-81: 5,7 %

Exportations 1985: 1 627,0 Mio USD   Importations 1985: 2 597,0 Mio USD
Exportations vers la CE 1984: 1 083,4 Mio USD   Importations de la CE 1984: 2 055,0 Mio USD
Élèves: enseign. primaire 1983: 1 198 447   Élèves: enseign. secondaire 1983: 387 445
Personnel/lit d'hôpital 1982: 469   Personne/médecin 1982: 3 618

	Unités	1981	1982	1983	1984
Commerce extérieur					
Exportations	75 = 100	292,4	231,7	218,6	209,8
Importations	75 = 100	266,0	239,5	218,6	219,7
Balance commerciale	Mio USD	− 1 267,2	− 1 412,2	− 1 228,0	− 1 318,6
Exportations/importations	%	66,4	58,4	60,4	57,7
Balance commerciale avec la CE	Mio USD	− 850,6	− 1 213,8	− 940,0	− 971,6
Export. vers la CE/import. de la CE	%	64,0	49,0	55,8	52,7
Exportations/PIB	%	41,4	36,8	35,2	33,9
Indicateurs financiers					
Balance des paiements	Mio DTS	60,0	147,0	32,0	− 98,0
Réserves internationales	Mio USD	536,1	606,5	567,3	406,3
Dette extérieure publique	Mio USD	5 301,7	5 381,2	5 724,7	5 591,2
Service de la dette/exportations	%	29,0	29,8	34,0	38,6
Aide publique au développement					
APD net total	Mio USD	239,5	209,6	205,4	184,2
APD net bilatéral	Mio USD	204,2	182,2	168,2	155,2
APD net CE/bilatéral	%	54,8	66,2	64,9	61,3
APD net multilatéral	Mio USD	35,4	27,4	37,2	29,0
APD net CCE/multilatéral	%	52,0	16,0	38,1	42,9
Aide alimentaire					
Céréales	000 t	87,9	105,9	87,5	142,1
Produits laitiers	000 t	0,8	0,9	1,4	7,4
Total	Mio USD	20,3	16,8	16,9	34,1
Origine du PIB					
Agriculture, forêts, pêche	%	15,6	15,0	14,2	15,2
Industrie	%	36,6	34,9	35,5	35,0
Services	%	38,0	40,4	:	:
Indice d'évolution des prix	75 = 100	166,6	192,8	210,9	226,0

TUNISIE

Productions et exportations	Unités	1981	1982	1983	1984
Principales productions					
Céréales, total	000 t	1 264	1 287	955	1 060
Tomates	000 t	380	260	360	430
Tubercules et racines	000 t	135	110	150	135
Huile d'olive	000 t	70	55	150	95
Bois rond	000 m³	2 588	2 641	2 692	2 751
Minerai de fer	000 t	212	147	165	165
Phosphates naturels	000 t	4 925	4 729	5 924	5 385
Pétrole brut	000 t	5 407	5 146	5 578	5 484
Gaz naturel	térajoule	18 196	19 267	17 540	18 096
Essence	000 t	163	176	182	211
Huiles légères	000 t	423	405	410	423
Huiles lourdes	000 t	658	532	591	591
Engrais phosphatés	000 t	474	495	527	503
Principales exportations					
CTCI 271.3 Phosphates naturels	Mio USD	46,0	41,2	38,3	35,8
	%	1,8	2,1	2,0	2,0
CTCI 331.01 Huile brute de pétrole	Mio USD	1 267,8	837,1	783,6	737,6
	%	50,6	42,2	41,9	41,1
CTCI 332 Produits pétroliers	Mio USD	84,6	74,0	68,0	57,9
	%	3,4	3,7	3,6	3,2
CTCI 421.5 Huile d'olive	Mio USD	101,7	96,2	38,5	73,7
	%	4,1	4,9	2,1	4,1
CTCI 513 Produits chimiques inorganiques	Mio USD	94,1	99,8	107,4	102,9
	%	3,8	5,0	5,7	5,7
CTCI 561 Engrais manufacturés	Mio USD	195,8	178,6	170,3	155,1
	%	7,8	9,0	9,1	8,6
CTCI 841 Vêtements	Mio USD	323,0	327,8	324,8	289,0
	%	12,9	16,5	17,4	16,1

Population 1985: 49 270 000	→ Taux de croissance 1970-85:	2,3 %
PNB 1985: 56 060,0 Mio USD	→ Taux de croissance 1970-85:	7,4 %
PNB/h 1985: 1 130,0 USD	→ Taux de croissance 1970-81:	2,6 %

Exportations 1985: 7 918,0 Mio USD	Importations 1985: 11 120,0 Mio USD
Exportations vers la CE 1984: 2 782,6 Mio USD	Importations de la CE 1984: 3 249,7 Mio USD
Élèves: enseign. primaire 1982: 6 497 308	Élèves: enseign. secondaire 1983: 2 540 636
Personne/lit d'hôpital 1982: 471	Personne/médecin 1983: 1 481

	Unités	1981	1982	1983	1984
Commerce extérieur					
Exportations	75 = 100	335,6	410,2	404,7	509,2
Importations	75 = 100	191,0	189,5	184,2	229,8
Balance commerciale	Mio USD	− 4 162,5	− 3 046,1	− 2 877,5	− 3 529,2
Exportations/importations	%	53,0	65,4	66,3	66,9
Balance commerciale avec la CE	Mio USD	− 1 018,5	− 728,9	− 292,7	− 467,1
Export. vers la CE/import. de la CE	%	60,6	71,2	87,5	85,6
Exportations/PIB	%	11,1	14,6	15,6	11,9
Indicateurs financiers					
Balance des paiements	Mio DTS	− 498,0	− 677,0	− 587,0	− 860,0
Réserves internationales	Mio USD	928,0	1 080,0	1 288,0	1 271,0
Dette extérieure publique	Mio USD	19 114,5	18 761,0	18 969,1	19 910,9
Service de la dette/exportations	%	38,8	33,3	52,7	30,9
Aide publique au développement					
APD net total	Mio USD	723,4	642,1	351,6	241,0
APD net bilatéral	Mio USD	675,4	621,8	318,7	219,1
APD net CE/bilatéral	%	54,5	23,8	23,9	18,3
APD net multilatéral	Mio USD	48,0	20,3	32,9	21,9
APD net CCE/multilatéral	%	48,9	54,4	84,4	79,3
Aide alimentaire					
Céréales	000 t	0,2	0,3	0,3	
Produits laitiers	000 t	0,0	0,0	0,7	0,3
Total	Mio USD	0,0	0,0	4,1	0,4
Origine du PIB					
Agriculture, forêts, pêche	%	22,0	20,7	19,5	19,4
Industrie	%	30,9	31,4	32,7	33,3
Services	%	47,1	47,9	:	:

TURQUIE

Productions et exportations	Unités	1981	1982	1983	1984
Principales productions					
Céréales, total	000 t	25 526	26 558	24 492	26 314
Blé	000 t	17 050	17 542	16 437	17 235
Maïs	000 t	1 200	1 360	1 480	1 500
Riz, paddy	000 t	330	350	315	280
Tomates	000 t	3 600	3 700	3 700	4 000
Tubercules et racines	000 t	3 000	3 000	3 050	3 200
Sucre centrifugé brut	000 t	1 521	1 860	1 770	1 655
Tabac brut	000 t	168	208	234	178
Oranges	000 t	687	668	744	776
Lait de vache	000 t	3 538	3 210	3 107	2 805
Lait de brebis	000 t	1 176	1 179	1 192	981
Viande de bovins	000 t	201	210	220	225
Bois rond	000 m³	21 878	21 878	20 737	18 927
Bois scié	000 m³	3 498	3 577	4 117	4 119
Engrais azotés	000 t	718	723	783	759
Engrais phosphatés	000 t	469	518	621	580

Population 1985:	23 120 000	→ Taux de croissance 1970-85:			0,8 %
PNB 1985:	47 900,0 Mio USD	→ Taux de croissance 1970-85:			7,3 %
PNB/h 1985:	2 070,0 USD	→ Taux de croissance 1970-81:			4,5 %

Exportations 1985:	10 641,5 USD	Importations 1985:	12 162,9 USD
Exportations vers la CE 1985:	2 632,3 Mio USD	Importations de la CE 1985:	3 764,4 Mio USD
Élèves: enseign. primaire 1983:	1 460 214	Élèves: enseign. secondaire 1983:	2 370 102
Personne/lit d'hôpital 1982:	167	Personne/médecin 1982:	644

	Unités	1981	1982	1983	1984
Commerce extérieur					
Exportations	75 = 100	268,4	264,0	243,4	251,8
Importations	75 = 100	204,7	183,1	157,9	155,8
Balance commerciale	Mio USD	− 4 828,0	− 3 347,6	− 2 241,0	− 1 741,5
Exportations/importations	%	69,4	76,3	81,6	85,5
Balance commerciale avec la CE	Mio USD	− 3 200,5	− 2 629,5	− 1 379,6	− 988,3
Export. vers la CE/import. de la CE	%	44,3	45,7	63,2	72,8
Exportations/PIB	%	21,9	22,0	29,0	30,9
Indicateurs financiers					
Balance des paiements	Mio DTS	116,0	− 856,0	345,0	
Réserves internationales	Mio USD	1 597,2	775,3	976,4	1 158,1
Dette extérieure publique	Mio USD	6 998,1	7 112,2	9 528,4	10 357,7
Service de la dette/exportations	%	10,4	10,3	9,1	
Aide publique au développement					
APD net total	Mio USD	− 14,8	− 7,6	2,6	2,9
APD net bilatéral	Mio USD	− 17,5	− 10,5	− 0,4	− 1,4
APD net CE/bilatéral	%	45,6	25,5	− 519,5	96,5
APD net multilatéral	Mio USD	2,8	2,9	3,0	4,3
APD net CCE/multilatéral	%				
Origine du PIB					
Agriculture, forêts, pêche	%	13,2	14,3	14,9	14,9
Industrie	%	:	:	:	:
Services	%	38,7	39,3	:	:
Indice d'évolution des prix	75 = 100	439,5	581,4	809,0	1 264,2

YOUGOSLAVIE

Productions et exportations	Unités	1981	1982	1983	1984
Principales productions					
Céréales, total	000 t	15 245	17 439	17 292	18 501
Blé	000 t	4 270	5 218	5 525	5 595
Sorgho	000 t	12	12	8	13
Maïs	000 t	9 807	11 137	10 719	11 312
Tomates	000 t	453	470	425	480
Tubercules et racines	000 t	2 774	2 636	2 580	2 458
Sucre centrifugé brut	000 t	870	697	940	1 011
Tabac brut	000 t	70	77	67	77
Lait de vache	000 t	4 484	4 602	4 610	4 580
Viande de bovins	000 t	323	343	345	350
Bois rond	000 m³	14 094	15 276	15 329	15 091
Bois scié	000 m³	4 229	4 432	4 413	4 658
Minerai de cuivre	000 t	111	119	130	137
Minerai de plomb	000 t	119	113	114	115

European Communities – Commission
Communautés européennes – Commission

ACP – Basic statistics
ACP – Statistiques de base

Luxembourg: Office des publications officielles des Communautés européennes

1987 – 217 p. – 10,5 × 14,8 cm

Theme 1: General statistics (midnight blue covers)
Series A: Yearbooks
Thème 1: Statistiques générales (couverture bleu nuit)
Série A: Annuaires

EN/FR

ISBN 92-825-7382-6

Cat.: CA-47-86-575-2A-C

Price (excluding VAT) in Luxembourg
Prix publics au Luxembourg, TVA exclue

ECU 9,30   BFR 400   DKR 73   DM 19,50   ΔPX 1 290   ESC 1 400   FF 64
HFL 22   IRL 7.10   LIT 13 400   PTA 1 280   UKL 6.60   USD 10

Selection of the most important statistics of the ACP countries, signatories with the Community of the Lomé Convention, and comparison with other developing countries. This selection covers the following areas: population, national accounts, production of industry, mining and agriculture, foreign trade, prices, finance, external aid, standard of living.

Sélection des statistiques les plus importantes des pays ACP, signataires avec la Communauté de la convention de Lomé, et comparaison avec d'autres pays en voie de développement. Cette sélection couvre les domaines suivants: population, comptes nationaux, productions industrielle, minière et agricole, commerce extérieur, prix, finances, aide extérieure, niveau de vie.